Agent-Based Software Development

Agent-Oriented Systems
Series Editor: Michael Luck (University of Southampton, United Kingdom)

Overview:
Agent technology has seen a dramatic growth of interest in recent years and is being given added impetus by the integration of new technologies and applications into the mainstream of commercial software. For example, the World Wide Web, e-commerce, Grid computing, and distributed object technologies all suggest that agent technology has an important role in modern computing. This is now also true at the level of commercial and industrial take-up of the technology, with an increasing number of companies investing in agent products and agent development solutions and a number of standards initiatives underway for some time.

The Agent-Oriented Systems Series aims to cover important advances in agent-based computing concerning development methodologies, tools and techniques, standards, and other aspects of agent-oriented systems development. This series will be of interest to all software engineers, IT personnel, computer scientists, and technologists working in the area of agent-based computing and in related application domains as well as related areas of distributed computing, semantic Web, Grid computing, and so forth. It should also provide a valuable set of resources addressing the state of the art in agent-oriented systems development. The series topics include, but are not limited to:

- Agent-oriented software engineering;
- Agent standards;
- Development case studies;
- Infrastructure for agent-based systems;
- Agent platforms and tools;
- Agent-oriented information systems.

For a listing of recent titles in the *Artech House Computing Library*,
turn to the back of this book.

Agent-Based Software Development

Michael Luck
Ronald Ashri
Mark d'Inverno

Artech House
Boston • London
www.artechhouse.com

Library of Congress Cataloging-in-Publication Data

A catalog record for this book is available from the Library of Congress.

British Library Cataloguing in Publication Data

A catalog record of this book is available from the British Library.

Cover design by Yekaterina Ratner

685 Canton Street
Norwood, MA 02062

International Standard Book Number: 1-58053-605-0

10 9 8 7 6 5 4 3 2 1

Contents

Preface

The field of agent-based computing is large and growing, and set to underpin much of the infrastructure of the next generation of computing that seeks to address issues in ambient intelligence, pervasive and ubiquitous computing, Grid computing, the semantic Web, e-business and many other areas. However, in order to take full advantage of the benefits that agent technology brings, the agent paradigm ought to be adopted at the stage of system design. This suggests the use of agent-oriented methodologies for the development of agent systems, adherence to standards intended to ensure interoperability, and the adoption of relevant tools and techniques to aid the process. This book provides a thorough exploration of all these areas, and brings together the different aspects of agent-oriented development in one coherent text.

OVERVIEW OF THE BOOK

Chapter 1 starts by discussing the key concepts underlying agent systems, and reviewing the motivation for their development through a consideration of the underlying computational context. In Chapter 2, these basic notions of agents are fleshed out through a review of several important agent architectures and key multiagent systems. The aim of this chapter is simply to provide an adequate grounding for the issues that are covered in the subsequent chapters on more specific development-oriented work. It can be taken simply as a necessary preliminary chapter, or as a broad review of the field in its own right.

The main part of the book begins in Chapter 3 with a description of a selection of tools that are available for use in agent systems development. These include commercial systems as well as more academic offerings, with each compared to the others along major axes. Complementing this, Chapter 4 presents a detailed analysis of the various different methodologies and notations that have been developed for the design of agent-based systems. It provides a review of the salient techniques, many of which are now mature, and some in regular use.

Chapter 5 addresses the context for the development of agent systems through the use of *standards*. It describes the work that has been done in the IT community to support interoperability, primarily through the efforts of the Foundation for Intelligent Physical Agents (FIPA), but also other standards organizations. Arguably, the development of such standards must occur before the widespread adoption of agent technologies. Chapter 6 similarly considers the context, but through the availability of standard technologies that can be used to provide much of the functionality that underlies systems of autonomous interacting agents. Technologies such as Jini and Web services all offer valuable aspects that can be leveraged in developing agent systems.

Finally, Chapter 7 ends the book by reviewing the different resources that are available for consultation for more detail on the various aspects of agent-oriented development, and on agent technologies more generally. In a fast-moving field, Web resources and other sources of information and support can be critically important. Fortunately, there are many possible places to seek further information. One of these is the Web site that accompanies this book, at `www.agentdevelopment.com`, which contains pointers to numerous reference sites, and a range of relevant resources.

ACKNOWLEDGMENTS

This book resulted from discussions with Tim Pitts of Artech House, in the context of the emerging maturity of the field of agent-oriented software development. Tim has provided support and encouragement, and we appreciate his efforts in pushing the project forward. Similarly, the day-to-day work of badgering the authors and dealing with our delays and problems was handled by Louise Skelding and Tiina Ruonamaa, who coped with us admirably during the development of the manuscript. We are grateful to them both for their patience.

Most of the work in producing this book has been undertaken by the three authors, but the book itself would not offer anything like the coverage and depth of analysis had the authors of Chapter 4 and Chapter 5 not agreed to contribute.

A special mention must be made of Serena Raffin, who gave up her own time to help generate many of the diagrams included in the chapters of this book. Without her, we would never have made it.

As is often the case, the environments in which we work provide excellent contexts in which to undertake an endeavor like the one here. We appreciate and recognize that our departments and universities not only enabled us to write this book, they also provided the experience of research and development that we describe throughout. Particular thanks should go to Paul Howells, Nick Jennings, Luc Moreau, Terry Payne, Mark Priestly, and Steve Winter, who provided support from within our own institutions. Thanks also to Florence and Musa for making the days working in London much more pleasant than they would otherwise have been.

Personally and individually, we must thank those around us for bearing with us during the stress and tension of writing late and early, when we should have been spending our time with them. And for those who didn't bear with us, we love you anyway. Special thanks to our parents, Harry and Dalia, Andreas and Photini, and Ray and Pauline.

Thanks also to Katia, Carla and Titta (and Lilly), Nikolas and Panikos, Daniel, Christos "Kozias" Markides, Alex and Olivia, Abha, Jo and Leo, Jeremy and Monica (and Francesca and Martina), Dan and Franky (and Poppy and Joseph), Alex, Rachel, Sharon and Ben (and Daniel, Jonathan, and Francesca), Orly, Dawn, Lucy, Olivia, John and Philly (and Cameron), Eileen, Susan, Nicky, Serena,

Liz, Jane, Clare, Lucia, Mary, Carla, Michelle, Dolly and Candy (and Tiger and Hector), Eli, Phil and Geddy (and Michael and Daisy), Paul Rooney, Gi and Philly (and Beany, Tatti, Oscar, Flo, and Rose), Andy and Mel (and Thomas and Max), Neil and Susi (and Alex and Olly), Tim and Lisa (and Joseph), Dave and Jo (and Saskia), Karen and Jason (and Tali), Val and Bill, Vijay and Lisa, Chris and Catherine (and Eliza), Emma Barrett, Ali and Dave, Chris and Secha, Nicki and Tony, Nicki and Giles, Chris and Sylvia, Tony and Leslie, Polly and Antonia, Eli, Lisa Rigg, Mike Freeman, Mike Bacon, Jenny Goodwin, Kellie Samuda, Mo City, Hutch, Gib, Lawso, Dicks and the Lab Bar in Soho, the Guinea Grill, the weekenders cricket club, and Choral Clench, all of whom have distracted us so easily.

Michael Luck, Ronald Ashri,
and Mark d'Inverno
Southampton and London
January 2004

Chapter 1

Agent-Based Computing

1.1 OPEN AND DYNAMIC COMPUTING ENVIRONMENTS

Computer systems in the twenty-first century are dramatically different from those that have been the norm over the last 50 years. Unlike previous changes, which have seen vast improvements in computing capacity and power, modern computing is essentially defined by the *interconnection* of computers, and all that it brings. The advent of the World Wide Web 10 years ago offered a radically new take on the *information society*, releasing information and making it available to all. Somewhat more crucially, it also provided the basic infrastructure for the dynamic provision of on-line *services*, which are only now beginning to take root with real substance and significance.

Against this technological background, 2003 was also the year in which Internet penetration in Western Europe and the United States was expected to pass 60%. In Europe, the European Commission has launched its *eEurope* initiative, which aims to bring every citizen, home, school, and business online to create a digitally literate Europe. In short, the maturity of the technology, and its penetration of all aspects of society, have converged to suggest not just new kinds of systems, but also their implementation and deployment on a scale that offers dramatic new opportunities and problems. This book is concerned with one way—and one that is being seen by many as a key underpinning technology for the next generation of computing—of meeting these opportunities and addressing these problems.

As indicated above, the move from a focus on the individual standalone computer system to a situation in which the real power of computers is realized through distributed, open, and dynamic systems has radically changed the nature of software and its development. The key difference now is that there is an environment made up of computers in the infrastructure, in support systems, and embedded in a vast array of devices, as well as on the traditional desktop. More importantly, these computers are typically networked and can interact dynamically to form new configurations of systems to suit current needs. The flexibility that such abilities offer, although increasingly taken for granted, is set to change the way we do business, undertake science, and manage our everyday activities. However, the characteristics of dynamic and open environments in which, for example, heterogeneous systems must interact, span organizational boundaries, and operate effectively within rapidly changing circumstances and with dramatically increasing quantities of available information, suggest that improvements on the traditional computing models and paradigms are required.

In particular, the need for some degree of autonomy, to enable components to respond dynamically to changing circumstances while trying to achieve overarching objectives without the need for user intervention, is seen by many as fundamental. In practical developments, Web services, for example, now offer fundamentally new ways of operating through a set of standardized tools, and support a service-oriented view of distinct and independent software components interacting to provide valuable functionality. In the context of such developments, *agent technologies* have become some of the most valuable tools that can be used to tackle the emergent problems, and to manage the complexity that arises.

Agents can be viewed as autonomous, problem-solving computational entities capable of effective operation in dynamic and open environments. They are often deployed in environments in which they interact, and possibly cooperate, with other agents (including both people and software) that may have conflicting aims. These are exactly the kinds of characteristics that are needed in the new computational environments. Agent-based systems have emerged over the past 10 to 15 years, from a convergence of technologies in distributed object systems and distributed artificial intelligence, and have seen rapid and dramatic growth both academically and commercially. Indeed, agent technologies are already providing real benefits in a diverse range of business and industry domains, spanning manufacturing, supply chain management, and B2B exchanges, for example.

1.2 OBJECT TECHNOLOGIES

The relation of agents to objects has caused difficulty for some in understanding what it is that makes agents distinct. While object-orientation as a programming paradigm has achieved much success, and offers a valuable abstraction for the development of complex systems, agents provide a different and *higher* level of abstraction. Like objects that provide encapsulation of state and behavior, agents also encapsulate these properties. However, objects are essentially passive in nature—they have no choice as to whether or not they interact, and are simply *invoked* by other objects to perform particular tasks or execute particular functionality. By contrast, agents have the ability to *decide* for themselves whether to participate in computational activity, and whether to perform the desired operation. This is the fundamental distinction that marks out agents as distinct by virtue of their *autonomy*. It is this autonomy that is also responsible for providing the flexibility that is needed for open and dynamic environments. If behavior is predetermined and is guaranteed when invoked, then the ability to provide flexible responses in the light of changing circumstances is severely curtailed, if not ruled out entirely.

In terms of modeling, objects can be regarded as a valuable way to view the world. Yet an agent-based approach offers a much more natural representation of real-world systems in which different individuals interact according to their own agenda and priorities. They then can come together to achieve overarching objectives that might not, or not as easily, be achieved by the individuals alone, but they do so when it is appropriate. When the goals of individual agents are closely aligned, and if they are completely benevolent and honest (or veracious) so that they always respond to requests made of them, and always provide information when queried, then the resulting systems may come close to resembling an object-oriented system. In these cases, the object-oriented paradigm may be adequate, but this is a particular configuration of agents that is unlikely to provide the flexibility that may be required in modern computing environments.

In short, agents can be distinguished from objects in that they are autonomous entities capable of exercising choice over their actions and interactions. Agents cannot, therefore, be directly invoked like objects. However, they may be constructed using object technology. Moreover, agents typically run in their own thread of control, as opposed to standard object systems, which have one thread.

Object orientation is also relevant when considering how to develop agent systems. The question of where agent development methodologies fit in, and the extent to which they are needed in addition to existing object-oriented methodologies, depends on the approach taken. If agents provide a *programming* paradigm to rival object-oriented programming, then methodology is clearly of central importance, since the program and the programming themselves are informed by the agent paradigm. If, instead, they provide a paradigm or metaphor for design, then methodology is certainly important, but the nature of that methodology is likely to be related to current object-oriented approaches. In this case, however, the agent approach will require significant modifications from a standard object-oriented approach to address the agent abstractions and interactions. In either case, however, methodology is a vital issue that must be considered in some detail in order to support agent-orientation. In particular, the object-oriented paradigm does not address issues of developing software that exhibits flexible autonomous behavior.

There has recently been a good degree of work aimed at addressing these concerns, which are the focus of Chapter 4, but more work remains to be done before the approach is accepted as part of the mainstream. Indeed, as the field matures, the broader acceptance of agent-oriented systems will become increasingly tied to the availability and accessibility of well-founded techniques and methodologies for system development.

1.3 BASIC NOTIONS OF AGENTS

The introduction of the notion of agents is partly due to the difficulties that have arisen when attempting to solve problems without regard to a real external environment or to the entity involved in that problem-solving process. Thus, though the solutions constructed to address these problems are in themselves important, they can be limited and inflexible in not coping well in real-world situations. In response, agents have been proposed as *situated* and *embodied* problem-solvers that are capable of flexible and effective operation in complex environments. This means that the agent receives input from its environment through some sensory device, and acts so as to affect that environment in some way through effectors. Such a simple but powerful concept has been adopted by many branches of computing because of its usefulness and broad applicability.

However, a recurrent theme that is raised in one form or another in many different contexts is the lack of consensus over what it is that actually constitutes an agent. Certainly, the immediately engaging concepts and images that spring to mind when the term is mentioned are a prime reason for the popularization of agent systems in the broader (and even public) community, and for the extremely rapid growth and development of the field. Indeed the elasticity in terminology and definition of agent concepts has led to the adoption of common terms for a broad range of research activity, providing an inclusive and encompassing set of interacting and cross-fertilizing subfields. This is partly responsible for the richness of the area and for the variety of approaches and applications.

Despite some healthy debate over precise definitions of agenthood, it is clear that there is now a generally accepted understanding of agents as computational entities that are capable of exhibiting flexible behavior in dynamic and unpredictable environments. This understanding is important, and it provides an operational basis for what this book is about, and motivates the effort directed towards the development of agent technologies and agent-based systems. In more specific terms, however, we can drill down and identify two distinct views of agents. The *weak notion* of agents provides a characterization that enumerates four properties regarded as necessary and sufficient for agenthood:

- Autonomy: agents must be self-starting and independent entities that are able to function without direct programmer or user intervention.
- Reactiveness: agents can monitor their environments and respond quickly and effectively to changes in those environments.
- Proactiveness: agents have overarching goals that direct behavior over longer periods of time towards achieving complex tasks.
- Social ability: since agents operate in dynamic and open environments with many other agents, they must have the ability to interact and communicate with these others.

Since this characterization of agents was originally provided in 1994 [1], it has been the subject of much discussion, and several authors have provided alternative characterizations with additional properties. These include, for example, the ability to learn, mobility, the requirement that agents are benevolent or honest (an unlikely requirement in open environments), that they are rational, and many others.

The *strong* or *intentional* notion of agents also requires agents to be based around control architectures comprising mental components such as beliefs, desires, and motivations. While the stance adopted throughout this book is broad and open, and avoids the dogma that can creep into these kinds of discussions, it will be seen very clearly, especially in the initial discussion of agent architectures, that these notions can be important and valuable as a metaphor that leads to the provision of effective and flexible control and behavior.

The broad area of understanding agenthood has merited several efforts that explore the area in some depth, including encompassing agent frameworks [2, 3] and agent taxonomies [4], which go some way to identifying the key features of agent systems and the characteristics of the different branches of the field. In attempting to distinguish agents from programs, Franklin and Graesser constructed an agent taxonomy [4] aimed at identifying the key features of agent systems in relation to different branches of the field. Their aim, amply described by the title of the paper, "Is It an Agent or Just a Program?", highlights the problem of whether there is value in the notion of agents. The definition provided, that an "autonomous agent is a system situated within and a part of an environment that senses that environment and acts on it, over time, in pursuit of its own agenda and so as to affect what it senses in the future," serves to distinguish some nonagent programs from agents through the introduction of such things as *temporal continuity*. Using this, Franklin and Graesser then move to classify existing notions of agents within a taxonomic hierarchy. The benefit of all these approaches is that the richness of the agent metaphor is preserved throughout its diverse uses, while the distinct identities of the different perspectives are highlighted and used to direct and focus research and development in different ways.

1.4 AGENT PROPERTIES

There is now a plethora of different labels for agents ranging from the generic *autonomous agents* [5], *software agents* [6], and *intelligent agents* [1] to the more specific *interface agents* [7], *virtual agents* [8], *information agents* [9], *mobile agents* [10, 11], and so on. The diverse range of applications for which agents are being touted includes operating systems interfaces [12], processing satellite imaging data [13], electricity distribution management [14], air-traffic control [15], business process management [16], electronic commerce [17], and computer games [18], to name a few. The richness of the agent metaphor that leads to such different uses of the term is both a strength and a weakness. Its strength lies in the fact that it can be applied in very many different ways in many situations for many different purposes. The weakness, however, is that the term *agent* is now used so frequently that it might be considered that there is no commonly accepted notion of what it is that constitutes an agent.

Typically, however, agents are *characterized* along certain dimensions, rather than defined precisely. For example, as described above, Wooldridge and Jennings [1], offer a *weak notion* of agency that involves *autonomy* or the ability to function without intervention, *social ability* by which agents interact with other agents, *reactiveness* allowing agents to perceive and respond to a changing environment, and *proactiveness* through which agents behave in a goal-directed fashion. As indicated, these characteristics are broadly accepted as representative of the key qualities that can be used to assess *agenthood*.

Similarly, Etzioni and Weld [19] summarize desirable agent characteristics as including *autonomy*, *temporal continuity* by which agents are not simply "one-shot" computations, believable *personality* in order to facilitate effective interaction, *communication ability* with other agents or people, *adaptability* to user preferences, and *mobility*, which allows agents to be transported across different machines and architectures. They further characterize the first of these, autonomy, as requiring that agents are *goal-oriented* and accept high-level requests, *collaborative* in that they can modify these requests and clarify them, *flexible* in not having hard, scripted actions, and *self-starting* in that they can sense changes and decide when to take action. Other characteristics are often considered, both implicitly and explicitly, with regard to notions of agency including, for example, *veracity*, *benevolence*, and *rationality*.

The difficulty with this approach of *characterizing* agents through identifying their properties is exemplified by considering *mobile agents* [10, 11], which are quite distinct and identifiable in the focus on movement of code between host machines. Here, the key characteristic is precisely this mobility, and indeed mobility has been regarded by some as an intrinsic agent property. A critical analysis of the area of mobile agents would, however, unearth a recognition that this mobility augments other, more central agent characteristics in mobile agents, so that mobility is valuable in identifying the kind of agent, rather than understanding all agents. Similarly, some of the more specific labels for agents describe other characteristics that do not impact on agents as a whole, but relate to a particular domain or capability. In this book, we will consider agents in general terms, avoiding any particular *definition* but adhering broadly to the *weak* notion described above. In particular, we will not consider domain-specific characteristics such as mobility. The key for us is the focus on flexible behavior.

1.5 HISTORY OF AGENTS

Agent-based computing is a multidisciplinary field which, as discussed earlier, is rooted in distributed artificial intelligence and distributed object technologies. At a conceptual level, the basic notions stem from the work of those who took issue with the traditional view of artificial intelligence as symbol manipulation, and argued for the construction of situated and embodied systems. As we will see in Chapter 2, they were concerned with the brittleness of existing systems that addressed only subproblems, and instead sought to build more flexible and robust complete systems that exhibited effective behavior in changing environments.

Work in distributed artificial intelligence (DAI) dates back to the mid- to late 1970s and was concerned with the development of mechanisms and methods to enable systems of interacting agents to pursue overarching goals in a cooperative fashion. For example, DAI gave rise to the Functionally Accurate, Cooperative (FA/C) paradigm, which first provided a model for task decomposition and agent interaction in a distributed problem-solving system. In this way, agents no longer needed to have all the necessary information locally to solve their subproblems, and interacted through the asynchronous exchange of partial results. The issues under investigation related to the integration of data, goal-directed control, and distributed planning. DAI evolved naturally into much of what is now the field of multiagent systems.

At the same time, advances in distributed object technologies provided an infrastructure without which the development of more general large-scale agent systems would become much more difficult and less effective. Indeed, agent techniques and technologies would have become less *transferable* and would certainly not have achieved the broader penetration they currently enjoy. For example, the CORBA distributed computing platform to handle low-level interoperation of heterogeneous distributed components can underpin the development of agent systems without the need for reinvention of fundamental techniques.

Many such areas have contributed to the development of agent-based computing. Indeed, the swell of interest in agents has typically been attributed to key changes and advances in the technological landscape over a number of years in recent times. As mentioned earlier, perhaps the most dramatic and most important of these changes has been the emergence of the World Wide Web which, on the one hand, has opened up a wealth of resources in an accessible way and provided ready technologies for remote distribution of information that brings with it, on the other hand, a new set of problems relating to information gathering. (That little more needs to be said about the Web itself is a mark of the impact it has made across technological domains and everyday life.) As far as agents are concerned, both the benefits and the difficulties that have arisen as a result of the Web have contributed to the progress of agent research and development. The distribution of information and associated technologies lends them almost ideally to use by, in, and for multiagent systems, while the problems that arise as a consequence suggest no solution quite as much as agents. The dual aspect of this interaction with the World Wide Web has thus been a major driving force. In fact, it might be argued that the success of agent systems is due to the timely coincidence of a maturity in some related fields and specific developments in others that have converged in a particular way, catalyzed by the agent metaphor, to describe the current state of the art.

At present, agent-based computing has achieved notable successes, but is still an emerging field. It offers great rewards, but there are still challenges that need to be met. One of the most fundamental obstacles to the mainstream deployment of agent technology is the lack of mature software development methodologies for agent-based systems. Clearly, basic principles of software and knowledge engineering need to be applied to the development and deployment of multiagent systems, but they also need to be augmented to suit the differing demands of this new paradigm. At a tool level, software developers will require sophisticated yet easy-to-use agent-oriented CASE (computer-aided software engineering) environments to help them in all aspects of the system development process, including the design, testing, maintenance, and visualization of agent-oriented systems. Some systems already have rudimentary elements of these.

Importantly, the success of future developments is likely to be ensured not by considering agents in isolation, but through their integration with evolving (and current) systems integration technologies (such as Jini and UDDI). Agent technologies are particularly relevant at higher levels of interaction relating to communication, ontologies, content, and semantics, whereas business integration frameworks focus on the provision of scalable and robust solutions to the lower levels, including protocols, syntax, distributed computing APIs, and directory services. It is important to build on current efforts to ensure that these are interoperable.

This book aims to provide an overview of the solutions to some of these problems, and to show that the challenges are indeed being met. This is important, and the success of the agent paradigm will itself be critical in providing the means to take advantage of the opportunities that several new and emerging application domains are raising. In the next and final section, we present a brief description of several of these domains, to demonstrate their range and diversity. Drawn from the sketches in the *AgentLink Roadmap* for agent-based computing [20], they indicate the potential impact of agent-related technologies on society, and the fact that agent technologies will play an increasingly important role in underpinning the transition to an information-intensive society and economy.

1.6 APPLICATION OPPORTUNITIES

1.6.1 Ambient Intelligence

The notion of ambient intelligence has largely arisen through the efforts of the European Commission in identifying challenges for European research and development in information society technologies. Aimed at seamless delivery of services and applications, it relies on three identified pillars of ubiquitous computing, ubiquitous communication, and intelligent user interfaces, yet it offers perhaps the strongest motivation for, and justification of, agent technologies. The ambient intelligence vision describes an environment of potentially thousands of embedded and mobile devices (or software artifacts) interacting to support user-centered goals and activity. This suggests a component-oriented view of the world in which the artifacts are independent and distributed. The consensus is that autonomy, distribution, adaptation, responsiveness, and so on, are the key characterizing features of these ambient intelligent artifacts, and in this sense they very strongly share the same characteristics as agents.

In particular, these ambient intelligence artifacts are likely to be function-specific (though possibly configurable to tasks) and will, of necessity, need to interact with numerous other ambient intelligence artifacts in the environment around them in order to achieve their goals. Interactions will take place between pairs of artifacts (in one-to-one cooperation or competition), between groups of artifacts (in reaching consensus decisions), and between artifacts and the infrastructure resources that comprise their environments (such as large-scale information repositories or other supporting resources, possibly through agent encapsulation). Interactions like these enable the establishment of electronic institutions or virtual organizations, in which groups of agents come together to form coherent groups able to achieve some overarching goals.

1.6.2 Grid Computing

The high-performance computing infrastructure, known as the Grid, for supporting large-scale distributed scientific endeavor has recently gained heightened and sustained interest from several communities, as a means of developing e-science applications such as those demanded by the Large Hadron Collider facility at CERN (the European Organization for Nuclear Research), engineering design optimization, and combinatorial chemistry. Yet it also provides a computing infrastructure for supporting more general applications that involve large-scale information handling, knowledge management, and service provision.

It is natural to view large systems in terms of the services they offer, and consequently in terms of the entities providing or consuming services. Grid applications, in which typically many services may be involved, spread over a geographically distributed environment, which new services join and existing ones leave, thus very strongly suggest the use of agent-based computing. In this view, agents act on behalf of service owners, managing access to services, and ensuring that contracts are fulfilled. They also act on behalf of service consumers, locating services, agreeing to contracts, and receiving and presenting results. Just as in the ambient intelligence vision, agents will be required to engage in interactions, to negotiate, and to make proactive run-time decisions while responding to changing circumstances. In particular, agents will need to collaborate and to form coalitions of agents with different capabilities in support of new virtual organizations. Such virtual organizations have been identified as the tool with which to unwrap the power of the Grid.

Initially geared towards high-performance computing, Grid computing is now being recognized as the future model for service-oriented environments, within and across enterprises. The impact will be larger than just virtual organizations—a global company is much like such a virtual organization and will require similar technology.

1.6.3 Electronic Business

To date agents have been used in the first stages of e-commerce, product and merchant discovery, and brokering. The next step will involve moving into real trading, negotiating deals, and making purchases. However, it can be argued that the real impact of electronic commerce will be on a dramatic change in the supply chain. If a consumer can contact directly the producer instead of a reseller it might produce an increase in efficiency of the overall supply chain. These changes in the supply chains will permit new markets to appear, old markets to change, and the participation of new players. These observations raise some broader questions about e-commerce in general, and the speeding-up effects of agents in particular. Consumers who are excluded from the e-commerce loop may find their prices and choices becoming worse.

In the short term, travel agencies and retailing will be the primary business-to-consumer application domains using agent technology in e-commerce. One of the current efforts aimed at driving this forward can be seen in the Trading Agents Competition (TAC), which offered a sophisticated problem domain of multiple auctions for agents to compile travel packages for customers. Such initiatives can highlight the potential of agent technology for a wider audience, while at the same time contributing to the more rapid development of the field in a specific application and problem domain. Here, one interesting segment is supply chain management for virtual and transnational enterprises. On the other hand, it can be foreseen that agent technology in this market will enable small and medium enterprises to collaborate and form coalitions in much more flexible ways, almost regardless of geographic location.

In the longer term, full supply chain integration is the aim. According to a Pricewaterhouse-Coopers report, there were more than 1,000 public e-markets and around 30,000 private exchanges at the beginning of 2001. Although the baseline domains exist, the lack of standards and uniformity of these platforms constrains what can currently be achieved, but offers a real challenge and opportunity for deployment of agent systems over the next 5 to 10 years.

1.6.4 Simulation

Multiagent systems provide a natural basis for training of decision-makers in complex decision-making domains. For example, defense simulations using multiagent systems can enable military planners, strategic defense staff, and even operational staff to gain experience of complex military operations through simulations and war games. These simulated experiences are obtained instead of, or in addition to, experiences gained in actual military operations. Similarly, decision makers in other complex and dynamic environments can gain valuable experience through exercises that simulate their real-world domain using multiagent systems. Applications include marketplaces subject to rapid change, such as telecommunications markets undergoing deregulation, and markets for fast-moving consumer goods, such as breakfast cereals, where consumer tastes and competitor activities can lead to market turbulence. In these applications, as for those in defense, multiagent systems may simulate over a few hours the dynamics of an actual market that could occur over several years, and so give trainee decision makers rapid exposure to many diverse experiences. In addition, as the military example reveals, the decision maker is allowed to learn through his or her mistakes without creating real-world consequences.

Social simulation is somewhat unusual in that it does not require many of the challenges listed earlier to be addressed for it to succeed in the time scales considered in this report. Since simulations are by their nature closed (even though they may model open systems), they are almost immediately enabled. However, there are many open issues to be resolved before agent-based simulation models can be applied more widely to public policy domains. For example, there is as yet no general understanding of what constitutes "good" performance by a multiagent system, except perhaps in some domains. There is no guarantee, for example, that an agent society in which different species of agents coevolve in the course of their interactions with one another will progress in any sense; later generations of a species may be less fit than earlier generations of that same species when pitted against earlier generations of their competitor species. In such a case, at which timepoint should the simulation be terminated? Different termination points may lead to different assessments of system performance and different recommendations to policy makers. Indeed, the question of performance assessment of multiagent systems is part of a larger, mostly open, question of performance assessment of decision support systems in general.

Multiagent systems as social simulations are also of increasing importance in entertainment applications. These applications range from single (human)-player computer games to multiplayer games, where the other players may be both humans and agents. Potential applications also exist in other interactive media, such as interactive movies, television, and even books, where viewers and readers may have their own avatar participate in the story and may interact with fictional characters directly. The film industry has already notched up several successes in this area, perhaps the most notable recent example being the film, *The Lord of the Rings: The Two Towers*. This film achieved visually impressive battle scenes by using agent technology to model individual characters, with the overall film sequence emerging from their interactions.

1.7 BOOK OVERVIEW

The book continues in Chapter 2 with an introduction to agents and multiagent systems by outlining key ideas and architectures on which many systems have been based. Chapter 2 reviews several single-agent architectures, both reactive and deliberative, before moving on to consider aspects of multiagent systems such as interaction protocols and coordination. It provides the context for the discussion in subsequent chapters. Chapter 3 builds on this through a discussion of different toolkits and systems that may be used to construct agent systems. The range covered is broad, and includes commercial offerings as well as freely available software. In particular, it compares the systems along various dimensions and provides pointers to other work. Then, in Chapter 4, the process of development itself is addressed, with a detailed analysis of several agent-oriented methodologies and notations to support development. As agent technologies become more mature and are deployed in an increasing number of applications, the role of standards will become increasingly important. Chapter 5 describes the work to date on the establishment of standards primarily in agent systems, but also in related areas, for supporting systems interoperability in particular. In Chapter 6, the relation of agent technology to other existing technologies is explored, outlining how existing middleware, for example, can be used to support agent systems development. Finally, in Chapter 7, a review of the various other resources that are available for agent systems is provided. This details the organizations, events, literature, and Web portals that can be used for further investigation of particular subareas, or simply for more general coverage of the broader field. The field of agent-based computing is large and varied, and Chapter 7 offers a way to move beyond the material presented in this book.

References

[1] Wooldridge, M. J., and N. R. Jennings, "Intelligent Agents: Theory and Practice," *Knowledge Engineering Review*, Vol. 10, No. 2, 1995, pp. 115–152.

[2] d'Inverno, M., M. Luck, and UKMAS Contributors, "Multi-Agent Systems Research into the 21st Century," *Knowledge Engineering Review*, Vol. 16, No. 3, 2001, pp. 271–275.

[3] Luck, M., and M. d'Inverno, "A Formal Framework for Agency and Autonomy," *Proceedings of the First International Conference on Multi-Agent Systems*, Menlo Park, CA: AAAI Press / MIT Press, 1995, pp. 254–260.

[4] Franklin, S., and A. Graesser, "Is It an Agent, or Just a Program? A Taxonomy for Autonomous Agents," *Intelligent Agents III — Proceedings of the Third International Workshop on Agent Theories, Architectures, and Languages, Lecture Notes in Artificial Intelligence,* J. P. Müller, M. Wooldridge, and N. Jennings, (eds.), Volume 1193 of *LNCS*, Springer, 1997, pp. 21–35.

[5] Johnson, W. L., and B. Hayes-Roth, (eds.), *Proceedings of the First International Conference on Autonomous Agents*, New York: ACM Press, 1997.

[6] Genesereth, M. R., and S. P. Ketchpel, "Software Agents," *Communications of the ACM*, Vol. 37, No. 7, 1994, pp. 48–53.

[7] Lashkari, Y., M. Metral, and P. Maes, "Collaborative Interface Agents," *Proceedings of the Twelfth National Conference on Artificial Intelligence*, 1994, pp. 444–449.

[8] Aylett, R., and M. Luck, "Applying Artificial Intelligence to Virtual Reality: Intelligent Virtual Environments," *Applied Artificial Intelligence*, Vol. 14, No. 1, 2000, pp. 3–32.

[9] Kuokka, D., and L. Harada, "Matchmaking for Information Agents," *Proceedings of the Fourteenth International Joint Conference on Artificial Intelligence*, 1995, pp. 672–679.

[10] Chess, D., et al., "Itinerant Agents for Mobile Computing," *IEEE Personal Communications*, Vol. 2, No. 5, 1995, pp. 34–49.

[11] Wong, D., N. Paciorek, and D. Moore, "Java-Based Mobile Agents," *Communications of the ACM*, Vol. 42, No. 3, 1999, pp. 92–102.

[12] Etzioni, O., et al., "The Softbot Approach to OS Interfaces," *IEEE Software*, Vol. 12, No. 4, 1995, pp. 42–51.

[13] Toomey, C., and W. Mark, "Satellite Image Dissemination Via Software Agents," *IEEE Expert*, Vol. 10, No. 5, 1995, pp. 44–51.

[14] Jennings, N. R., and T. Wittig, "ARCHON: Theory and Practice," *Distributed Artificial Intelligence: Theory and Praxis*, N. Avouris and L. Gasser, (eds.), ECSC, EEC, EAEC, 1992, pp. 179–195.

[15] Kinny, D., M. Georgeff, and A. Rao, "A Methodology and Modelling Technique for Systems of BDI Agents," *Agents Breaking Away: Proceedings of the Seventh European Workshop on Modelling Autonomous Agents in a Multi-Agent World, Lecture Notes in Artificial Intelligence 1038*, Y. Demazeau and J.-P. Müller (eds.), New York: Springer, 1996, pp. 56–71.

[16] Jennings, N. R., et al., "Agent-Based Business Process Management," *International Journal of Cooperative Information Systems*, Vol. 5, Nos. 2 & 3, 1996, pp. 105–130.

[17] Guttman, R. H., A. G. Moukas, and P. Maes, "Agent-Mediated Electronic Commerce: A Survey," *Knowledge Engineering Review*, Vol. 13, No. 2, 1998, pp. 147–159.

[18] Grand, S., and D. Cliff, "Creatures: Entertainment Software Agents with Artificial Life," *Autonomous Agents and Multi-Agent Systems*, Vol. 1, No. 1, 1998, pp. 39–57.

[19] Etzioni, O., and D. Weld, "Intelligent Agents on the Internet: Fact, Fiction, and Forecast," *IEEE Expert*, Vol. 10, No. 4, 1995, pp. 44–49.

[20] Luck, M., P. McBurney, and C. Preist, *Agent Technology: Enabling Next Generation Computing (A Roadmap for Agent Based Computing)*, Southampton, England: AgentLink, 2003.

Chapter 2

Agent Architectures

2.1 INTRODUCTION

Although much of the value of the agent paradigm relates to the ways in which multiple agents come together to achieve complex tasks, the starting point of agent-based computing comprises the individual agents themselves. Exactly what kind of computational entity is an agent? In Chapter 1, we considered agents in a broad sense, but didn't really delve into their design or architecture.

There are two key reasons why agent architectures are important. The first is that we want to both predict and explain the behavior of an agent system based on its current state and that of the environment. The second is concerned with providing a methodology or blueprint of how to go about building real agent systems. In this chapter, therefore, we provide a general background to agent systems by showing some of the variety of ways in which the agent metaphor has been interpreted and implemented. We aim to discuss the benefits and limitations of each approach and thereby provide the reader with an insight into the issues involved in developing agent-based software in general.

We identify four agent architecture categories and review key examples we consider to be representative of each. The categories are *reactive architectures*, *deliberative architectures*, *hybrid architectures*, and *distributed agent architectures*. In general, *architectures* provide information about essential data structures, relationships between these data structures, the processes or functions that operate on these data structures, and the operation or execution cycle of an agent.

Typically, *single* agent architectures fall into one of three categories based on their architectures [1], as follows:

- *Reactive agent systems* act by means of stimulus-response rules and do not symbolically represent their environment.
- *Deliberative agent systems* symbolically model their environment and manipulate these symbols in order to act.
- *Hybrid agent systems* can act both deliberatively and reactively.

Single-agent architectures result from what is referred to as the *microlevel* design perspective where the focus is on the individual agent. The *macrolevel* design perspective, on the other hand, describes the stance taken when dealing with the social or global dimensions of a distributed agent system. Such systems are designed at a holistic level as well as at the microlevel of individual agents. In particular, consideration of the macrolevel of agent design is used in the construction of *distributed* agent systems. In order to introduce the basic issues involved in constructing distributed intelligent systems, in this chapter we focus on perhaps the best-known technique for dynamically managing task allocation in a distributed system, the *contract net protocol*. We also outline the more recent Agentis framework for building interactive multiagent applications, which is based upon an agent interaction model whose central elements are services and tasks. Key to the operation of the Agentis system is the set of protocols that permits reliable concurrent request and provision of services and tasks from and to agents, based on an underlying asynchronous point-to-point messaging infrastructure.

In this chapter, we provide overviews of example systems and highlight the most relevant benefits and limitations. Sections 2.2, 2.3, and 2.4 consider examples of reactive, deliberative, and hybrid single-agent architectures, respectively, all designed at the microlevel. Distributed agent architectures are described in Section 2.5. These systems, which include a macrolevel design perspective, are collections of agents that interact in some prespecified way to fulfill the *global goals* of the system as well as the agents' own local goals. The next section considers several other approaches to building agent systems not covered previously. The final section discusses issues relating to the construction of agent systems in general and presents some conclusions about the current state of agent technology.

2.2 REACTIVE AGENT ARCHITECTURES

The traditional AI view is that in order for software agents to exhibit intelligent behavior, they need an internal (symbolic) representation of their environment. The agents then can manipulate and reason about this internal representation in order to determine what to do next. However, some have argued that effective behavior does not necessarily require symbolic representation and manipulation, a view strengthened by the problems that have emerged in mainstream artificial intelligence such as the complexity and, in some cases, intractability, of some symbolic manipulation problems such as planning. (Essentially, planning is the process of constructing a sequence of actions which, when performed in order, will achieve some of its goals.) This is because symbolic reasoning is very resource- and time-intensive in determining the best action to perform next, so that by the time the action is performed, the environment may have changed in such a way that the action is no longer useful. In this case, the agent could be said to have failed. The opposite view is that effective behavior is only achieved when systems are *situated* and *embodied* in the real world, and can respond to events in the environment in a timely fashion. In this view, agent behavior is directly coupled with the world, typically incorporating *stimulus-response* rules; the environment provides a stimulus that causes a rule to fire and the agent to respond in specified way.

Agents that do not maintain a symbolic representation of their environment are known as *reactive agents*, and their architectures as *reactive* architectures. Such reactive systems were originally proposed by Brooks, who developed the *subsumption architecture* for controlling the behavior of a robot. In a similar fashion, Maes, a former colleague of Brooks, developed the *agent network architecture*, built upon the principle that intelligent behavior is an emergent phenomenon arising from the interaction of "societies of nonintelligent systems." Both architectures are considered next.

2.2.1 Subsumption Architecture

Brooks proposed the subsumption architecture as a means of controlling the behavior of a mobile robot in real time, with three basic requirements [2], as follows:

- Agents should be able to cope with multiple goals. For example, an agent might have the goal of moving to a certain location in its environment, directly ahead of it, as quickly as possible, while at the same time also possessing the goal to avoid obstacles. Clearly, when there is an obstacle in the path of an agent, these goals conflict, and any control mechanism for the robot needs to determine which of the goals takes priority.
- Agents should have multiple sensors. In general, physical agents have several different sensors (including infra red cameras and acoustic range-finders, for example) each with the possibility of giving erroneous or conflicting readings. Agents must be able to make decisions in these difficult circumstances.
- Agents should be robust. Essentially, this refers to two aspects: first, agents must be able to function (albeit possibly less effectively) when some sensors fail; second, agents should be able to behave effectively when the environment is changing drastically around them.

The approach taken by Brooks is not a functional one in which component parts are isolated according to perception, action, reasoning, planning, and so on, with some overarching central control mechanism. Instead, it is achieved using an entirely different approach, the *layered approach*. Here, the architecture comprises several *task-achieving behaviors*, each of which is implemented separately and arranged as shown in Figure 2.1. The hierarchy of layers reflects how specific a behavior is; the more specific the task, the higher the layer. In the case of the mobile robot, there are eight layers of behavior, from 1 to 8, as follows.

1. Avoid contact with objects in the environment;
2. Wander aimlessly;
3. Explore the environment;
4. Build a map of the environment and plan routes within it;
5. Notice change in the environment;
6. Reason about and identify objects in the world, and perform certain tasks related to certain objects;
7. Build and execute plans that involve changing the world in some desirable way;

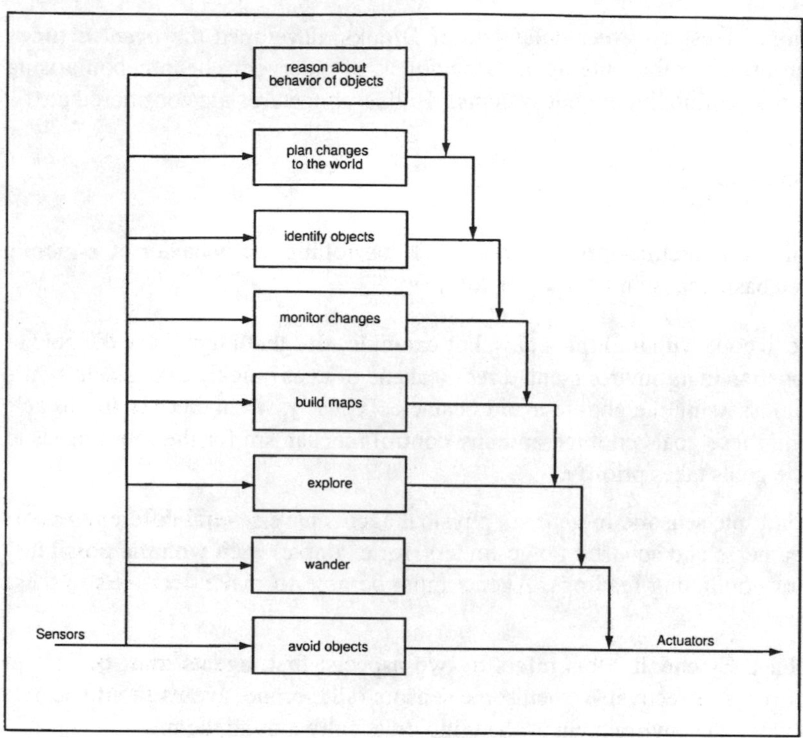

Figure 2.1 The subsumption architecture.

8. Reason about the behavior of other objects and how it might impact on plans, and consequently modify plans.

The different layers exist in parallel, with each unaware of the other layers that are above it, but able to examine data from lower layers. Each layer is connected to the sensors and actuators, but extracting only those aspects of the world (from the sensors) that are relevant to its function. In addition, layers can prevent lower layers from trying to control the behavior of the agent by suppressing their inputs and inhibiting their outputs.

The first step in the agent's construction is to build the *0th* control layer and, once this has been tested, to build the *1st* control layer on top of the 0th layer. The 1st layer has access to the data at layer 0 and can also inject data to suppress the normal activity of the 0th layer. The 0th layer continues to execute, unaware that there is a higher layer intermittently influencing its behavior. This process can then be repeated for each successive layer, with each layer competing to control the behavior of the robot. In this way, the control system functions at a very early stage of system development, with higher layers being added as required without having to change the existing lower-layer architecture.

The robot architecture showed that robots could be designed by decomposing the control problem by *behavior* rather than using *functional* modules. The approach combines a modular structure with a clear control methodology, and supports a neat way of modeling the different levels of abstraction of the world and the reasoning required at each level. In this sense, it has had a significant impact on agent architectures in general, forming the basis for many hybrid architectures such as INTERRRAP [3] and TouringMachines [4]. These latter architectures, which we consider later in this chapter, also contain different levels of abstraction, each of which competes for control over an agent's actuators.

By itself, however, the subsumption architecture does not support any *explicit* reasoning, and it is not clear that it can be scaled up to domains requiring more sophisticated problem-solving behavior. In addition, the design of its layers was done on a rather ad hoc basis, and led by intuition rather than a clear methodology or set of guiding principles. Systems built on the subsumption architecture are quite complex and idiosyncratic, and it is almost impossible for any formal investigation of the properties of such systems. This makes it difficult to predict or explain such an agent's behavior in a given environmental scenario.

2.2.2 Agent Network Architecture

Building on some of the ideas of the subsumption architecture, and on those of Minsky [5], who has argued that intelligent systems consist of societies of mindless interacting systems, Maes developed the agent network architecture (ANA) [6]. The ANA consists of a collection of *competence modules*, each of which competes to control behavior. This competition depends on the *activation* of a module which, in turn, depends on both *external* and *internal* considerations. The former includes whether a module is executable, the agent's perception of the environment, and the current goals of the agent. However, the novelty of ANA lies in the internal mechanism by which modules affect the activation of other modules through *links* between them. Activated modules increase the activation of their *successors*, nonexecutable models activate their *predecessors*, and all modules decrease the activation of their *conflictors*.

For example, Maes considers modeling the behavior of an agent in drinking from a cup. She supposes that the agent has two permanent goals, to relieve its thirst and to be polite, the latter requiring the agent to move the cup to its mouth rather than its mouth to the cup. If the agent is thirsty in a situation in which the data observed includes the presence of a cup, then two modules, *drink* and *recognize-cup*, are activated. Once the external activation is calculated, the internal activation is considered. Then, since in this scenario the *recognize-cup* module is currently executable, activation spreads from this module to its successors, from all other modules to their predecessors, and from every module to all their conflictors. Finally, the activation of each module is inspected and, if one surpasses a threshold value, it becomes activated and controls the behavior of the agent.

Like Brooks, Maes argues that such an architecture is attractive because it is distributed, modular, and robust. However, while it represents a novel approach for constructing autonomous agents, and does provide some evidence that cognitive functions can be implemented in terms of simple behaviors, just like the subsumption architecture, it is difficult to see how it could be extended to achieve more rational behavior, or to provide a paradigm for designing agent applications in general.

2.3 DELIBERATIVE AGENT ARCHITECTURES

Agent systems able to maintain and manipulate representations of the world, without stimulus-response rules of the kind described above, are often called *deliberative agents* [1]. In order to model *rational* or *intentional* agency in these kinds of agents, mentalistic notions, or *mental attitudes* are used to describe and characterize behavior. These attitudes include beliefs, goals, desires, knowledge, plans, motivations, and intentions, and are commonly grouped into three categories: informative, motivational, and deliberative [7]. The first category refers to that which a system considers to be true about the world, and includes knowledge, beliefs, and assumptions; the second refers to the *wants* of a system, including goals, desires, and motivations; and the third concerns how an agent's behavior is directed and includes plans and intentions. The distinction between the second and third categories is subtle, since it is possible that a system may *desire* a certain state without planning for it, or without *intending* it to happen.

There are several compelling reasons why agents defined using mental attitudes might be useful. First, if an agent can be described in terms of what it knows, what it wants, and what it intends, then, since it is modeled on familiar concepts, it becomes possible for users to understand and predict its behavior. Second, understanding the relationship between these different attitudes and how they affect behavior can provide the control mechanism for *intelligent action* in general. Third, computational agents designed in this way may be able to interpret the behavior of others independently from any implementation.

As stated in Chapter 1, this book does not adhere to any particular stance on the nature of agents or their mental attitudes. However, many agent systems include a deliberative architecture to support reasoning at the mental-attitude level. Moreover, many of these deliberative architectures are based on the *belief-desire-intention* (BDI) model of rational agency.

2.3.1 BDI Architecture

Although not a system, the BDI model provides a foundation for many systems and we therefore consider it separately as an abstract architecture in its own right. Arguably, the most successful agent architectures are founded on the BDI model, in which agents continually monitor their environments and act to change them, based on the three mental attitudes of belief, desire, and intention, representing informational, motivational, and decision-making capabilities. Architectures based on the BDI model explicitly represent beliefs, desires, and intentions as data structures, which determine the *operation* of the agent.

The intuition with BDI systems is that an agent will not, in general, be able to achieve *all* its desires, even if these desires *are* consistent. Agents must therefore fix upon some subset of available desires and commit resources to achieving them. These chosen desires are *intentions*, and an agent will typically continue to try to achieve an intention until either it believes the intention is satisfied, or it believes the intention is no longer achievable [8].

Many *formal* models have been devised in order to investigate and analyze the relationships between belief, desire, and intention. Much of this work investigates how *modal* and *temporal* logics can be used to specify theories of agent behavior. For example, Cohen and Levesque [8], Kinny et al. [9], Jennings [10], Haddadi [11], and Wooldridge [12] have all proposed such models. These models are often underpinned using the *possible-worlds* semantics first proposed by Hintikka [13]. Using this as a basis, it is possible to develop BDI modal logics that determine how different relationships between the mental attitudes produce different agent behavior.

As well as the formal models of BDI agents that specify desired behaviors of BDI agents, generic BDI architectures that encapsulate the BDI model have been constructed to support the design of practical agents [14], and programming languages have been proposed that can be used to implement BDI agents that satisfy some of the formal BDI properties [15]. In addition, BDI agents have been used extensively in real-world applications [16]. Many of the architectures and systems that are discussed in this chapter have been influenced by models of BDI, including the *Intelligent Resource-Bounded Machine Architecture* (IRMA) [17] and, arguably the best known and most established architecture, the *Procedural Reasoning System* (PRS). Both of these agent systems can be considered to be *deliberative*, and are considered next.

2.3.2 Procedural Reasoning System

Since the mid-1980s, many control architectures for practical reasoning agents have been proposed. Most of these have been deployed only in limited artificial environments; very few have been applied to realistic problems, and even fewer have led to the development of useful field-tested applications. The most notable exception is the Procedural Reasoning System (PRS). Originally described in 1987 [18], PRS has progressed from an experimental LISP version to a fully fledged C++ implementation known as the *distributed MultiAgent Reasoning System* (dMARS), which has been applied in perhaps the most significant multiagent applications to date [16].

For example, Oasis [19] is a system for air traffic management that can handle the flow of over 100 aircraft arriving at an airport. It addresses issues of scheduling aircraft, comparing actual progress with established sequences of aircraft, estimating delays, and notifying controllers of ways to correct deviations. The prototype implementation comprised several different kinds of agents, including aircraft agents and coordinator agents, each of which was based around PRS. Oasis successfully completed operational tests at Sydney Airport in 1995. Similarly, dMARS has been used as the basis of an agent-based simulation system, Swarmm, developed for Australia's Defence Science and Technology Organisation to simulate air mission dynamics and pilot reasoning. More recent work has sought to apply dMARS to represent different roles in an organization in more general business software for running call centers or Internet services. The Agentis system allowed the generation of fully automated, server-side customer-service applications, and the first major installation aimed to use 4,000 dMARS agents.

The PRS architecture has its conceptual roots in the BDI model of practical reasoning developed by Bratman and colleagues [17]. As Figure 2.2 shows, a BDI architecture typically contains four

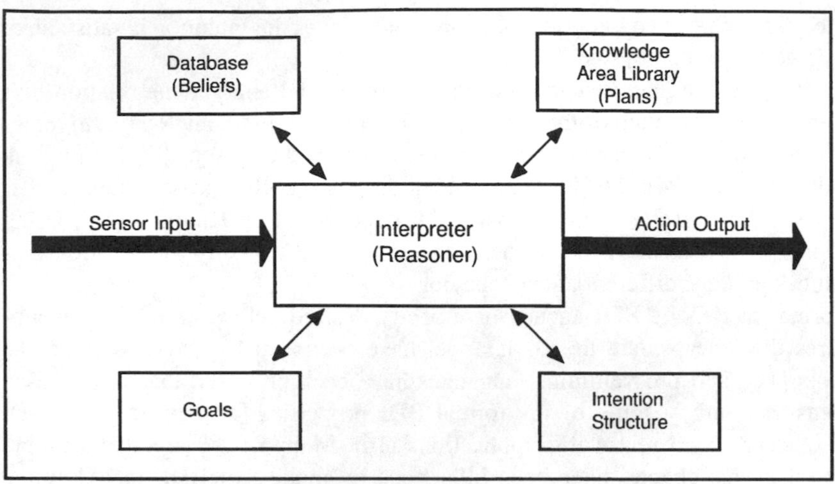

Figure 2.2 The PRS architecture.

key data structures: beliefs, goals, intentions, and a plan library. An agent's *beliefs* correspond to information the agent has about the world, which may be incomplete or incorrect. An agent's *desires* (or goals, in the system) intuitively correspond to the tasks allocated to it. Beliefs, desires, and intentions of PRS are represented explicitly in the *Database*, *Goalbase*, and *Intention Structure*, respectively. PRS agents continually respond to perceptions, or *events*, which represent new beliefs and goals, by selecting plans to become intentions.

In PRS agents, the BDI model is operationalized by *plans*. Each agent has a *plan library*, which is a set of plans, or *recipes*, specifying courses of action that may be undertaken by an agent in order to achieve its intentions. An agent's plan library represents its *procedural knowledge*, or *know-how*: knowledge about how to bring about states of affairs. Plans are designed by a programmer before run time to capture the procedural knowledge of the agent as recipes detailing courses of action. They are the main feature of PRS systems and comprise several components that we describe here.

The *trigger* or *invocation* specifies what an agent must perceive in order for a plan to become a contender for execution selection. For example, the plan *make tea* may be triggered by the event *thirsty*. In addition, the plan's *context* must be believed by the agent before the plan can be adopted for execution. For example, the plan *make tea* might have the context *have tea bags*. The *plan body* captures procedural knowledge as an OR-tree with arcs labeled with formulas that may be primitive external actions such as C++ function calls, internal actions such as adding a fact to its database, query goals that are matched to the agent's beliefs, or, finally, achieve goals that generate new subgoals. This *make tea* plan might have the body *get boiling water; add tea bag to cup; add water to cup*. Here, *get boiling water* is a subgoal (something that must be achieved when plan execution reaches this point in the plan), whereas *add tea bag to cup* and *add water to cup* are primitive actions (i.e., actions that can be performed directly by the agent).

At the start of execution, agents are initialized with a set of plans, goals, beliefs, an empty event buffer, and no intentions. The *operation* of the agent can then be enumerated as follows:

1. Perceive the world, and update the set of events.
2. For each event, generate the set of plans whose trigger condition matches the event. These are known as the *relevant* plans of an event.
3. For each event, select the subset of relevant plans whose context condition is satisfied by the agent's current beliefs. These plans are known as *active* plans.
4. From the set of active plans, select one for execution so that it is now an intention.
5. Include this new intention in the current intention structure either by creating a new intention stack or by placing it on the top of an existing stack.
6. Select an intention stack, take the topmost intention, and execute the next formula in it.

In this way, when a plan starts executing, its subgoals will be posted on the event queue, which in turn will cause plans that achieve this subgoal to become active, and so on. Once the intention stack executes successfully, the event is removed from the event queue. This is the basic execution model of dMARS agents. Note that agents do no first-principles planning at all, as all plans must be generated by the agent programmer at design time. The planning performed by agents consists entirely of context-sensitive subgoal expansion, which is deferred until a point in time at which the subgoal is selected for execution.

As mentioned above, a whole range of practical development efforts relating to BDI systems have been undertaken, and can be divided into those that are almost straightforward reimplementations and refinements of PRS and dMARS on the one hand, and those that are more loosely based on broader BDI principles. The former category includes systems such as UM-PRS developed at the University of Michigan, a freely available reimplementation of PRS [20], PRS-Lite developed at SRI by Myers [21], Huber's JAM system [22], and the commercial JACK system [23], which are respectively increasingly sophisticated. The latter category includes Bratman's IRMA architecture [17], Burmeister and Sundermeyer's COSY [24], and the GRATE* system developed by Jennings [25]. Nevertheless, PRS and dMARS remain as the exemplar BDI systems.

2.3.3 AgentSpeak(L)

Rao's AgentSpeak(L) [15] is an attempt to provide an operational and proof-theoretic semantics for a language that can be viewed as an abstraction of an implemented BDI system. Essentially, it captures the essence of a PRS system; the only PRS constructs not included in AgentSpeak(L) are simply those that have been designed to make programming tasks more efficient.

As we have seen above, agents have beliefs (about themselves, others, and the environment) and intentions, which are sequences of plans (called *intended means*). Each agent has a library of plans, and each plan comprises a trigger, context, and body, which is a *sequence* of *actions* and *goals* (collectively called *formulas*).

The basic operation of an AgentSpeak(L) agent is similar to PRS and has two aspects. The first concerns agents responding to internal events (new subgoals) and external events (new beliefs) by selecting appropriate plans. If the event queue is nonempty, an event is selected and those plans whose trigger matches the event are identified as relevant plans. Those relevant plans whose context is satisfied by the current beliefs become the *active* plans. From this set, one plan, called the *intended means*, is selected nondeterministically. Now, if the event that generated the intended means is external, the intended means creates a new intention. If the event is internal, then the intended means is pushed onto the intention whose top plan's current formula is the subgoal that generated the event.

The second aspect of the agent's operation is the execution of intentions. First, an intention is selected, and the next formula in the top plan of that intention is evaluated. If the formula is an action, it is placed in a buffer. If the formula is a *query goal*, and if it is satisfiable with respect to the beliefs using a substitution, the substitution is applied to the rest of the executing plan. Alternatively, if the formula is an *achieve goal*, then a new goal event is added to the set of events to be processed.

The AgentSpeak(L) language is a significant attempt to unite the theory and practice of BDI agents, but again, the link between mental attitudes as data structures in implemented systems [as modeled by AgentSpeak(L)] and as modal operators in the theoretical model is weak. Rao simply suggests that we, as designers, should *ascribe* these theoretical notions to implemented agents, rather than suggesting that there is an approach to defining a formal relationship between them.

In the next section, we briefly discuss IRMA, which is important because it was the first attempt, by Bratman himself among others, to build an architecture that captured the ideas to explain the BDI theory of resource-bounded reasoning. It also offers an alternative view of instantiating the BDI model.

2.3.4 IRMA

In considering the problem of enabling agents to perform means-ends reasoning, to weigh competing alternative plans of action, and to cope with interaction between these two forms of reasoning in a resource-bounded way, Bratman proposed a high-level architecture, subsequently implemented as IRMA [17]. This architecture, based on the BDI model, recognizes that agents will always be computationally limited or *resource-bounded*, and that suboptimal decisions may have to be made.

As with PRS, IRMA explicitly represents the beliefs, desires, and intentions of an agent as data structures in the system. In IRMA, once a plan has been selected for execution it becomes an *active* plan, and therefore an intention. IRMA's reasoning cycle is based around five key processes, comprising the *opportunity analyzer*, the *means-end reasoner*, the *compatibility filter*, the *filter override mechanism*, and the *deliberation process*, described below.

Initially, IRMA perceives its environment and updates its beliefs. Then, using the *opportunity analyzer* it must check whether its current goals have been inadvertently achieved, whether existing intentions can no longer be realized, or whether new alternative plans can be proposed. Goals are achieved by presenting them to the *means-end reasoner*, which attempts to generate new subplans. Plans from both the opportunity analyzer and the means-end reasoner are passed to the filtering process made up of the *compatibility filter* and the *filter override mechanism*, which run in parallel.

The role of the compatibility filter is to ascertain whether new plans are consistent with the existing intentions of the agent. Typically, incompatible plans are discarded but, in some cases, if they satisfy certain properties, they can be passed to the *deliberation process* by the filter override mechanism instead. When the override mechanism intervenes in this way, existing incompatible intentions are suspended. Next, the deliberation process determines how the plans it is passed after filtering affect the current intention structure. This intention structure simply comprises plans that have been selected for execution, and may be updated to accommodate new plans, when appropriate.

IRMA has been demonstrated and tested in the Tileworld simulation environment [26], which showed that given appropriate overriding mechanisms, committing to plans by means of intentions is a useful strategy for effective agent behavior in a dynamic environment.

The real benefit of both IRMA and PRS is that they are built from a clear conceptual model of the relationship between beliefs, goals, intentions, and plans. One problem, however, is that neither architecture provides designers with guidance on *how* an agent makes decisions based on its mental state, nor do they provide general rules of how to construct agent plans before run time. In addition, although it is possible to simulate reactive behavior by building plans appropriately, this is not an efficient or effective way of doing so, since reactive responses can only take place at the end of each (quite long-winded) operation cycle of these agents.

The inherent limitations of both the reactive and the deliberative approach have led to *hybrid* architectures, in which the two are combined. We consider these next.

2.4 HYBRID AGENT ARCHITECTURES

In general, agents can be neither totally deliberative nor totally reactive. If they are only reactive, they cannot reason about their actions and will not be able to achieve any sophisticated behavior; if they are just deliberative they may never be able to act in time.

It is now generally recognized, therefore, that if agent systems are to survive in real and complex environments they need to be reactive in order to respond to environmental changes with sufficient speed, *and* be deliberative in order to achieve complex goals without deleteriously affecting longer-term options [27]. If environments change rapidly or unexpectedly, agents may need to act in a reactive manner, whereas more stable environments may allow agents time to deliberate on the best course of action. Architectures containing both deliberative and reactive components are *hybrid* architectures, of which two key examples, TouringMachines [4] and INTERRRAP [28], are discussed next.

2.4.1 TouringMachines

Ferguson proposed *TouringMachines* as an architecture for controlling and coordinating the actions of autonomous agents situated in dynamic multiagent worlds. He argued that agents operating in the real world would inevitably have to deal with several issues that had not—at that time—been considered in the vast array of architectures that exhibited quite well-defined preprogrammed behavior. Such architectures would need to address a number of possibly conflicting issues, as follows:

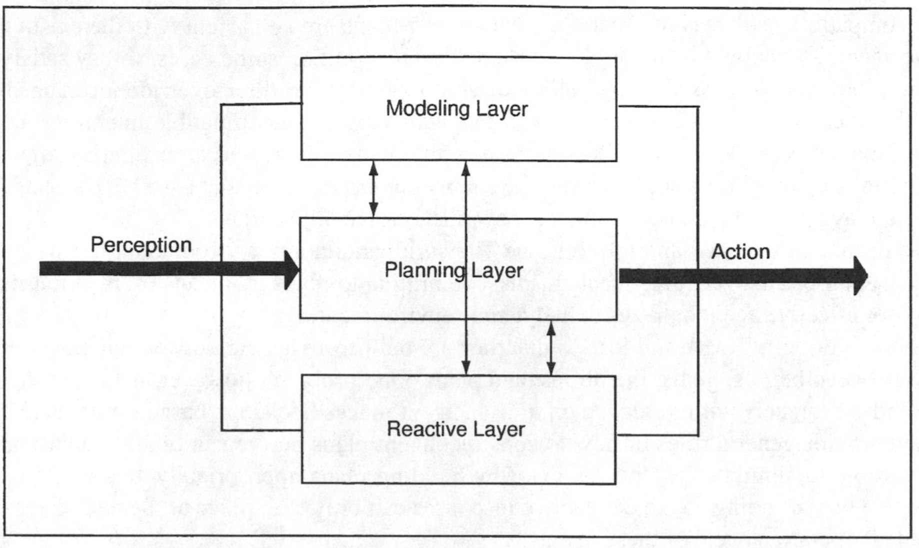

Figure 2.3 The TouringMachines architecture. (*After:* [27].)

- They need the ability to deal with unexpected events in the real (physical or electronic) world, and do so at different levels of granularity.
- They need to deal with the dynamism in the environment created by the actions of other agents.
- They must pay attention to environmental change.
- They need to reason about temporal constraints in the knowledge that computation is necessarily resource-bounded.
- They must reason about the impact the short-term actions may have on long-term goals.

In response, Ferguson proposed the TouringMachines architecture, illustrated in Figure 2.3 [27]. The architecture is similar to the subsumption architecture in that it consists of a number of layers, the *reactive layer*, the *planning layer*, and the *modeling layer*, which continually compete to control the agent's behavior. The reactive layer responds quickly to events not explicitly programmed in the other layers, such as when a new agent or obstacle is perceived. Generating, executing, and modifying *plans*, such as constructing a route in order to move to a target destination, are the responsibilities of the planning layer. Finally, the modeling layer is used for building and maintaining models of entities in the environment (including the agent itself), which are used to understand the current behaviors of others and make predictions about their future behaviors.

Each layer models the agent's world at a *different* level of abstraction but, unlike the subsumption architecture, each is directly connected to both the action and perception of the agent, and any two layers can communicate with each other. Since these layers are each modeled at different abstraction levels, they each have an incomplete view of the world, encoding different strategies and tactics for responding to events. Conflicts over action-selection therefore inevitably arise, so the architecture includes a set of global context-dependent control rules to achieve coherence between these layers, which work by suppressing either the input to, or the output from, a layer.

Ferguson showed that this architecture was feasible and appropriate for agents operating in dynamic environments. Moreover, he demonstrated that it was possible to integrate expensive deliberative reasoning mechanisms with reactive behavior-based components in a resource-bounded agent. The architecture is important because it showed that it could successfully produce a wide variety of behaviors from reactive through to goal-directed, all required of a sophisticated agent embedded in a complex environment.

2.4.2 INTERRAP

Müller et al. [3] also argued that layered hybrid architectures are beneficial as they support the modeling of an agent's environment at different levels of abstraction, the different times taken to respond to an action (responsiveness), and the levels of knowledge and reasoning sophistication required by an agent. However, they also acknowledge that the design of individual layers is often quite personal and not guided by any general theory of agency.

In response, they proposed an architecture that combines the advantages of BDI-style architectures and those of layered ones. This architecture, called INTERRAP, used the BDI model to guide the construction of each of the individual layers within the architecture.

The state of each layer is represented by beliefs, goals, and intentions, and each layer can receive what is known as *perceived propositions*. This means that each layer can perceive information from the environment, and from other layers, but this information is always in the form of simple propositions such as *at* (*agent* (*A*, *B*)). The architecture implements three basic functions at each layer, thus providing a uniform control structure for each layer. These are enumerated here:

- *Belief revision* maps an agent's current perception and current beliefs to a set of new beliefs. For example, an agent may perceive that an object has moved, and belief revision updates the agent's current beliefs accordingly.
- *Situation recognition and goal activation* take the current beliefs and goals and generate a new set of goals for the agent to try to achieve.
- *Planning and scheduling* derive a new set of intentions (what the agent is committed to doing) from the current set of beliefs, goals, and intentions of the agent.

The motivation for this kind of architecture is based around the interfaces between each of the three layers, and the ways in which layers can communicate with other layers. The developers of INTERRAP categorized Ferguson's TouringMachines architecture as *horizontally layered*—each layer can interact with every other layer, as well as with the perceptions and actions. In this kind

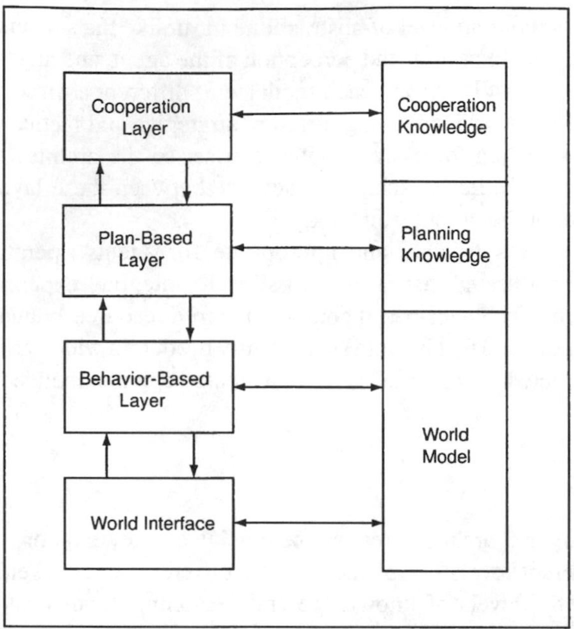

Figure 2.4 The INTERRRAP architecture. (*After:* [3].)

of architecture, many communication paths have to be considered and any centralized control would therefore need to be very sophisticated. In response, INTERRRAP is a *vertically layered* architecture in which layers are configured similarly, but where communication is only possible between *adjacent* layers. Clearly, in this model, fewer communication channels have to be designed. Consider a system with n layers, for example. If each layer can only communicate with adjacent layers in *both* directions, at most $2(n-1)$ channels will be required. In a horizontal architecture, the first layer alone requires $2(n-1)$ paths to communicate in both directions with every other layer, the next layer needs $2(n-2)$ paths to ensure communication with all succeeding layers, and so on. An n-layered horizontal architecture may therefore require anything up to $2n!$ communication paths. The disadvantage of vertically layered architectures is that for a layer to control behavior, the control must necessarily pass through all lower layers.

As indicated above, the INTERRRAP agent architecture [14] is an example of a vertically layered architecture and is shown in Figure 2.4, adapted from [3]. It comprises four layers that can communicate in both directions with adjacent layers. INTERRRAP was developed to model resource-bounded autonomous agents that interact with others in dynamic environments, while implementing a pragmatic BDI architecture. The control of the agent is contained in three different *hierarchical* layers known as the *behavior-based layer*, the *plan-based layer*, and the *cooperation-based layer*. While the behavior-based layer is always carefully modeled for specific domains, the others contain more generic information pertaining to goal-directed and social behavior.

The agent's knowledge base is correspondingly split into three layers. At the lowest level, the agent's *world model* comprises beliefs about the environment. At the next level, the *mental model* contains knowledge about the agent itself, including its goals, plans, and intentions. The *social model* is the highest level containing information about others and the current state of joint-plans, joint-goals, and joint-intentions. These three knowledge bases are respectively accessed and updated by the *behavior-based component*, *plan-based component*, and *cooperation component*. The lowest level allows agents to react to unforeseen events and to quickly execute routine tasks without any explicit deliberative reasoning. The plan-based layer allows nonsocial goal-directed behavior. Plans are either hierarchical templates that call other plans or are directly executable behaviors. Finally, the social level enables the agent to interact with others by coordinating actions and forming joint-plans.

The essential operation of the agent is simple; in response to events in the environment, control spreads upwards until the appropriate level is reached and the functions described earlier are applied accordingly. The benefits of decentralizing knowledge and behavior into layers must be weighed against the cost of communication between, and coordination of, these layers; this is analogous to problems determining the number of agents required for building multiagent applications. Extending this analogy—that the design of layered architectures is analogous to designing multiagent systems by treating each layer as an autonomous agent—the contract net protocol is proposed as a useful mechanism for coordinating the concurrent execution of symbolic reasoning at different layers. We discuss the contract net in more detail later in this chapter.

2.4.3 Other Hybrid Architectures

In more recent work on building agent development tools and architectures, agents typically have both reactive and deliberative components.

For example, the Sensible Agent Testbed, a set of tools for the building, running, monitoring, and testing of complex multiagent systems [29], involves hybrid agents. The agent architecture contains a *perspective modeler* that maintains an explicit model of an agent's subjective view of its environment. The model includes both the *behavioral* (reactive) and *intentional* (proactive) models of itself and others. Similarly, the *autonomy reasoner* dynamically determines the appropriate decision-making framework for the agent. One such framework is categorized as *command driven*, where the agent does not function deliberatively but simply obeys orders directly from a master agent without deliberating.

In another recent example, the DECAF agent toolkit (Distributed, Environment-Centered Agent Framework), which allows a well-defined software engineering method to be used in building multiagent systems, also uses a hybrid agent architecture [30]. On one hand, the deliberative element is incorporated using a plan editor that builds a symbolic representation of a plan to achieve some objective. On the other hand, the reactive component is the *executor* that simply takes a set of enabled actions and produces a set of low-level commitments to very specific courses of action.

(Note that there are counterexamples to the hybrid approach. One such is the CMUnited simulated soccer clients constructed to play in the RoboCup Soccer competitions [31]. Even the very basic primitive movement commands such as kicking and dribbling are *predictive* in that they take into account predicted world models as well as predicted effects of future actions to determine which primitive movement they should do next.)

2.5 DISTRIBUTED AGENT ARCHITECTURES

The architectures described above may enable agents to interact with other agents. However, the design of these systems is concerned with the individual agents and the dimensions required to interact effectively with others. The *macro*level, conversely, considers a multiagent system from a *holistic* perspective, where interaction, coordination, and cooperation between agents are designed in advance of run time. The concern here is with the global system structure and mechanisms to support interaction, including agent communication protocols, and to enable effective coordination [32]. Although coordination is not the focus of this chapter, it is appropriate in the context of considering agent architectures to review at least some common mechanisms that are useful in providing such a holistic viewpoint.

2.5.1 Contract Net Protocol

Almost certainly, the most commonly employed coordination mechanism for controlling the problem-solving behavior of a collection of distributed agents is the *contract net protocol* [33]. This is concerned with the dynamic configuration and coordination of agents to form hierarchies that can achieve complex, distributed tasks.

In the examples of architectures above, there is generally no consideration of issues of coordination. In many systems in which agents interact, the forms of interaction and the relationships between agents are static, representing an unalterable structure. Since much of the value of agent-based computing derives from its ability to address the issues that arise from dynamic and open environments, however, this is inadequate. By contrast, the contract net protocol (CNP), proposed by Smith and Davis [33], provides a mechanism by which nodes (or agents) can *dynamically* create relationships in response to the current processing requirements of the system as a whole, thereby enabling *opportunistic task allocation.*

In the contract net framework, a node with a task to be achieved forms *contracts* with others who proceed to accomplish this task. The steps to forming and maintaining a contract are defined by the *contract net protocol*, described as follows, and shown in Figure 2.5:

1. A node decomposes a task into a number of subtasks. For each subtask, the node issues a *task announcement* describing what needs to be performed, along with *eligibility* requirements detailing the necessary processing requirements to complete the task.

2. Once a node receives a task announcement, if it fulfills the eligibility specification, it may *bid* for the task. Essentially, nodes evaluate their interest using *task evaluation procedures* specific to the problem at hand. If a node has sufficient interest in a task announcement, it will submit a bid to undertake to perform the task. A node will not bid unless it is free to perform the task.

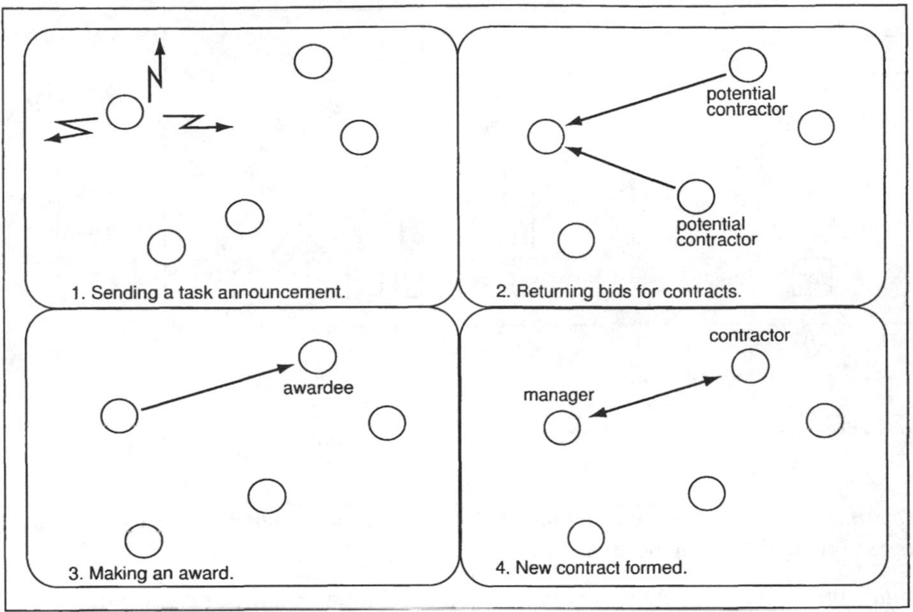

Figure 2.5 The contract net protocol.

3. Once all bids have been received by the original (potential manager) node, it ranks them according to criteria associated with the task, and *awards* a contract to the bidder with the highest ranked bid.

4. There is now a *contract* between the *manager* who made the task announcement and the bidder (the *contractor*) with the highest ranked bid. Over time, the manager monitors the problem-solving of the contractor, requesting progress reports or canceling the contract if necessary. The manager also integrates partial results from completed contracts to provide a complete solution to the original task.

5. The contractors issue reports to the manager, which may be *interim* reports, or *final* reports containing a result description. Finally, the manager terminates a contract with a *termination* message.

The messages passed between the agents include information relating to the task, so that other nodes can evaluate whether they are suited to perform that task. For example, when the CNP is applied to the simulation of a distributed sensing system, a task announcement includes three types of information [34], as follows:

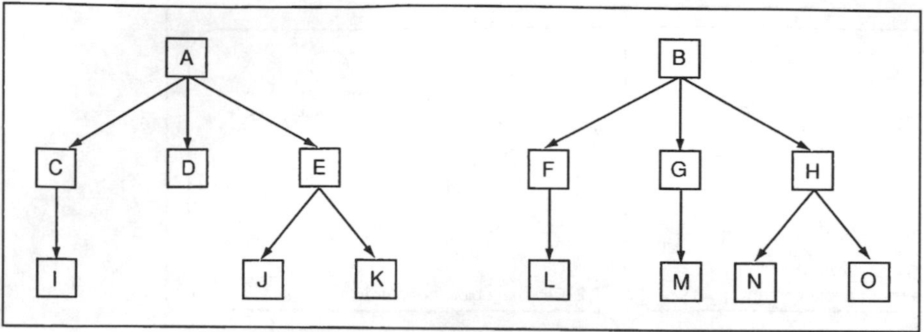

Figure 2.6 The contract net manager-contractor hierarchy.

- The *Task Abstraction Slot* specifies the identity and position of the manager that enables potential contractors to reply to the task announcement;
- The *Eligibility Specification* specifies the location and capabilities required by any bidders;
- The *Bid Specification* indicates that a bidder must specify its position and its sensing capabilities.

Contractor nodes may, in turn, subcontract parts of their task by announcing their own task announcements. In this way, the CNP is repeated with the contractor eventually becoming a manager for these subcontracts. This leads to a hierarchical configuration in the contract net, as shown in Figure 2.6.

The contract net protocol was a novel means for dynamically allocating tasks in distributed systems, and it is still commonly found in many agent systems. However, it should be pointed out that it offers a very simple coordination mechanism, and does not provide any strategies for global coherence. It is thus only suited to situations in which the tasks are easily decomposable into independent subtasks. In addition, it is only suitable if agents are not in conflict, since it does not support mechanisms for *bargaining* or *negotiating* in general. However, it does serve to illustrate the general principles involved when considering the design of systems from the macrolevel perspective.

2.5.2 Agentis

Agent communication languages (ACLs) occupy a central position in the field of multiagent systems, underpinning the ability of different and heterogeneous agents to effectively interact. Efforts to develop and specify such languages continue, with perhaps the most significant languages to date being FIPA's ACL (see Chapter 5) and KQML, which have received much attention and interest for the last few years. At a basic level, communication languages do not encode information about how a particular message is received and used by a recipient in the context of a broader interaction—the higher-level structure that is required for effective and coherent agent interaction also needs to be investigated. (Some languages, such as FIPA ACL, are also tied to particular interaction protocols; Chapter 5 considers this further.)

The Agentis system is a framework for building interactive applications, and employs a set of just such protocols to ensure the reliable concurrent request and provision of services and tasks from and to agents. This is achieved in the context of an underlying asynchronous point-to-point messaging infrastructure (i.e., the standard one provided by dMARS [35]).

Agentis incorporates an *agent interaction model* that is based on well-defined notions of *services* and tasks. Services are units of work performed by Agentis agents. The usual flow of control is that a human user of the system requests one or more services, via a *user interface process*, from an agent dedicated to serving that user. Agents may also request and provide services from and to other agents, or from other interface processes such as database servers. Tasks are smaller units of work whose performance is part of the *service contract* that is created when an agent accepts a service request. For example, a user may be obliged to perform one or more information provision tasks to enable an agent to successfully complete a service.

In an Agentis system, a set of standard agents provide predefined services for process control and monitoring, user login and session management, and event logging. There are also user-configurable agents that provide user-defined services (specified in a high-level, dMARS-like, graphical process description language). In addition, a system may contain nonagent interface processes, such as user, database, or WWW interfaces that can request services from, or provide services to, Agentis agents. The framework is designed to be flexible and scalable, and to decouple the specification of custom application-dependent behavior from standard functionality. This makes it easy to design, configure, modify, and extend application systems whose key characteristic is that their behavior may be specified as sets of interactive event-driven or goal-driven processes.

The protocol set provides the ability to request, accept, or decline services and tasks, to return execution status information and output values progressively as they become available, and to cancel, suspend and resume services and tasks prior to completion. In addition, it is designed to guarantee that protocol message collisions are benign, that deadlocks do not occur, and that other constraints, such as the requirement that a task request only occurs in the context of a service provision, are enforced. It also includes a registration facility that provides service description, access control, and the ability for a service provider to inform a requestor about changes in service availability, as well as the ability to send simple notices or queries.

2.5.3 Other Approaches to Macrolevel Organization

Building agents that work together in a society for both individual and social value is clearly fundamental to building robust and effective multiagent systems in general. One such architecture, mentioned earlier, is DECAF, a software environment for the rapid design, development, and execution of intelligent agents to function together effectively in complex domains. This platform provides a means to evaluate such key social concepts as communication, planning, action scheduling, execution monitoring, coordination, and learning [30]. The focus of DECAF is not on implementing specific agent architectures nor on building the basic communication primitives but rather on how generic behaviors can be reused, how plans can be easily built using a graphical editor, and how various existing middle-agents can be used.

Similarly, RETSINA [36] is a multiagent infrastructure that comprises a set of services, conventions, and knowledge that enable complex social interactions such as negotiation to take place. In this infrastructure the architecture of the individual agent is not considered, and all that is required is that the agent be "socially aware" and can communicate and interact with others and with the various infrastructural components supplied by RETSINA. It is claimed that the infrastructure can support any coordination scheme such as team behavior (see below), negotiation, and contract nets. What is deliberately not included in the architecture is any notion of *social norms* [37–40], which are rules or conventions that a society of agents abide by such as, for example, driving on the correct side of the road in a particular locality. RETSINA does not consider such norms as part of the infrastructure but as being particular to the design of specific multiagent systems. RETSINA is considered in more detail in Chapter 3 in terms of its role as a toolkit.

A final example of macrolevel approaches can be seen in *Teamcore*. The key motivating principle behind the Teamcore architecture is that an agent integration infrastructure (a set of services and conventions) based on theoretical principles of coordination can automate robust coordination among heterogeneous agents in distributed systems [41]. Existing theories of teamwork on joint intentions and shared plans provide the analytical model for designing coordination that can be used to provide certain guarantees of system behavior. Even with a set of diverse heterogeneous agents, as long as they act as team members, each member acts responsibly to others, covers for execution failures, and exchanges key information as required. Other related work includes the open agent architecture (OAA) [42], a centralized integration architecture, and the adaptive agent architecture (AAA) [43], which provides a distributed extension to OAA.

2.6 OTHER APPROACHES

2.6.1 AGENT0 and PLACA

In the examples so far, the focus has been on agent architectures to support the design of agent-based systems. Another approach to building agents is to design a programming language with semantics based on some theory of rational or intentional agency, such as the BDI model, and to program the desired behavior of individual agents directly using mental attitudes. Such a technique is referred to as *agent-oriented programming* (AOP). An agent-oriented program comprises a set of transition rules that specify how an agent in a given mental state will respond to an input, which may be a set of messages from other agents, by defining its new mental state and any outputs.

The language we describe here is PLACA [44], which extends the expressive power of AGENT0 [45] developed by Shoham, who introduced the concept of agent-oriented programs. We do not describe PLACA in detail, but include it simply as an example of an alternative approach, especially because of its formal nature, which provides a counterpoint to the earlier architectures in this chapter. This section thus only includes brief summaries, and the interested reader can explore further through the references.

When it was first introduced, AGENT0 (and later its successor, PLACA) represented a new programming paradigm that supported the notion of a *societal* view of computation in which agents would interact with each other in order to achieve their individual goals. Shoham asserted that an approach that could enable a system of agents to be built in this way needs three particular elements, as follows:

1. It requires a formal logical language to describe the mental state of each agent. Such mental state consists of beliefs and intentions, as we have seen in other systems described in this chapter.
2. It also needs a programming language with which to specify the agents and their behavior.
3. Finally, it needs a method for adapting nonagent legacy systems so that they can be incorporated into an agent system, thereby allowing agents to communicate with them by attributing beliefs and intentions.

A program in PLACA is defined by an initial mental state and a set of mental-state rules specifying how the mental state changes in various scenarios. At run time, an agent's state consists of *capabilities* and its mental state, which comprises *beliefs*, *intentions*, and *plans* (where plans, and possibly intentions, are initially empty). At every step, an agent collects messages that have been received from others from the *input buffer*, clears this buffer, and updates its mental state according to its defining program.

At the beginning of each execution step, those transition rules that are satisfied in the current state are identified, and applied to the current mental state and messages collected from the *input buffer*. Once the mental state is updated, messages that need to be sent are placed in the *output buffer*, and actions that need to be performed are recorded and executed in the next step. If there is sufficient time before the next tick of the *clock*, the *planner* may construct and refine current plans for satisfying intentions. A basic representation of the PLACA interpreter is shown in Figure 2.7.

PLACA is based on a modal logic specification of the relationship between the mental-state components. Its designers claim that PLACA agents satisfy all the axioms provided, but the relationship between the logic and the programming language is not well-defined. This is a persistent problem in the agent field: how to determine the correspondence between computational systems on the one hand, and formal models, typically constructed in modal logic, on the other. One approach to this problem is to carefully design temporal logics so that agents can be described using logic formulas that are directly executable, as we will see next.

2.6.2 Concurrent METATEM

The same societal view of computation as in AOP is also present in Concurrent METATEM [46], a programming language in which each agent is defined as a concurrently executing process, communicating with other such processes via message-passing. The distinct characteristic of this work is that agents are specified using a temporal logic that is directly *executable*. To directly execute a specification written in a temporal logic formula, the interpreter attempts to construct a model structure in which the agent specification is satisfied. However, since the environment is dynamic, it may

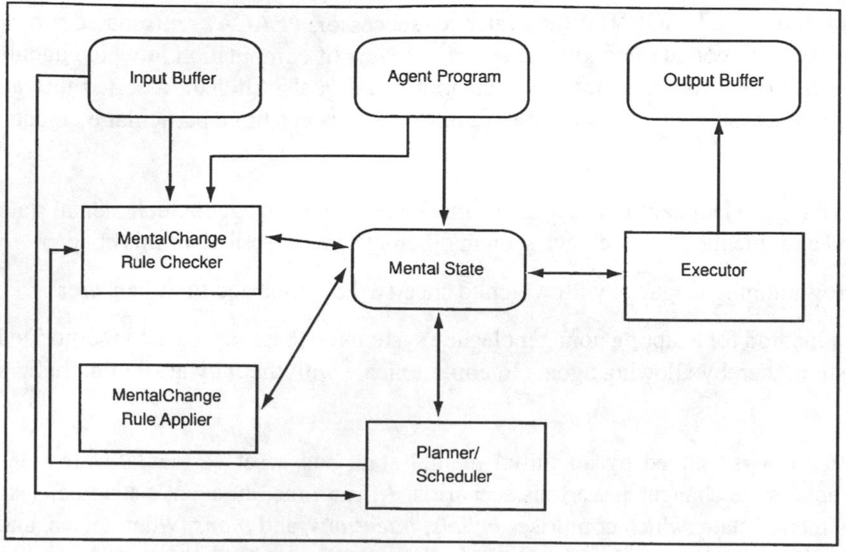

Figure 2.7 The PLACA interpreter. (*After:* [44].)

constantly be altering that model, so that responses must be made to what has just become true or untrue because of this dynamism.

The way in which the model is constructed in a dynamic environment is referred to as the *execution strategy*. When a Concurrent METATEM program is executed, it produces a sequence of temporally ordered states, each labeled with a model structure stating those propositions that are true. This trace provides Concurrent METATEM specifications with a concrete computational interpretation.

The basic form of a specification in Concurrent METATEM is as follows: "on the basis of what has happened in the past do something in the future." Thus, each agent is specified by a set of rules of the form:

$$past_i \Rightarrow future_j$$

and at each cycle, the precedent of each rule is matched against an internal history, firing if a match can be found. Once a rule fires, the agent is committed to the antecedent, which typically involves trying to make some predicate true.

As an example, consider the following Concurrent METATEM program, specifying the behavior of a controller agent solely responsible for supplying an infinitely renewable resource [47]. While the resource cannot be used by two agents at the same time, it is possible that the controller may be asked by two different agents for the resource simultaneously. The predicates $ask(x)$ and $give(x)$ mean that agent x has been asked for the resource, and that agent x has been given the resource, respectively.

In temporal logic, the formula, $\circ Form$, is satisfied at present if $Form$ is satisfied at the *next* time moment. Similarly, $\diamond Form$ is satisfied at present if $Form$ is true at some time in the future, and $F \mathcal{Z} G$ is satisfied if F is true *since* G has been true.

The specification of the controller agent is defined in Concurrent METATEM as follows:

$$\circ ask(x) \Rightarrow \diamond give(x) \tag{2.1}$$

$$(\neg ask(x) \mathcal{Z} (give(x) \wedge \neg ask(x))) \Rightarrow \neg give(x) \tag{2.2}$$

$$give(x) \wedge give(y) \Rightarrow (x = y) \tag{2.3}$$

These three formulas can be interpreted in English as follows:

1. If an agent asks, then eventually give the resource to that agent;
2. Do not give to anyone unless they have asked since you last gave to them;
3. If you give to two people, then they must be the same person.

Concurrent METATEM is attractive because it is directly executable so that no time-consuming and error-prone refinement is required in the process from specification to implementation. In addition, specifications have a concrete computational semantics defined by the sequence of models that arise through the constant interplay of the dynamic environment and the action of the agent. However, since the execution of Concurrent METATEM is based on theorem-proving, some standard problems arise such as the undecidability of first-order logic and the complexity involved in simple propositional logic. In addition, it is not clear how other modal operators commonly associated with agents such as belief, desire, and intention could be incorporated into the language while maintaining its directly executable property.

2.7 DISCUSSION

Agent designers generally recognize that agents require both deliberative and reactive architectural components in order to act effectively and efficiently in dynamic and uncertain environments with multiple conflicting goals. Indeed, as many have argued, from a practical viewpoint the difference between these architectures lies simply in the stage of the development process at which the system must reason; the design of the behavior of reactive agents occurs during their construction, whereas with deliberative agents it occurs at run time.

Similarly, multiagent systems may be developed incorporating both a microlevel and macrolevel design perspective. The distinction between the microlevel and macrolevel views is analogous in some respects to the distinction between deliberative and reactive architectures. The more a macrolevel stance is taken, the more the relationships and interactions are developed at design time. Alternatively, it is implicit in a microlevel stance that agents will form their own group relationships dynamically and participate in interactions in order to achieve their individual goals at run time.

In this chapter, we have described systems that have been successful in producing desirable aspects of agent behavior from different architectural paradigms. Our aim has been to show the range of architectures, and to outline the key aspects of each. Although we have not provided a detailed assessment of the different mechanisms, these are easily found in the literature. What we aim to have done is to provide a computational perspective on agents that will facilitate the discussion of the aspects covered later in the book.

There are many other sources for more details on these aspects. For example, Wooldridge and Jennings provide a comprehensive survey of theoretical and practical agent research [1], while Bond and Gasser [48], and more recently, Moulin and Chaib-draa [49], consider systems and theories in distributed artificial intelligence (DAI). Complementing this is a survey of software agents by Nwana [50] and industrial applications of DAI techniques by Parunak [32]. In this chapter, our aim has been more specific, providing a general background to agent systems by showing some of the variety of ways in which the agent metaphor has been interpreted and implemented. See Chapter 7 for details of relevant sources on agent-based computing in general.

References

[1] Wooldridge, M., and N. R. Jennings, "Agent Theories, Architectures, and Languages: A Survey," *Intelligent Agents: Theories, Architectures, and Languages,* M. Wooldridge and N. Jennings, (eds.), Volume 890 of *LNCS*, New York: Springer, 1995, pp. 1–39.

[2] Brooks, R. A., "A Robust Layered Control System for a Mobile Robot," *IEEE Journal of Robotics and Automation*, Vol. 2, No. 1, 1986, pp. 14–23.

[3] Müller, J. P., M. Pischel, and M. Thiel, "Modelling Reactive Behavior in Vertically Layered Agent Architectures," *Intelligent Agents: Theories, Architectures, and Languages, Lecture Notes in Artificial Intelligence 890,* M. Wooldridge and N. Jennings, (eds.), New York: Springer, 1995, pp. 261–276.

[4] Ferguson, I. A., "TouringMachines: An Architecture for Dynamic, Rational, Mobile Agents," Ph.D. thesis, Clare Hall, University of Cambridge, England, 1992 (also available as Technical Report No. 273, University of Cambridge Computer Laboratory).

[5] Minsky, M., *The Society of Mind*, New York: Simon and Schuster, 1985.

[6] Maes, P., "The Agent Network Architecture (ANA)," *SIGART Bulletin*, Vol. 2, No. 4, 1991, pp. 115–120.

[7] Kiss, G., "Goal, Values, and Agent Dynamics," *Foundations of Distributed Artificial Intelligence,* G. O'Hare and N. Jennings, (eds.), New York: John Wiley and Sons, 1996, pp. 247–268.

[8] Cohen, P. R., and H. J. Levesque, "Intention Is Choice with Commitment," *Artificial Intelligence*, Vol. 42, 1990, pp. 213–261.

[9] Kinny, D., et al., "Planned Team Activity," *Artificial Social Systems — Selected Papers from the Fourth European Workshop on Modelling Autonomous Agents in a Multi-Agent World, MAAMAW-92 (Lecture Notes in Artificial Intelligence 830),* C. Castelfranchi and E. Werner, (eds.), New York: Springer, 1992, pp. 226–256.

[10] Jennings, N. R., "On Being Responsible," *Decentralized AI 3 — Proceedings of the Third European Workshop on Modelling Autonomous Agents in a Multi-Agent World,* E. Werner and Y. Demazeau, (eds.), New York: Elsevier, 1992, pp. 93–102.

[11] Haddadi, A., "Towards a Pragmatic Theory of Interactions," *Proceedings of the First International Conference on Multi-Agent Systems*, Menlo Park, CA: AAAI Press / MIT Press, 1995, pp. 133–139.

[12] Wooldridge, M., "This Is MyWorld: The Logic of an Agent-Oriented Testbed for DAI," *Intelligent Agents: Theories, Architectures, and Languages, Lecture Notes in Artificial Intelligence 890,* M. Wooldridge and N. Jennings, (eds.), New York: Springer, 1995, pp. 160–178.

[13] Hintikka, J., *Knowledge and Belief,* Ithaca, NY: Cornell University Press, 1962.

[14] Fischer, K., J. P. Müller, and M. Pischel, "A Pragmatic BDI Architecture," *Intelligent Agents II,* M. Wooldridge, J. P. Müller, and M. Tambe, (eds.), Volume 1037 of *LNCS*, New York: Springer, 1986, pp. 203–218.

[15] Rao, A. S., "AgentSpeak(L): BDI Agents Speak out in a Logical Computable Language," *Agents Breaking Away: Proceedings of the Seventh European Workshop on Modelling Autonomous Agents in a Multi-Agent World,* W. Van de Velde and J. Perram, (eds.), Volume 1038 of *LNCS*, New York: Springer, 1996, pp. 42–55.

[16] Georgeff, M., and A. Rao, "A Report on AAII," *IEEE Expert (Intelligent Systems and Their Applications)*, Vol. 11, No. 6, 1996, pp. 89–92.

[17] Bratman, M. E., D. J. Israel, and M. E. Pollack, "Plans and Resource-Bounded Practical Reasoning," *Computational Intelligence*, Vol. 4, 1988, pp. 349–355.

[18] Georgeff, M. P., and A. L. Lansky, "Reactive Reasoning and Planning," *Proceedings of the Sixth National Conference on Artificial Intelligence*, Menlo Park, CA: AAAI Press / MIT Press, 1987, pp. 677–682.

[19] Kinny, D., M. Georgeff, and A. Rao, "A Methodology and Modelling Technique for Systems of BDI Agents," *Agents Breaking Away: Proceedings of the Seventh European Workshop on Modelling Autonomous Agents in a Multi-Agent World,* Y. Demazeau and J.-P. Müller, (eds.), Volume 1038 of *LNCS*, New York: Springer, 1996, pp. 56–71.

[20] Lee, J., et al., "UMPRS: An Implementation of the Procedural Reasoning System for Multirobot Applications," *CIRFSS94, Conference on Intelligent Robotics in Field, Factory, Service and Space*, Cambridge, MA: MIT Press, 1994, pp. 842–849.

[21] Myers, K. L., "A Procedural Knowledge Approach to Task-Level Control," *Proceedings of the 3rd International Conference on Artificial Intelligence Planning Systems (AIPS-96),* B. Drabble, (ed.), Menlo Park, CA: AAAI Press, 1996, pp. 158–165.

[22] Huber, M. J., "JAM: A BDI-Theoretic Mobile Agent Architecture," *Proceedings of the Third International Conference on Autonomous Agents (Agents'99)*, Seattle, WA, 1999.

[23] Busetta, P., et al., "JACK Intelligent Agents—Components for Intelligent Agents in Java," *AgentLink News*, No. 2, 1999, pp. 2–5.

[24] Burmeister, B., and K. Sundermeyer, "Cooperative Problem Solving Guided by Intentions and Perception," *Decentralized AI 3 — Proceedings of the Third European Workshop on Modelling Autonomous Agents in a Multi-Agent World,* E. Werner and Y. Demazeau, (eds.), New York: Elsevier, 1992, pp. 77–92.

[25] Jennings, N. R., "Specification and Implementation of a Belief Desire Joint-Intention Architecture for Collaborative Problem Solving," *Journal of Intelligent and Cooperative Information Systems*, Vol. 2, No. 3, 1993, pp. 289–318.

[26] Pollack, M. E., and M. Ringuette, "Introducing the Tileworld: Experimentally Evaluating Agent Architectures," *Proceedings of the Eighth National Conference on Artificial Intelligence (AAAI-90)*, Boston, MA, 1990.

[27] Ferguson, I. A., "Integrated Control and Coordinated Behaviour: A Case for Agent Models," *Intelligent Agents: Theories, Architectures, and Languages*, M. Wooldridge and N. Jennings, (eds.), Volume 890 of *LNCS*, New York: Springer, 1995, pp. 203–218.

[28] Müller, J. P., and M. Pischel, "Modelling Interacting Agents in Dynamic Environments," *Proceedings of the Eleventh European Conference on Artificial Intelligence*, 1994, pp. 709–713.

[29] Barber, K. S., et al., "Infrastructure for Design, Deployment and Experimentation of Distributed Agent-Based Systems: The Requirements, the Technologies and an Example," *Autonomous Agents and Multi-Agent Systems*, Vol. 7, No. 1/2, 2003, pp. 49–69.

[30] Graham, J. R., K. S. Decker, and M. Mersic, "DECAF — A Flexible Multiagent System Architecture," *Autonomous Agents and Multi-Agent Systems*, Vol. 7, No. 1/2, 2003, pp. 6–27.

[31] Noda, I., and P. Stone, "The Robocup Soccer Server and CMUnited Clients: Implemented Infrastructure for MAS Research," *Autonomous Agents and Multi-Agent Systems*, Vol. 7, No. 1/2, 2003, pp. 101–120.

[32] Parunak, H. V. D., "Applications of Distributed Artificial Intelligence in Industry," *Foundations of Distributed Artificial Intelligence,* G. O'Hare and N. Jennings, (eds.), New York: Wiley, 1996, pp. 139–164.

[33] Smith, R. G., "The Contract Net Protocol," *IEEE Transactions on Computers* Vol. 29, No. 12, 1980, pp. 1104–1113.

[34] Smith, R. G., "The CONTRACT NET: A Formalism for the Control of Distributed Problem Solving," *Proceedings of the Fifth International Joint Conference on Artificial Intelligence*, 1977, p. 472.

[35] d'Inverno, M., et al., "A Formal Specification of dMARS," *Intelligent Agents IV: Proceedings of the Fourth International Workshop on Agent Theories, Architectures, and Languages, Lecture Notes in Artificial Intelligence 1365,* M. Singh, A. Rao, and M. Wooldridge, (eds.), New York: Springer, 1998, pp. 155–176.

[36] Sycara, K., et al., "The RETSINA MAS Infrastructure," *Autonomous Agents and Multi-Agent Systems*, Vol. 7, No. 1/2, 2003, pp. 29–48.

[37] Lopez y Lopez, F., M. Luck, and M. d'Inverno, "Constraining Autonomy Through Norms," *Proceedings of the First International Joint Conference on Autonomous Agents and Multi-Agent Systems*, New York: ACM Press, 2002, pp. 674–681.

[38] Grosz, B., et al., "The Influence of Social Norms and Social Consciousness on Intention Reconciliation," *Artificial Intelligence*, Vol. 142, No. 2, 2002, pp. 147–177.

[39] Castelfranchi, C., "Prescribed Mental Attitudes in Goal Adoption and Norm Adoption," *Artificial Intelligence and Law*, Vol. 7, No. 1, 1999, pp. 37–50.

[40] Conte, R., and C. Castelfranchi., "From Conventions to Prescriptions: Towards an Integrated View of Norms," *Artificial Intelligence and Law*, Vol. 7, No. 4, 1999, pp. 323–340.

[41] Pynadath, D. V., and M. Tambe, "An Automated Teamwork Infrastructure for Heterogeneous Software Agents and Humans," *Autonomous Agents and Multi-Agent Systems*, Vol. 7, No. 1/2, 2003, pp. 71–100.

[42] Martin, D. L., A. J. Cheyer, and D. B. Moran, "The Open Agent Architecture: A Framework for Building Distributed Software Systems," *Applied Artificial Intelligence*, Vol. 13, No. 1/2, 1999, pp. 92–128.

[43] Kumar, S., P. R. Cohen, and H. J. Levesque, "The Adaptive Agent Architecture: Achieving Fault-Tolerance Using Persistent Broker Teams," *Proceedings of the International Conference on MultiAgent Systems*, 2000, pp. 159–166.

[44] Thomas, S. R., "The PLACA Agent Programming Language," *Intelligent Agents, ECAI-94 Workshop on Agent Theories, Architectures, and Languages*, M. Wooldridge and N. Jennings, (eds.), Volume 890 of *LNCS*, New York: Springer, 1995, pp. 355–370.

[45] Shoham, Y., "Agent-Oriented Programming," *Artificial Intelligence*, Vol. 60, No. 1, 1993, pp. 51–92.

[46] Fisher, M., "A Survey of Concurrent METATEM — The Language and Its Applications," *Temporal Logic—Proceedings of the First International Conference (Lecture Notes in Artificial Intelligence 827),* D. Gabbay and H. Ohlbach, (eds.), New York: Springer, 1994, pp. 480–505.

[47] Wooldridge, M., "Agent-Based Software Engineering," *IEE Proceedings on Software Engineering*, Vol. 144, No. 1, 1997, pp. 26–37.

[48] Bond, A. H., and L. Gasser, (eds.), *Readings in Distributed Artificial Intelligence,* San Mateo, CA: Morgan Kaufmann, 1988.

[49] Moulin, B., and B. Chaib-draa, "An Overview of Distributed Artificial Intelligence," *Foundations of Distributed Artificial Intelligence,* G. O'Hare and N. Jennings, (eds.), New York: Wiley, 1996, pp. 3–56.

[50] Nwana, H. S., "Software Agents: An Overview," *Knowledge Engineering Review*, Vol. 11, No. 3, 1996, pp. 205–244.

Chapter 3

Agent Toolkits

3.1 INTRODUCTION

Agent-based applications need a significant amount of enabling infrastructure before even one message is exchanged between agents. A large set of supporting services must be made available throughout an agent-based system before the application developer can move on to focus on the application domain, be it e-business, Grid computing, or Ambient Intelligence. Such services range from basic communication to discovery, coordination, security, and so on, and come together to provide an environment that can support agent-based computing. In this way, they can be considered as providing the *operating system* for agents. There are also issues that span domain-independent infrastructural services and application-specific services, relating to the architecture of individual agents within the environment and specific coordination mechanisms that deal with issues such as negotiation [1, 2] or the creation of agent teams [3] and organizations [4–6].

Crucially, mainstream development would not be able to practically adopt agent-based approaches if the underlying operating systems had to be rewritten each time or if new agent architectures and complex coordination mechanisms were redesigned for every new application. It has been realized, and has become widely accepted, that a necessary precondition for agent technologies to move from research laboratories to mainstream development, as part of the application developer's set of technologies for designing and implementing distributed applications, is the development of appropriate toolkits that would provide the necessary support for developing agents and deploying the infrastructure required to support agent applications [7, 8]. As a result, recent years have seen significant efforts being undertaken into the development of appropriate infrastructure for agent-based systems (and there has been much debate on identifying the appropriate concepts to support the development of agent-based infrastructure (for an example, see [9]). Such development efforts often do more than just design and develop an enabling infrastructure; they also provide the necessary tools to aid in the development of applications that operate using that infrastructure. Tools of this kind range from graphical development environments to management and monitoring services.

In this chapter, we use the term *agent toolkits* to describe software for deploying an agent infrastructure and for aiding in the development of agent applications. Agent toolkits are intended to provide a significant proportion of the basic building blocks required to support an operational agent-based system. Ideally, this should allow the application developer to focus on those issues that are specific to the particular application being developed instead of issues relating to how the concepts of agents and multiagent systems can find practical realization. Of course, like operating systems development, each toolkit represents the designer's particular beliefs or philosophy about how agent-based systems should operate.

The main aim of this chapter is to compare and contrast some of the most widely used and influential toolkits for agent-based systems development. At the same time, it also aims to illustrate some of the main challenges in developing such toolkits and the variety of methods with which these challenges have been tackled. As is seen from the reviews within the chapter, the richness of the agent paradigm makes it especially hard to strike the right balance between what should be implemented within the toolkits and what must be considered application-specific.

The form of such toolkits is as varied as the large number of toolkits available (for example, `www.agentlink.org` lists more than 100). Some are integrated development environments that provide a graphical interface; others include networking capabilities providing some form of middleware, while still more are simply sets of application programming interfaces (APIs) that a programmer can integrate into his or her own solutions. Either way, they all necessarily employ some form of agent model and some even prescribe a particular methodological approach.

The chapter begins by outlining a set of criteria that are used to select the toolkits reviewed in this chapter, as well as a generic framework for comparing and contrasting them. Subsequently, each toolkit is presented, and the ways it tackles each of the issues identified in the generic agent toolkit are discussed. Six toolkits are investigated in some detail, but there are also brief outlines of several other important toolkits. The chapter concludes with a discussion on the main toolkits, drawing some conclusions about the current state of the art and possible future directions.

3.2 REVIEW METHOD

3.2.1 Selection Criteria

The toolkits described here have been selected based on three criteria. First, they should tackle as wide a range of issues as possible in relation to application development in distributed, heterogeneous, and dynamic computing environments, and should lead to realistic applications rather than the simulation of applications or simplified prototypes. This allows us to touch on as many of the related subjects as possible and provide a wide range of examples of how similar problems are tackled through different approaches. Second, they should be well documented, and there should be several examples of their use in significant applications. Examples of the application of toolkits are essential since this is currently the only way to ensure some appropriate feedback on the viability of the toolkit beyond its conceptual structure. Finally, the toolkits should have a significant user community as evidence of their acceptance within the wider field of agent-based systems.

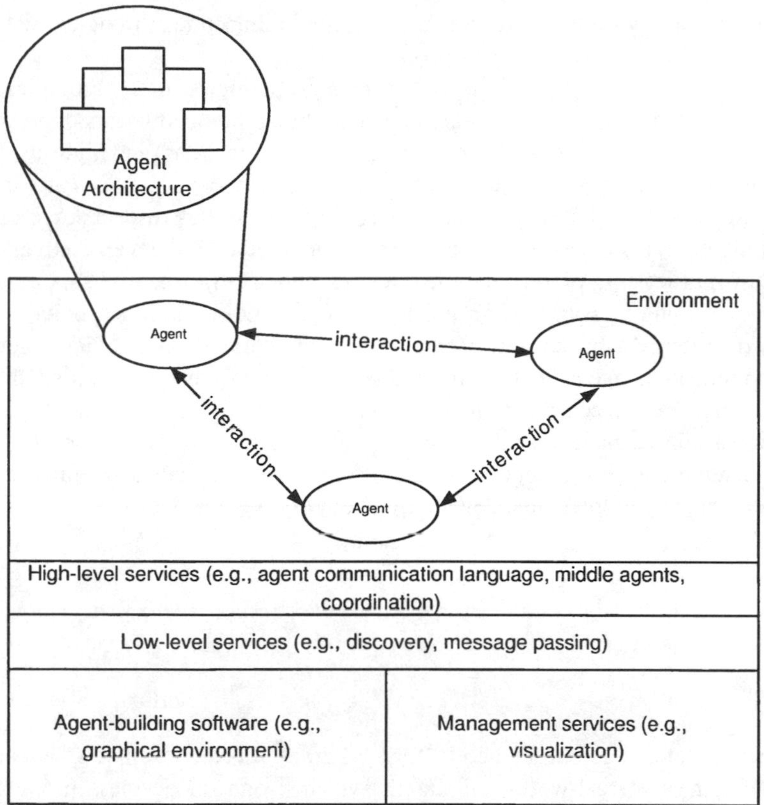

Figure 3.1 Generic toolkit framework.

3.2.2 Generic Toolkit Framework

In order to evaluate the various toolkits, a consistent method of describing them, and eventually comparing and contrasting them, is required. Towards this end, a *generic toolkit framework* is proposed, which imposes a specific structure within which to place and relate the various issues that must be addressed. This structure is imposed with the caveat that there is a great variety of possible divisions of concerns and one view may favor a specific set of toolkits and disadvantage others. However, for the purposes of an effective comparison, it is necessary to commit to one. A division of concerns, as illustrated in Figure 3.1, is employed and detailed next.

The first step is to separate the development of individual agents and their interface to the environment from coordination and communication between multiple agents. For each toolkit, therefore, we need to define how a single agent can be constructed and how that agent can perform actions that will affect its environment. The capabilities that are provided for individual agents are examined at this stage, such as planning or logical reasoning, as well as the specific architectures through which such capabilities are expressed.

When considering multiagent systems, the focus is on discovery, communication, ontologies, and any coordination mechanisms there may be for the agents. Capabilities provided in this context are divided into low-level services (e.g., enabling middleware, basic security functions) and high-level services (e.g., coordination mechanisms, complex security infrastructure). Low-level services are, in essence, generic services that any distributed system infrastructure requires. In this respect some of the important issues are the ability to transfer messages from one agent to another, low-level discovery mechanisms, such as the use of multicasting protocols to discover essential infrastructural services, and security mechanisms for encrypting messages. High-level services are those that are specific to the operation of an agent-based system. At this level, the focus is on agent communication languages and protocols to support communication, agents that facilitate the discovery of other agents (usually termed *middle agents* [10]), ontologies, and coordination mechanisms.

Finally, we investigate the available management services for any resulting applications relating to the monitoring of the application and debugging, and the software that is specifically aimed at aiding the development process, such as an integrated development environment.

3.3 ZEUS

3.3.1 Background

The Zeus agent toolkit has been under development since 1997 at BTexact. It is the result of practical experience gained while developing two real-world multiagent systems: one for business process engineering [11] and the other for multimedia information management [12]. At the time of this writing, Zeus is an open source project available under a license similar to the Mozilla public license and is written entirely in Java. A dedicated Web site maintains more information about the toolkit, including manuals and developed examples, as well as links for downloading the toolkit itself.[1]

According to the Zeus philosophy, there are five issues that represent the main infrastructural problems that need to be tackled by an agent toolkit [13]:

Information Discovery Information discovery refers to the methods that agents have at their disposal to find out information about other agents. It is usually addressed by providing services similar to the white pages and yellow pages that we use in everyday life to find addresses and telephone numbers of other people or companies. In Zeus, this issue is tackled through what are called utility agents that provide just such services.

Communication For agents to be able to exchange messages, they require a common way of formulating messages. This is something that agent infrastructure should provide through the definition of an appropriate agent communication language. Zeus uses the FIPA agent communication standard (described in more detail in Chapter 5).

1 http://193.113.209.147/projects/agents/zeus/index.htm

Ontology In addition to a common language for formulating messages, agents also need common methods for describing their application domain. Exactly which ontologies are used in any situation is an application-specific issue. Zeus aids by providing tools for defining ontologies.

Coordination Although it could be argued that coordination is clearly an application-specific task, Zeus provides some of the most widely used coordination mechanisms. These can significantly aid the development process if the provided coordination mechanisms are applicable to the domain in question.

Integration with legacy software Agent-based systems are often proposed as ideal solutions for integration of new systems with legacy software. Agents can act as the interlocutor between legacy software and new systems. Zeus addresses this issue by providing a means for Zeus agents to interface with external programs.

Beyond these issues, the Zeus design follows a set of basic guidelines: a clear separation between domain-specific problems and agent-level functionality; a user-friendly graphical interface for development; an open and extensible design; and strong support for standards and standardized technologies as evident by its compliance with the FIPA standards.

3.3.2 Agents

According to the Zeus perspective, agents are deliberative, so they reason explicitly about which goals to select and which actions to perform. They are goal directed, so any action performed is in support of a specific goal. They are versatile, so they can perform a number of goals and engage in more than one task. They are truthful, so when dealing with other agents they always state the true facts. Finally, agents are temporally continuous, so they have a notion of time and can synchronize based on a clock.

Based on this approach, the Zeus toolkit provides a set of components that represent specific agent functionalities such as planning and scheduling algorithms, agent communication language capabilities (using the FIPA ACL), and communication protocol implementations, ontology support, and coordination.

The assembly of these components readily leads to the construction of what is termed a *generic Zeus agent*, illustrated in Figure 3.2. Agents can send and receive messages, through *mailbox* and *message handler* components. A *resource database* component has a list of the resources available to the agent, with the possibility to directly interface with external databases. Through the *execution monitor* component, agents can interface with external systems such as legacy systems and also keep track of actions. The *coordination engine* component handles the agent's goals, deciding which to follow or abandon. It also handles interaction with other agents based on the available interaction protocols. Information about other agents, such as name and abilities, is kept in an *acquaintance database* component. Finally, the *planner/scheduler* component has the task of producing plans and the timings for when actions defined in the plans should be performed in reference to specific goals, as requested by the coordination engine.

This generic agent has all the rudimentary tools necessary to form the base of an agent functioning in a variety of domains. Although it is possible to provide different implementations for these buildings blocks, and therefore obtain different types of generic agents, it does not seem possible to deviate significantly from the organizational structure of the intercomponent relationships.

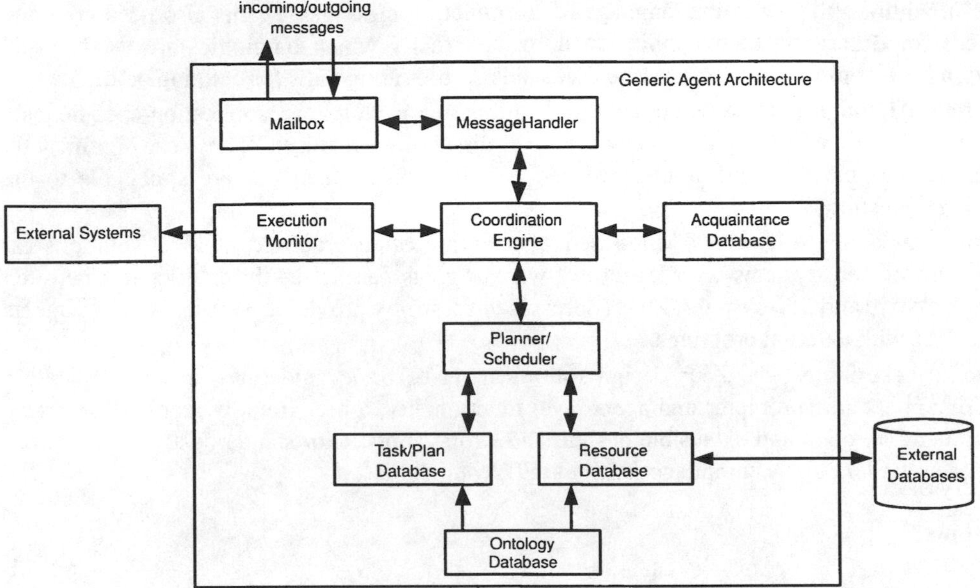

Figure 3.2 Generic Zeus agent architecture.

Nevertheless, since the code for each of these components is provided as part of the overall Zeus package, it is possible to configure them in any manner desired or add or replace existing components. Crucially, the Zeus development environment assumes this particular configuration for enabling development via a graphical interface and without direct interaction with these components at the code level.

3.3.3 Multiagent Systems

Low-Level Services

All communication in Zeus is based on message exchange using the TCP/IP protocol and ASCII messages. This is done to allow for maximum portability of agents. As a result, all services are high-level services that depend on the FIPA ACL and ontologies.

High-Level Services

Infrastructure support for a multiagent system in Zeus revolves around *utility agents*. The term *utility agent* is used to differentiate between those agents that provide supporting infrastructure and those that perform the actual application tasks, which are called *task agents*. There are two types of such utility agents, as follows:

The *agent name server* (ANS) (or white pages) maintains a registry of all known agents and provides a mapping between an agent's name and its logical network location. It is necessary to have at least one ANS, since without it no agent would be able to communicate with any other. (In larger applications it may be necessary to have a number of ANS agents in order to support all the agents.) However, there is always a root ANS agent to bootstrap the system, and other utility or task agents must be provided with the network address of this agent. This root ANS agent also provides a system-wide clock that other agents refer to so that they can synchronize on registration with the ANS. The *facilitator* (or yellow pages) agent maintains a list of abilities for those agents registered with it. Such a facilitator agent is needed to deal with dynamic changes in the capabilities of agents.

The operation of a multiagent system starts with the registration of each agent with the ANS. Subsequently, agents can retrieve the network addresses of other agents they wish to communicate with from the ANS. This implies that the agents have prior knowledge of other agents' names and abilities and just need the actual network addresses. Alternatively, if they do not have this prior knowledge, the application requires a facilitator, which maintains its information by querying the ANS about registered agents and then queries each agent in turn about its abilities. This approach for discovery of other agents restricts the flexibility of the system by the need for a root ANS agent, so some prior knowledge is always required. Furthermore, the facilitator design is rudimentary and does not allow more sophisticated behavior like dynamic registration and deregistration of agent capabilities.

Agent communication in Zeus is based on the exchange of FIPA ACL messages. This is supported through specific implementations of the mailbox and message handler components that can parse such messages and handle the protocols relating to their receipt and transmission. The content of messages is formulated according to the ontologies describing the domain of operation of the agent. Ontologies are supported through the ontology database component, which allows developers to equip agents with ontologies for use in formulating plans and goals, and in describing resources.

Coordination in Zeus is supported through a variety of approaches. The central approach is based on variations of the contract net protocol [14], where there is a call for proposals by an initiator agent followed by replies from responding agents, and a negotiation phase that can proceed based on a number of strategies. In addition, Zeus allows for the definition of roles, such as peer, subordinate, and superior. Through the definition of such roles, multiagent systems can be given an organizational structure that can aid coordination between agents. Finally, Zeus allows for multiagent planning by enabling each agent to factor tasks that depend on other agents into its planning responses.

3.3.4 Agent-Building Software

Zeus provides a graphical environment that allows for the development of an entire multiagent system application with almost no need to code anything except the interfaces to external systems. This development environment also suggests a certain method for the development of applications.

Development begins with the definition or import of the ontologies that are to be used in the application, and an *ontology editor* is provided for this purpose. Then, through the *Zeus agent editor*, each task agent is configured by defining planning parameters, tasks, available resources, acquaintances, roles, and interaction protocols. At this point, agents are linked to external programs or resources such as databases and legacy software. Finally, the utility agents are configured so that code generation for each agent can now take place and the agents can be distributed on the platforms from which they will operate.

3.3.5 Management Services

Zeus enables the monitoring and control of a multiagent system through a variety of perspectives, using utility agents that interrogate other agents about their operation and then collate and present the information in an appropriate manner:

- The society tool provides visual information about the exchange of messages between agents.
- The report tool shows the progress on the main tasks and execution state of each subtask.
- The agent viewer allows the monitoring of the internal state of each agent.
- The control tool allows this state to be altered.
- The statistic tool collects statistics on individual agents and the society as a whole.

The sum of these services provides a powerful tool for the debugging of applications. However, by its nature, it creates a significant amount of traffic within a system and places resource demands on each individual agent. Furthermore, certain types of information, such as the internal state of each agent, may not be available at all in an environment in which agents come from, or represent, different organizations. These services, therefore, should be considered as viable in settings in which the multiagent system is relatively closed, where security concerns are low, and where the number of agents is not too large.

3.4 RETSINA

3.4.1 Background

RETSINA (reusable environment for task-structured intelligent network agents) is a multiagent systems toolkit developed over a period of years, and at least since 1995, at the Intelligent Software Agents Laboratory of Carnegie Mellon University's Robotic Institute. RETSINA has been used extensively in a range of applications such as financial portfolio management, e-commerce, and mobile communications. The toolkit, available as the RETSINA Agent Foundation Classes, can operate under Windows, Unix, and mobile platforms, and uses a variety of languages (Java, C++, C, Python, LISP, Perl) that are tailored to the specific environments. However, the main infrastructural components are written in Java. A limited version of RETSINA is freely available for noncommercial use, under license by Carnegie Mellon University.[2]

The design of RETSINA is based on two central assumptions about agent applications development [15]. First, multiagent systems infrastructure should support complex social interactions

2 http://www-2.cs.cmu.edu/~softagents

between agents through the provision of services that are based on predefined conventions on how social interaction will take place. These predefined conventions refer mainly to the use of a common communication language, protocols, and ontologies. From the perspective of the multiagent system infrastructure, agents are seen as black boxes, but they are expected to be able to participate in social interactions based on these conventions. Second, agents in a multiagent system engage in peer-to-peer relationships. Any societal structures, such as hierarchies, should emerge through these peer-to-peer interactions, and should not be imposed by a centralized approach. This is in recognition of the need to avoid a reliance on centralized control, and allow for truly distributed structures to emerge. These assumptions for multiagent systems development lead to a very clear separation between individual agents and the supporting infrastructure.

3.4.2 Agents

An agent in RETSINA is understood, in abstract terms, as a stand-alone survivable piece of code with communicative and intelligent behavior. In real terms, it is understood as any piece of software that is able to interact with other agents and with the RETSINA multiagent system infrastructure, following the conventions defined in RETSINA.

All agents are derived from a *BasicAgent* class, which provides the main functions required for operation in a RETSINA multiagent system, such as message handling, logging, visualization, and discovery of other agents. This agent-specific functionality is separated from operation within specific operating environments by placing agents in an *AgentShell*, which provides the necessary interfaces for interaction with the underlying operating system. The AgentShell also provides basic management functionalities such as starting up or shutting down the agent and a timer module.

The reasoning and planning for agents is handled by the RETSINA Agent architecture, shown in Figure 3.3. It is based around the interactions between a *communication* module that handles messages from other agents, a *planner* that derives plans based on a provided set of goals and a plan library, a *scheduler* that uses the output from the planner to schedule when tasks will be performed, and an *execution monitor* that handles the actual performance of actions. These modules are supported by appropriate knowledge and beliefs, which are divided into *objectives*, *task structures*, *schedules*, *current actions*, and a *domain facts and beliefs database*.

RETSINA divides agent functionality into four main classes that are built on top of the BasicAgent and represent specializations of the basic architecture to deal with different types of functionalities:

- *Interface agents* interact with users by receiving inputs and displaying results.
- *Task agents* carry out the main problem-solving activities by formulating plans and executing them by coordinating and exchanging information with other agents.
- *Information agents* interact with information sources such as databases or Web pages. The task agents provide the queries, and the information agents are specialized in retrieving the required information by interfacing with databases, the Web, and so on.
- *Middle agents* provide the infrastructural support for the discovery of services between agents.

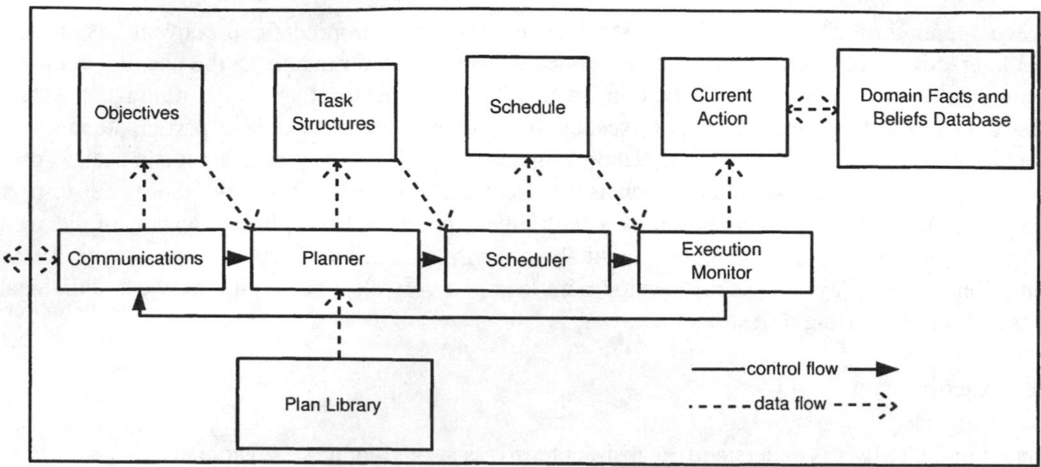

Figure 3.3 RETSINA agent architecture.

Although it is possible for developers to provide their own extensions of the BasicAgent class, it is suggested that application development begins from the specialized extensions already provided.

3.4.3 Multiagent Systems

Low-Level Services

Communication in RETSINA is facilitated by two types of low-level services. First, the RETSINA communicator module in individual agents enables agent-to-agent communication and abstracts beyond the underlying physical transmission layer and network type. This allows developers to focus on communication at the agent level. Second, dynamic discovery of high-level infrastructure services is enabled via the use of a multicast protocol. Once agents enter a multiagent system application, they multicast their presence and can be detected by high-level infrastructural services that then communicate directly with them. This multicast discovery is based on the Simple Service Discovery Protocol, which was developed as part of the Universal Plug-n-Play[3] ad hoc networking effort. It is a lightweight protocol that is intended to be used by service providers to announce the availability (or otherwise) of a service, and by service requesters to query for specific services. In RETSINA, a reply to a multicast query is a TCP/IP address and port number that can be used for communication with the discovered service.

The RETSINA multiagent system provides some basic security services for the authentication of agents, and for the protection of communication between agents. A certificate authority system is used for identity protection, through which each agent is guaranteed by a trusted authority. Communication

3 http://www.upnp.org

between agents is protected through the use of a public-private key system and support for the SSL protocol.

High-Level Services

RETSINA views infrastructure as something that should be cleanly separated from multiagent system applications and individual agent behavior. As a result there is no support for specific coordination mechanisms, organizational structures, or any regulatory policies, as these are deemed to be application-specific issues. Although there is no support for specific coordination mechanisms, protocol specification and interpretation are supported through a protocol engine and language that is based on finite input-output automata.

Agents exchange messages that are divided into two parts. First, an envelope defines the sender, receiver, thread of conversation, ontology, and ACL used. Within this envelope, content could be specified using any ACL and appropriate ontologies. RETSINA directly supports the KQML ACL (described in Chapter 5), by enabling agents to parse KQML messages, and an ontology derived from the Wordnet Ontology [16]. This functionality is implemented in the BasicAgent.

The basic high-level infrastructural support is provided through ANSs. An ANS maps agent identifiers to logical network addresses. There is also support for multiple name servers and redundant name servers in order to provide robustness and fault tolerance. Each agent is provided, through the BasicAgent class, with an ANS component that enables registration, deregistration, and lookup for name servers. Agent name servers can be discovered dynamically through multicast requests. As a result, a multiagent system can survive without the presence of an ANS and without the need for prior knowledge of an ANS.

Middle agents provide the second level of infrastructure support. The main type of middle agent is the *matchmaker*, which provides a mapping between agents and services. This mapping is created through advertisements that matchmakers receive from service provider agents. The matchmaker then matches a request to service providers and leaves them to handle all subsequent interactions. Both the advertisements of service availability and the requests for services are described using a specialized language, called LARKS (language for advertisement and request for knowledge sharing) [17]. LARKS is required to provide a standardized description of each service, such as input and output, preconditions and postconditions, the context, and a textual description of the service. The result is a KQML message that contains a LARKS advertisement, which uses the appropriate application ontology to describe the available service. The RETSINA toolkit also provides broker and blackboard middle agents. Brokers completely hide service providers from the service requestor by mediating all interactions. Blackboard agents simply provide a basic blackboard service where requests are posted for everyone to see, but capabilities are only known by the service providers who can then choose to reply to service requestors directly. A useful categorization of middle agents can be found in [10].

3.4.4 Agent-Building Software

The RETSINA Agent Foundation Classes are integrated within the Microsoft VisualStudio development environment. A RETSINA Agent AppWizard is available that provides some basic support for agent development, but there is no step-by-step guidance and the bulk of development involves direct interaction with code.

For debugging, RETSINA provides a useful graphical tool that enables developers to receive, compose, and send KQML messages to agents in order to test their ability to respond to messages.

3.4.5 Management Services

RETSINA considers management as an issue that should be actively supported through the multiagent system infrastructure. For this purpose it provides three types of management. The *logger* is a service that is able to record the main state transitions between agents for inspection by developers. Agents provide this information through the logger module that is implemented in the BasicAgent class. This logging service can be connected to an *activity visualizer*, which provides a graphical representation of the activity in a RETSINA application. Finally, a *launcher* service is provided that can coordinate the configuration and startup of infrastructural components and agents on diverse machines, platforms, and operating systems from a single control point.

A graphical tool is available specifically for managing ANSs, which allows the direct inspection of the information currently registered with an ANS, and the configuration of the ANS itself.

As mentioned earlier, these tools are only effective in what are very controlled situations, in which all agents fall under the same organizational domain, and where there are no issues concerning the misuse of information on the state of agents.

3.5 IMPACT

3.5.1 Background

IMPACT (interactive Maryland platform for agents acting together) is a joint research project between the University of Maryland in the United States, Bar Ilan University in Israel, the University of Koblenz-Landau in Germany, the University of Vienna in Austria, and the University of Milan in Italy. IMPACT has been used extensively in military applications, such as in the visualization and analysis of army logistics operations, the simulation of complex combat situations, and the provision of support for controlled flight. The development environment and the core of the infrastructural components are written in Java. At the time of writing, IMPACT was not available for use outside the project developers, but more information, including user manuals, can be found on-line at the project Web site.[4]

The view of what constitutes appropriate infrastructure support and software agent development is illustrated through 10 desiderata that the IMPACT project aims to meet [18]:

- It should always be possible to agentize nonagent programs.
- The methods in which data is stored should be versatile in recognition of the current diversity in data storage mechanisms.

4 http://www.cs.umd.edu/projects/impact

- The theory of agents should be independent from the specific actions any agent may perform. Such actions are a parameter of the agent.
- The decision-making mechanisms of each agent should be clearly articulated in order to enable modification at any point of an agent's life.
- It should be possible to reason about beliefs, uncertainty, and time.
- Security mechanisms are critical to protect the infrastructure from malicious agents, and to protect agents from other agents assuming false identities.
- There should be some method of providing guarantees as to the performance of agents.
- A theory of agents needs to be accompanied by an efficient implementation and should be such as to *allow* for an efficient implementation.
- Infrastructure reliability is paramount.
- Testing a theory through practical applications is essential.

3.5.2 Agents

Agents in IMPACT are divided into two parts:

- The software code, which consists of data types and functions that can manipulate those data types.
- The wrapper, which provides the actual intelligent agent functionality.

The software code could be any software program, and represents the actual interface to the environment through which the agent effects change in it. The wrapper represents the actual agent functionality that is able to manipulate the software code according to the behavior dictated by the wrapper's programming. This division is the IMPACT solution to the requirement for being able to agentify any program through a wrapper.

The wrapper is further divided into a set of basic components that come together to provide the IMPACT agent architecture, illustrated in Figure 3.4. All actions are regulated by the *agent program* that specifies which actions an agent should or should not perform in specific situations; the agent program defines what IMPACT terms the agent's *operating principles*. The agent program itself is defined according to an *agent program language* that allows for a wide set of regulatory modalities (do, obliged, forbidden, waived, and permitted). An *action base* component maintains descriptions of all the actions an agent can perform, together with the preconditions that are required for the execution of actions.

It is important to stress that IMPACT takes a wider view of what represents an action than many others. Everything an agent does, including tasks that are traditionally taken for granted or considered an integral part of the architecture, such as planning or timing, are considered actions that must be explicitly defined within the action base. Actions can be performed concurrently, and are regulated by a *concurrent action mechanism* component that decides, based on the current agent state and desired

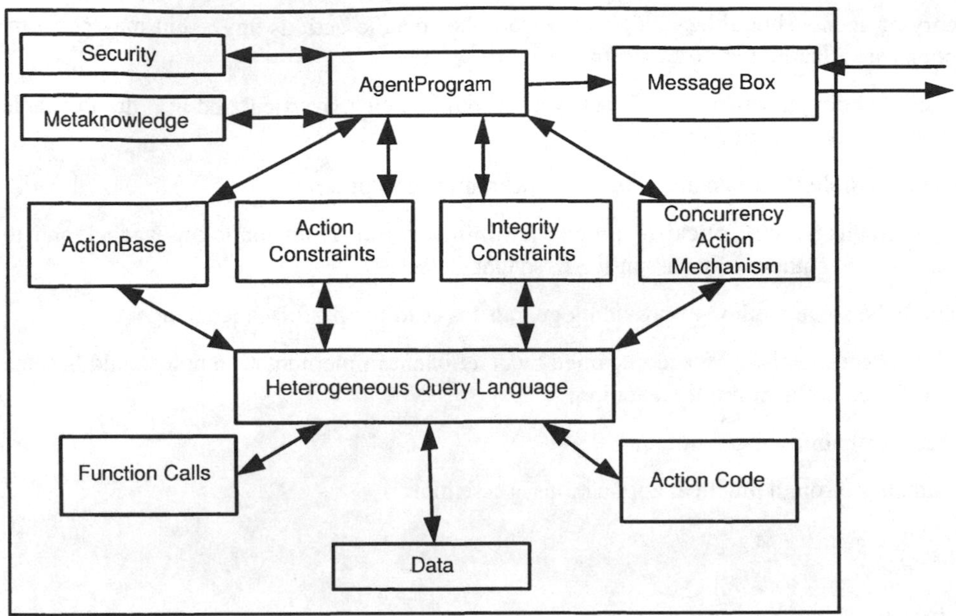

Figure 3.4 IMPACT agent architecture.

actions, whether a composite action can be defined to achieve the desired actions. Concurrency is also regulated by a set of *action constraints* that explicitly define when certain actions cannot be performed concurrently. A set of *integrity constraints* specify which agent states are legal in a given context and ensure that the agent does not perform any actions that may violate these constraints. A *heterogeneous query language* component provides the interface with the software code part of the agent.

Finally, an agent is equipped with *metaknowledge* that includes descriptions of the services the agent is able to provide, and beliefs about other agents, and a *message box* component that handles communication with other agents.

The most interesting feature of the IMPACT agent architecture, which clearly distinguishes it from other architectures, is the emphasis on ensuring that the agent operates within very well-defined parameters. The agent architecture clearly stipulates the actions that are allowed, integrity constraints, action constraints, and so on. This provides a multilayered solution to the problem of being able to guarantee "correct" behavior. Furthermore, the development process of agents in IMPACT also includes several consistency checks that ensure there are no conflicting rules, such as both forbidding and permitting an agent to do something. We will not elaborate on the details of these consistency checks here, but the interested reader can refer to the extensive articles on IMPACT elsewhere (see, for example, [19–21]).

3.5.3 Multiagent Systems

Low-Level Services

Agents in IMPACT operate within a dedicated platform, called an *agent roost*, which provides network connectivity and manages the agents operating within it. It is written in Java and uses Java Remote Method Invocation (RMI) to communicate with other agent roosts, so IMPACT agents can operate from any platform that can handle Java RMI. The agent roost handles the incoming and outgoing messages for each agent within it and can *wake* agents when a message arrives so that they can process it.

Communication with systems outside the agent roosts is achieved through a generic connections module, which is then specialized to enable connections to specific systems, such as Oracle servers.

High-Level Services

Infrastructure support is based on IMPACT servers, which provide yellow pages services, a type service, a thesaurus service, and a synchronization module. All agents providing services must register with the IMPACT server. Services are described in a standardized HTML-like language, and the service specification requires a service name in terms of a verb-noun expression (such as *rent:car[Japanese]*), input and output variables, and service attributes (such as cost, response time, and so forth). Only authorized developers can introduce new agents in the system and the process is semiautomatic, since the developer can use a graphical interface to describe the services provided by the agent at the moment of its introduction into the system.

The yellow pages service is a matchmaking service that matches service requests to service providers. This matchmaking service is enhanced through a similarity matching algorithm that is able to match a service request to a service provider even if the service request is not defined in the precise terms with which the service provision has been defined. For example, a request for a *car_purchase* can be matched to a *car_seller* service provider. This is achieved by maintaining two term hierarchies within the IMPACT server, one for nouns and one for verbs, and an agent table. The term hierarchies contain sets of synonyms that can be used to compute the similarity between two terms, and the agent table contains, for each service provider, a noun term, a verb term, and the agent name. If there is no direct match between the service request and an entry in the agent table, the term hierarchies are used to discover if there is another service that is sufficiently similar to the service request. The term hierarchies can be updated each time a new service type is registered. This approach attempts to provide a more robust service to agents since it can anticipate inconsistencies between service descriptions and service requests, and deal with them.

The type and thesaurus services are, in essence, services in support of the yellow pages service. The type service allows developers to define relationships between types that can then be used to aid the service discovery process. For example, a *japanese_car* type can be defined as a subtype of *car*. The thesaurus service allows the matchmaking algorithms to discover that the term *car* and *automobile* are synonyms and update the relevant term hierarchy.

The issue of reliable infrastructure is tackled by mirroring IMPACT servers, to ensure that if one server is not available, others can provide essential services. The synchronization module has the task of ensuring that updates in one server are mirrored on other servers.

Communication between agents in IMPACT is not considered as something that should be standardized at the infrastructure level. The message box is intended to parse any message and allow the rest of the agent architecture to handle the message in a standardized way. As a result, it is up to the application developer to provide an appropriate implementation of the message box component. There is also no specific support for coordination between agents.

3.5.4 Agent-Building Software

The IMPACT toolkit provides an agent development environment, called AgentDE, that allows developers to define every aspect of the agent that forms part of the agent wrapper. The AgentDE can maintain a library of actions, agent programs, service descriptions, and other definitions used during development so that they can be quickly recalled and reused. Various connections to external databases are also defined using the AgentDE. Once an agent has been defined, the AgentDE can perform a number of checks to ensure that the agent fulfills the requirements for consistency and safety. It then produces a binary file, called the agent metadata file (a serialized set of Java objects), which must then be copied to the target agent roost initialization directory. There it is deserialized by the agent roost and placed into operation. A more automated process, where the AgentDE can communicate directly with active agent roosts and transfer the agent metadata file over a network connection, is under development.

3.5.5 Management Software

Management in IMPACT revolves around managing agent roosts, and it is possible to access both through graphical interfaces. The agent roost interface allows developers to monitor the state of individual agents in the roost and the incoming and outgoing messages in the roost.

3.6 JADE/LEAP

3.6.1 Background

The JADE (Java agent development environment) toolkit provides a FIPA-compliant agent platform and a package to develop Java agents. It is an open source project distributed by TILab (Telecom Italia Labs) that has been under development since 1999 at TILab and through contributions by its numerous users. At the time of writing, version 3.01b1 is available, which implements the FIPA2000 specifications. The platform has undergone successful interoperability tests for compliance with the FIPA specifications.

LEAP (lightweight extensible agent platform) is the result of a research project funded by the European Commission and undertaken by a consortium of organizations coordinated by Motorola and including Broadcom, BT, TILab, Siemens, ADAC, and the University of Parma. The aim of the project was to provide an agent platform that is suitable for limited capability devices, such as PDAs and mobile phones.

The relationship between the two projects is that LEAP is a lightweight implementation of the core functionalities of the JADE FIPA platform, and can be used in conjunction with the JADE libraries for agent development. The latest release of JADE integrates LEAP so as to provide a unique toolkit that enables the development of FIPA-compliant agent applications on devices ranging from limited capability mobile devices to desktop computers.

The JADE toolkit has been widely adopted throughout the world, and there is an active community that contributes to its development and offers additional tools. Some examples of applications involving JADE are the development of a multiagent information system supporting the consultation of a corporate memory based on XML technology, communicating agents for dynamic user profiling, collective information dissemination and memory management, and agent-based health care services.

In a relatively recent development, a JADE Board has been established, governed by Telecom Italia Labs and Motorola, which is open to all companies and organizations that have an interest in using and further developing JADE. More information about the JADE Board, additional documentation, and links to downloading the JADE toolkit can be found at the JADE Web site.[5]

3.6.2 Agents

The JADE toolkit facilitates the development of agents that can participate in FIPA-compliant multiagent systems. It does not define any specific agent architectures but provides a basic set of functionalities that are regarded as essential for an autonomous agent architecture [22]. These are derived by interpreting the minimum concrete programming requirements for satisfying the characteristics of autonomy and sociality. Autonomy is interpreted as an implementation of agents as active objects (that is, with their own thread of operation). The requirement for sociality leads to enabling agents to hold multiple conversations on a peer-to-peer basis through an asynchronous messaging protocol.

This basic single-agent infrastructure is provided through an agent class, which developers then extend to provide their own implementations of agents. Programs extending the agent class operate within JADE containers that manage the agent life cycle. Agents can be started, stopped, removed, suspended, and copied. Each agent has access to a private message queue, where messages are stored until the agent chooses to retrieve them, and access to a set of APIs that allow the formulation of FIPA ACL messages. An outline of the main aspects of the agent class is illustrated in Figure 3.5.

Specific agent actions take place through a concurrent task model. Each task, or behavior as it is termed in JADE, is an extension of the behavior class of the JADE toolkit. Each agent has a behavior task list, and the agent class provides methods for adding or removing behaviors. Once an agent is placed within a container and set into operation, behaviors are executed based on a round nonpreemptive scheduling policy. Of course, complex tasks require a more sophisticated scheduling of behaviors as well as the conditional execution of behaviors. JADE provides models that are divided

5 http://sharon.cselt.it/projects/jade

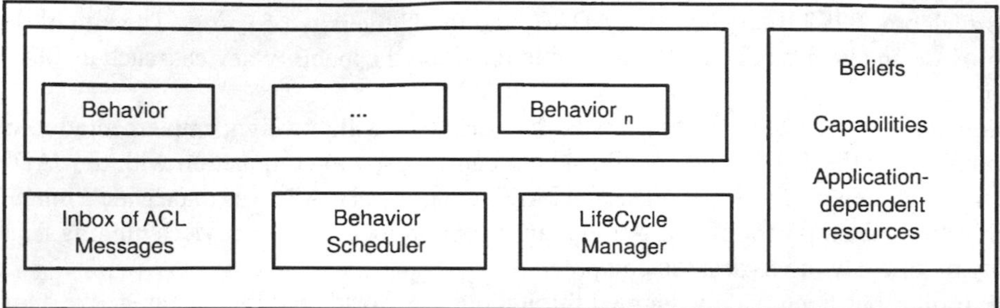

Figure 3.5 JADE agent components.

along the lines of simple behaviors, to address tasks not composed of subtasks, and composite behaviors, to address tasks made up through the composition of several other tasks. There are also cyclic and one-shot implementations of simple behaviors, and parallel, sequential, and finite-state machine implementations for composite behaviors. Development is further aided by the provision of specific implementations of behavior to handle basic tasks such as receiving or sending messages, and support for the set of interaction protocols defined by FIPA.

The LEAP core for JADE offers a lightweight version of the JADE container that can operate on PDAs. LEAP agents use a device-specific communicator module, which handles the specific connectivity protocols of the device and network at hand. Agents for limited devices use the same task-based model as JADE agents, within the limitations of the device at hand.

3.6.3 Multiagent Systems

Low-Level Services

Multiagent systems in JADE can be divided into three first-order components. A JADE platform is made up of a number of containers that operate on individual machines. Each container can have a number of agents within it. A platform can be thought of as defining a common application domain, and agents within this platform have access to the same infrastructural services. Containers handle the communication between agents and access to platform services. Communication within JADE platforms is based on Java RMI.

Communication between platforms is based on the FIPA-defined Message Transport Protocol (MTP) over which ACL messages can be sent. The actual implementation of the MTP can vary, and FIPA provides specifications for a number of different technologies. As a result, JADE provides a pluggable MTP framework along with concrete implementations that include an Internet InterOrb Protocol (IIOP) and an HTTP implementation.

Agents on mobile devices can communicate within the JADE platform through a gateway workstation that provides a translation of messages coming from limited devices into either IIOP or Java RMI.

High-Level Services

The high-level services offered by JADE follow the FIPA specifications, but we will avoid a long description here as these specifications are covered in detail in Chapter 5. Each JADE platform has access to an agent management system, which manages the platform and supervises access to it and provides white pages services. Yellow pages services are offered by directory facilitators and several can exist within a FIPA platform. JADE provides implementations of the SL-0 content language and agent management ontology that is used by the AMS and DF services to communicate. Finally, FIPA-defined interaction protocols are also supported.

JADE supports the development of user ontologies through a Java package that offers a set of classes providing common high-level terms for any ontology, such as Action, Result, TruePreposition, and so on.

In JADE, agents can take advantage of support for mobility to move between containers. At the time of writing, only interplatform mobility is supported. Agents can be completely removed from one container and placed in another, or they can be cloned across many containers. Mobility introduces the notion of location and other related issues, so JADE provides a mobility ontology that allows agents to describe such concepts.

3.6.4 Agent-Building Software

JADE is a set of APIs that can be used to deploy an agent platform and develop agents. Although no software is provided to guide this process, there is extensive documentation of the APIs, a detailed programmer's guide, and a wealth of examples.

3.6.5 Management Services

A significant number of utilities are provided for managing and monitoring the activity of an agent platform. A remote monitoring agent (RMA) provides control of the platform life cycle and all the registered agents within the platform. It provides a GUI which, among other functions, allows access and control to individual agents, such as starting and stopping them and sending custom ACL messages to them. Through the RMA, a separate GUI that allows management of directory facilitators can also be launched. A dummy agent utility is a graphical tool that enables developers to perform all the main activities any agent can perform (behaving like an agent in the platform). As such, it is a useful debugging tool that can help indicate where communication between agents is not developing in the desired manner. A sniffer agent allows the monitoring of messages exchanged between a group of agents. Finally, an Introspector Agent provides information about and control of the life cycle of a single agent.

3.7 JACK

3.7.1 Background

JACK is an agent development environment produced by the Agent Oriented Software Group, which has its headquarters in Melbourne, Australia. JACK was first released in 1998 and is currently at Version 4.0. It has a wide user base both in commercial and academic environments. It is commercially available, with special licenses for research purposes. A demonstration version is freely available.

There are two guiding principles underpinning the development of JACK. First, agent-oriented development can be thought of as an extension of object-oriented development. As a result, JACK operates on top of the Java programming language, acting as an extension that provides agent-related concepts. JACK developers compare it to the relationship between C and C++, where the latter is an extension of the former for providing object-oriented concepts. Second, agents in JACK are intelligent agents in that they are based on the BDI architecture. JACK is also supportive of agent standards and FIPA-compliant systems can be produced using JACK.

The JACK development environment can be divided into three main components:

- The JACK Agent Language is a superset of the Java language, and introduces new semantical and syntactical features, new base classes, interfaces, and methods to deal with agent-oriented concepts.
- The JACK Compiler compiles the JACK Agent Language down to pure Java, so that the resulting agents can operate on any Java platform.
- Finally, the JACK Agent Kernel is the run-time program within which JACK agents operate, and provides the underlying agent functionality that is defined within the JACK Agent Language.

More information about JACK, including documentation and access to the toolkit itself can be found at the AOS Web site.[6]

3.7.2 Agents

Although JACK can, in principle, support a wide variety of agent architectures, the default architecture, and the one that is clearly supported through appropriate concepts in the JACK Agent Language, is the BDI architecture (described in Chapter 2).

The *Agent* base class is the central artifact of the JACK Agent Language and, through it, developers define beliefs, plans, external and internal events, and capabilities. This class must be extended to implement application-specific agents. Agents schedule actions, including concurrent actions, using the *TaskManager*. A timer can provide different notions of time, such as a real-time clock (through the system clock) and a dilated clock that can be fast-forwarded, slowed down, or even stopped. Finally, the Agent class provides support for sending and receiving messages.

6 http://www.agent-software.com

Beliefs represent the knowledge that an agent possesses about the world. A *BeliefSet* is a database of beliefs that represents beliefs through a first-order, tuple-based relational model. Although agents can store information outside a BeliefSet, it is recommended that BeliefSets are used, since they can provide logical consistency and automatic update of beliefs based on events, and they also allow powerful queries on beliefs.

Plans are sequences of actions that agents execute on recording an event. Each plan in JACK corresponds to a single event, and multiple plans can be declared to handle the same event. Reasoning capabilities are provided to aid in outlining the required decision-making for deciding which plan to perform when an event occurs. This reasoning is based on the plan's relevance to a given situation and permitted context based on the agent's beliefs.

Events within the agent architecture are divided into external events (such as messages from other agents), internal events initiated by the agent itself, and motivations (described as goals that the agent wants to achieve). Events kickstart action in JACK by activating the required plans that may, in turn, raise other internal events or cause external events.

Capabilities provide a means for structuring a set of reasoning elements into a coherent cluster that can be plugged into agents. This enables the creation of libraries of capabilities that the developer can use to provide agents with particular functionality. Capabilities can contain within them the relevant plans, beliefs, and events, as well as the final code to implement the actions required by the plans. Through these concepts, JACK promotes a high level of code reuse and the incremental development of agents.

3.7.3 Multiagent Systems

Low-Level Services

Networking capabilities in JACK are based on UDP over IP, with a thin layer of management on top of that to provide reliable peer-to-peer communication.

High-Level Services

Agent communication between agents is handled by the JACK Kernel. Agents can exchange messages by specifying the name of the agents they wish to communicate with, assigned at the time of creation, and the JACK Kernel takes care of routing the message to the appropriate agent. If an agent resides on a remote host, then a portal name must be specified along with the agent name, to indicate to the JACK Kernel the logical network address of the remote host. Finally, a rudimentary ANS is provided that can provide the required portal name in case it is not known. As mentioned earlier, JACK supports interoperability with other FIPA-compliant agent systems and, to this end, the FIPA ACL is supported. However, there is some flexibility to change communication languages, since the MessageEvent objects simply define the message as a string.

JACK provides support for coordination between agents based on team-oriented programming, which views a group of agents as a whole and assigns goals to a team of agents, which must then coordinate their activity to achieve the team goal. In order to enable this, JACK offers a plugin to the main JACK development environment called SimpleTeam. It does not specify specific team management techniques (such as hierarchies) but allows developers to assign roles, specify concurrency constraints, and define team plans.

3.7.4 Agent-Building Software

JACK provides a comprehensive, graphical agent development environment. A high-level design tool allows a multiagent system application to be designed by defining the agents and relationships between them, in a notation similar to UML. Details of individual agents can also be specified at this level. This design can then be used to generate code outlines. In addition, a plan editor allows plans to be specified as decision diagrams. Along with these high-level tools, there is a component browser that allows developers to specify the actual agent code using the JACK Agent Language. Finally, a plan tracing tool and an agent interaction tool allow developers to visualize the monitoring of an application.

3.7.5 Management Services

An application can be monitored through an agent tracing controller. This graphical tool allows a developer to choose which agents to trace and provides a visual representation of the agents stepping through their plans.

3.8 LIVING MARKETS

3.8.1 Background

The *living markets* toolkit is produced by Living Systems AG, which has its headquarters in Donaueschingen, Germany. The company has been developing agent-based solutions since 1996 and their toolkit is being used in a variety of settings, including complex trading processes, logistics and distribution, and voice and bandwidth trading and settlement. They have a wide client base and have won several awards, including Leading Technology Pioneer as recognized by the World Economic Forum and Best German Internet Company.

The living markets toolkit is divided into a base agent server, which handles the application domain-independent issues relating to agent development, and specific solutions for specific markets (ranging from transportation to intraenterprise production and deal flow optimization) are built on top of the agent server. Similarly to JACK, agent development in living markets is considered as a natural progression from object-oriented techniques to role and goal-oriented programming techniques. As such, the adoption of an agent approach to building systems represents to them a *paradigm shift* in dynamic systems development, rather than simply an alternative pattern of object-oriented development. The base agent server is programmed using Java and the default communication is done through remote method invocation (RMI). However, there is also support for a range of industry standards such as XML, Secure Sockets Layer (SSL), Hypertext Transfer Protocol (HTTP), and the Common Object Request Broker Architecture (CORBA).

Living Systems is primarily a solutions company, so they adapt their toolkit to specific customer needs as opposed to marketing the toolkit directly. As a result, it is harder to identify specific features as we have done with other toolkits since there is a range of features adapted to, and developed for, specific markets. However, it still presents an interesting showcase of a *pragmatic* agent system. More information about the company and the toolkit can be found at their Web site.[7]

3.8.2 Agents

From an abstract perspective, agents in living markets are understood as proactive, goal-directed entities able to perform actions and perceive the environment. They have specific domain expertise and may adopt roles. As with RETSINA, agents are specialized into four generic types according to functionality:

Application agents are domain-specific agents and represent the main core functionality of the system.

Integration agents are dedicated to integrating the rest of the system with existing systems outside of the living markets environment.

Interface agents handle interaction with people for the system as a whole.

System agents are the agents that handle the management of the living markets system itself, performing tasks such as performance monitoring and load balancing.

At the practical, implementation level, agents generally operate within the agent base server, the living agents run-time system (LARS), and communicate by exchanging XML messages. Within LARS servers, agents occupy their own thread of operation so that multiple agents can operate concurrently. *Remote agents* that operate outside a LARS server (for example, on a mobile client) are also supported, albeit within the limitations of the environment within which they operate. In reflection of the application of living markets in financial domains, there is strong support for message encryption using the RSA encryption algorithm (which allows encryption of a message using a *public key* and decryption only by the holder of a *private key*) and the Blowfish key algorithm (a fast symmetric block cipher). Once decrypted, the XML messages are stored in a message box that can then be processed by the agent based on a set of logic rules, the agent's *standard logic* that defines its basic behavior. This handles application domain-independent activities such as requests as to the status of the agent or requests for moving to another LARS server. The living markets agents also have a set of business rules, which define the *business logic*. This is where the logic for dealing with specific business processes is encoded. The business logic interfaces with a *persistence layer* that can allow agents to store or retrieve information from the file systems or databases.

Beyond the distinction between business and standard logic, there is relative freedom in developing agent architectures within the living markets. The business rules can be coded to access a set of *capabilities* made available by the server that they can use to achieve their specific tasks. Such capabilities can also include components that allow interfacing with external applications.

7 http://www.living-systems.com

3.8.3 Multiagent Systems

Low-Level Services

The low-level services provided by the living markets toolkit are primarily concerned with enabling access to external systems and communication between agents. The LARS servers provide a dedicated communication channel that enables communication between agents within a single server as well as a special message router agent, which is able to route messages to other message routers residing on other LARS servers. When agents reside on the same server, messages are Java objects passed by reference between the agents. When communicating externally, the default communication method is Java RMI, although a variety of alternative channels, including strings over basic sockets, can be supported.

There is strong support for integration of agents with external systems, either through file transfer or HTTP messages, or through application programming interfaces that can be connected to agents. The support for integration extends to Enterprise Java Beans (EJBs) servers through customized beans that link EJB servers to LARS servers.

The living markets system attempts to address the issue of scaling agent systems to deal with potentially hundreds or thousands of agents interacting (a very realistic expectation in a financial environment). To this end, LARS servers are designed so as to take advantage of multiprocessor environments and can also be arranged into clusters. In addition, since there is support for mobility of agents between servers, agents can be moved automatically to the right servers to improve performance.

High-Level Services

The living markets toolkit offers a wide range of high-level services for agent applications reflecting the range of application environments in which it has been used. For the purposes of this review, we focus on the support offered for business-to-business applications, although several of these issues apply to other domains as well.

The toolkit divides the required services into four tiers based on functionality:

- First, agents need to be able to search for partners in deals, for products, or for services. The toolkit supports a means for describing this information and making it available to agents.
- Second, service providers and service requests need to be matched. The living markets toolkits support a method they term *softmatching*, through which results of searches can be returned based on their similarity to the actual request. The level of similarity required can be specified by the agent.
- Third, the toolkit supports a range of dynamic pricing mechanisms that allow agents to decide on the price for service provision. These mechanisms include English, Dutch, Reverse, and Vickrey auctions (descriptions of which, in the context of agent-mediated e-commerce, can be found in [23]), as well as bilateral and multilateral negotiations.

- Fourth, the last tier deals with the clearing and settlement of deals supporting physical and financial settlements.

Agent communication is based on the FIPA ACL packaged within XML messages. The message channel within the LARS servers and the message router take care of delivering the message to the appropriate recipient. Finally, there is also support for transaction management across platforms and databases.

3.8.4 Agent-Building Software

Agent development is supported by an integrated graphical agent development environment, the living markets Development Suite. This software allows application developers to visually design *agent scenarios*, which are representations of the main agents in the system, and the communication flows between them. For each agent, the developer can provide a description of the agent, a list of the main goals and their relative importance, and the services the agent must provide. Based on these scenarios, agents can be created and business logic defined in detail.

3.8.5 Management Software

Management in a living markets system is divided between day-to-day management of entire systems and more detailed management of the agents and the servers.

General management capabilities are provided through a living markets management console, which provides a Web-based interface that allows the day-to-day administration of the application. More detailed management and control of individual agents is provided through a control center that allows detailed access to each LARS server and the agents residing on the server. Individual messages can be scrutinized, and settings relating to communication infrastructure can be controlled.

3.9 OTHER TOOLKITS

This chapter focuses on and analyzes in some detail six significant toolkits for agent-based development. These six can be considered as representative of the range of ideas currently prevalent. However, they are by no means the only ones. In this section, we very briefly describe several other toolkits that have also had significant use to provide a more comprehensive view of the wide range of systems available.

agentTool [24] is a toolkit developed at Kansas State University in direct support of the multiagent systems engineering (MASE) methodology [25] (described in Chapter 5), also developed at KSU. The methodology specifies seven stages starting from identifying the system goals and then applying use cases and deriving roles based on them. Subsequently, agent classes are created, conversations constructed and agent classes assembled. Finally, the overall system deployment takes place. The agentTool software supports the construction and assembly of agent classes and conversations, through graphical tools, that lead to the generation of the actual agent code.

The architecture of the multiagent system and individual agents is supported through a notion of *concurrent tasks*, where each task defines a certain decision-making capability. Tasks are designed graphically as finite state automata and can integrate both intra-agent and interagent relationships.

Agent Factory [26] has been developed at the Practice and Research in Intelligent Systems and Media (PRISM) Laboratory of the University of Dublin. It provides extensive support for development through a graphical environment and a distributed run-time platform that scales from workstations to limited capability PDAs. There are some FIPA-compliant aspects such as Directory Facilitators and FIPA management agents. Development is supported by a structured methodology that leads to the implementation of BDI-type agents. The definition of agents is achieved through an interpreted programming language based on a formal logical model.

BOND is a FIPA-compliant multiagent system developed at the University of Central Florida. The main motivating concept behind the BOND agent infrastructure system is the view of agents as active mobile objects with some level of intelligence [27, 28]. Another significant design decision is to enable the dynamic reconfiguration of agents [29], to answer to the dynamically changing requirements placed on agent applications. Agents are built using BOND objects, which represent an extension of conventional Java objects through the addition of a unique identifier, dynamic properties, communication support, registration with a local directory, serialization and cloning, multiple inheritance, and support for editing via a graphical interface. A BOND agent is viewed as a finite state machine with an agenda to follow (or goals to achieve) based on strategies that are made available to the agent. There are two possibilities for the creation of a BOND agent. They can be created statically based on the BOND agent framework APIs or dynamically using what is called the BOND *Blueprint* language. Through this language, the various components of a BOND agent can be described and are assembled dynamically via a *bondAgentFactory*. BOND agents can also be serialized back to Blueprint for persistent storage or transfer to other hosts where they can resume operation.

CoABS (Cooperating Agent Based Systems) is a project[8] funded by the Defense Advanced Research Projects Agency (DARPA) with the goal of building enabling infrastructure that will allow the integration of agent-based systems developed with other toolkits. In order to achieve this, it makes use of Jini middleware technology, and offers wrappers for each agent that provide basic infrastructure services in a Jini context such as subscription, security, visualization, and logging. Chapter 5 provides more details on CoABS.

DECAF (Distributed Environment Centered Agent Framework) is a toolkit developed at the University of Delaware [30]. It focuses on the individual agent architectures rather than the underlying distributed infrastructure, although basic ANS services are provided. Agents in DECAF can be programmed using a purpose-built DECAF language that allows developers to program agents using coarse-grained concepts such as agent actions that abstract away from the finer grained Java programming languages method calls that implement the functionality. DECAF agents also benefit from carefully considered planning (based on TAEMS [31]) and execution scheduling facilities [32].

8 http://coabs.globalinfotek.com

Open Agent Architecture (OOA) [33] is developed at the Artificial Intelligence Center of SRI International. Agent communication and coordination is handled by specialized *Facilitator* agents, which can handle the distribution of tasks to other agents, enabling the execution of complex goals, as well as act as global data stores for the agents. Other agents in the system are divided into application agents, interface agents, and meta-agents. Meta-agents are similar to facilitators in that they offer coordination support, but whereas facilitators are domain-independent, meta-agents are domain-dependent. Communication between agents is based on an OOA-specific interagent communication language. Finally, the toolkit comes with a range of useful agents already configured, such as a Google agent that implements the Google APIs for programmatic access and a Wordnet agent.

Sensible Agents [34] is a toolkit being developed by the Laboratory of Intelligent Processes and Systems at the University of Texas at Austin. It provides a distributed environment for agent operation and communication. The main focus is on developing agents that are able to aid in decision-making in environments with limited resources. There is extensive support for modeling capabilities to provide the appropriate knowledge for agents to reason about the environment, and powerful planning capabilities. Agents are able to plan and make decisions on goal and action priorities. Furthermore, the level of control given to an agent to take decisions can be adjusted at a global level through appropriate restraining structures ranging from command-driven, slave-master relationships to each agent being locally fully autonomous.

SoFAR The Intelligence, Agents, Multimedia Group at the University of Southampton has developed the SoFAR (Southampton Framework for Agent Research) toolkit [35]. The focus of SoFAR is on providing a reliable infrastructure that supports agent communication and discovery in the domain of distributed information management (for example, handling metadata streams synchronously with multimedia streams over a wide area network [36]). The main contributions are a robust communications layer that abstracts away the low-level details from the actual agents, extensive support for managing and integrating ontologies into the agent-based system, and registration and subscription of agents to services based on contracts. Agents and ontologies can be specified in XML files (facilitating reuse and abstracting away from programming language issues), which are then processed by tools provided with the framework to generate the appropriate code for agents and supporting ontologies.

So far, this chapter has not touched on toolkits focused on providing infrastructure for mobile agent systems. There are several such toolkits (such as D'Agents [37], Aglets [38], Mole [39], and SOMA [40]), but their focus is on enabling mobility and dealing with the inevitable security issues [41–43] rather than on the wider issues of agent-based systems development. The main aim of mobile agent research is to automate the process of moving code from one computer to another. In traditional software, the decision of whether to migrate is external to the code that will eventually migrate while in mobile agents the decision of whether to migrate can be contained within the mobile code unit that may eventually migrate. Much has been written about the merits of mobile agents (see, for example, [44, 45]), with the most important advantages being locality of reference, a high degree of adaptability, and fault tolerance. Such systems, however, have also faced significant resistance due to security concerns and doubts about their true advantages. Despite such fears, however, the increase in mobile users is making the issues tackled by mobile agent systems very relevant. For example, a mobile phone or PDA entering a new office and seeking services for its user is very similar to a mobile agent moving to a new host. Even more complicated is the situation in which a user travels to an area where service provision is provided by a different organization (*roaming*). The concepts of agents and mobility are now coming together to provide solutions for such problems [46, 47]. As such, it can be expected that future agent-based systems toolkits will have to exploit the lessons learned from mobile agent research and relate them to the issues dealt with so far.

3.10 DISCUSSION

The six toolkits outlined in this chapter form a representative sample of the current state of the art in the field. All have a history of at least 3 years of development and have been used in a significant number of applications that have proved that agent-based system development can bring true benefits to the appropriate application domains. As such, they can all be described as *successful* attempts at providing an agent toolkit. Nevertheless, few guides exist to aid in ascertaining which of these is better. For example, there is no clear answer to the question of how exactly an agent communication language should be structured and what makes one better than another [48, 49], despite some efforts to evaluate languages (for example, [50]). Another similar issue relates to questions of determining appropriate agent architecture [51].

This section attempts to draw some links between the six main toolkits reviewed in this chapter, while a summary of their features is provided in Tables 3.1 and 3.2. The different approaches that each toolkit takes for each of the aspects considered are discussed, along with some of the relative advantages and disadvantages they offer.

3.10.1 Agents

Of the six toolkits, the only one that does not provide significant structure for an agent architecture is JADE. However, the task-based model it supports provides an effective framework upon which to build agent architectures, and it provides some basic pieces of functionality such as handling messages and participating in coordination protocols. Of the other five architectures, three (Zeus, RETSINA, JACK) are essentially variations of the BDI approach, with JACK offering the most "faithful" interpretation of the architecture. It is difficult to argue which of the three offers the best implementation, since there are relative advantages for each. Zeus provides a more consistent separation of issues of resources and models of other agents; JACK offers an effective and efficient system for managing beliefs through the BeliefSet; and, finally, RETSINA provides significant supporting infrastructure through the Logger module and powerful scheduling and monitoring capabilities. To a large extent, the choice might depend on how well specific application requirements can translate to the exact definitions provided by each.

IMPACT departs from the traditional approaches and places a lot of emphasis on the ability to guarantee that agent behavior will follow certain constraints. As such, IMPACT can be considered a pioneer from this point of view. At the same time, some analysis is necessary to verify whether

Table 3.1
Review of Features for Zeus, RETSINA, and IMPACT Toolkits

Toolkit Name	Agents	Multiagent Systems: Low-Level Services	Multiagent Systems: High-Level Services	Agent-Building Software	Management Services
Zeus	Goal-directed Multitask Planning and scheduling Support for coordination protocols	TCP/IP Communication	FIPA ACL Agent Name Server Matchmaking services (yellow pages) Coordination protocols based on contract net variations	Graphical agent development environment Automatic code generation	System visualization Statistics on system performance
RETSINA	Goal-directed Planning and scheduling Agents specialized in information agents, interface agents, task agents, and middle agents	Communicator module abstracts underlying network protocols Support for a variety of protocols within the toolkit Multicast discovery based on the Simple Service Discovery Protocol Security based on public keys and certificate authorities	KQML Agent name server Matchmaker services (yellow pages), Broker and Blackboard LARKS Service Description Language WordNet Ontology	Integration with Microsoft Visual Studio	Agent activity visualization Agent name server management
IMPACT	Agent Program Language with regulatory modalities Reasoning for concurrent actions Strong safety checking (operating principles, integrity constraints)	Agent Roosts act as containers for agents RMI-based communication between Agent Roosts	Yellow pages Thesaurus Type server Synchronization Service similarity matching algorithm	Basic agent development environment	Agent Roosts managed through graphical interface

Table 3.2

Review of Features for JADE, JACK, and living markets Toolkits

Toolkit Name	Agents	Multiagent Systems: Low-Level Services	Multiagent Systems: High-Level Services	Agent-Building Software	Management Services
JADE	Task-based model with simple, cyclic, parallel, sequential, and finite state machine behaviors Communications support based on FIPA standards	Agent containers RMI-based communication FIPA Message Transport Protocol: IIOP and HTTP support	Fully compliant with FIPA specifications	Application programming interfaces with no graphical support	Remote monitoring agent Directory facilitator GUI Dummy agent Sniffer agent Introspector agent
JACK	Agent language as extension of Java BDI model Planning capabilities Modular structures allowing grouping of plans and actions	UDP communication with thin management layer	FIPA ACL Basic agent name server Support for team-oriented programming	Fully integrated graphical development environment Graphical representation of plans	Agent tracing controller Plan execution visualization
living markets	Standard and business logic Persistence layer EJB integration	RMI-based communication Support for CORBA, SSL, HTTP, and Sockets RSA and Blowfish encryption Load balancing	FIPA ACL Negotiation strategies Auction protocols support	Fully integrated graphical development environment Agent scenario development	Back office Web-based management console Detailed administration of agents and servers

the added complexity introduced in the architecture is worth the guarantees offered for behavior. The living markets approach is perhaps the closest to current industry practice in enterprise application systems, since the notion of *business logic* and *standard logic* will resonate with similar notions in more standard technologies such as Enterprise Java Beans.

A final point of interest in terms of developing an agent architecture is the issue of equipping agents with appropriate functionality to ease the task of monitoring and managing them later on. A good example of differing approaches is given by Zeus and RETSINA. In Zeus, agents are queried using the normal agent communication path about their status in order to create a visualization of the world. This means that the information is "pulled" from the agent by an external component. In RETSINA, each agent is equipped with the appropriate functionality so that it can "push" the information about its status to the monitoring application. Other toolkits, such as JADE and living markets, which have agents operating within platforms, can monitor the agent activities through the platform and need not bother with contacting the agent directly.

The only real conclusion that can be drawn is that in order to choose between them, a developer should carefully weigh the advantages and disadvantages in relationship to the specific application being developed and the expertise available to the developer. For example, if one is not familiar with the BDI approach or artificial intelligence planning techniques, the effort required for them may not be worth the more direct results achievable through a different approach. It is also worth noting that in domains in which there are limited capability devices, the more lightweight architectures of JADE and living markets could prove much more suitable.

3.10.2 Multiagent Systems

Low-Level Services

Of the systems reviewed, Zeus and JACK offer the most lightweight solutions, using the TCP and UDP protocols, respectively, over IP networks. This provides flexibility at the cost of a lack of features, and means that the toolkit developers need to implement appropriate solutions, such as JACK's thin management layer on top of UDP, and must also provide the required functionality. The IMPACT, living markets, and JADE toolkits use the more heavyweight Java RMI (and, although alternatives are possible even within these toolkits, RMI is the default and most well-supported approach). To a certain extent, this is a limiting factor, since RMI consumes resources and can complicate the deployment process. In general, it can be argued that remote method invocation techniques run counter to the philosophy of multiagent systems, where agents should call on other agents to perform tasks using a high-level communication language. RMI is perhaps more suitable for traditional distributed systems where the purpose is to abstract network issues and allow the remote invocation of methods in a manner that appears similar to local method invocation.

RETSINA and living markets provide a more balanced use of low-level services. RETSINA makes interesting use of the relatively lightweight SSDP discovery protocol for dynamic infrastructure discovery, and allows direct communication between agents. The RETSINA approach indicates how new generation middleware technology can be highly effective in providing the low-level services required by multiagent systems.

RETSINA and Zeus allow agents to operate as standalone programs with all the required functionality to support participation in, and communication with, other agents being contained in each agent. This provides significant flexibility, and allows the developer to choose which infrastructural services an agent needs to participate and, as a consequence, support. JACK, JADE, IMPACT, and living markets all provide some sort of container within which agents should operate. On the one hand, the benefits of a container are obvious, since the container can contribute significantly to the required supporting services for all agents, provide a standardized means for handling communications, and seems to be the only way to support mobility for agents. On the other hand, using a container brings with it related costs and limits developers significantly in how much liberty they can have in employing alternative approaches. Perhaps the best solution would be for toolkits to support both modes of operation to give developers the best of both worlds, as the living markets toolkit does to a certain extent for agents operating on limited capability devices.

High-Level Services

The system review has revealed that the single most important high-level service functionality is the discovery of other agents. The solutions revolve mainly around white pages and yellow pages services. Zeus, RETSINA, and JADE provide both, while IMPACT provides only a yellow pages service, and JACK focuses on a white pages service. The living markets toolkit provides something similar to a yellow pages service along with the notion of *softmatching*, which allows a relaxation of the matching criteria, a feature that is very appropriate in business settings.

IMPACT differentiates itself from the others through an alternative approach for yellow pages services by using a simple service description language and a powerful similarity matching algorithm. This acknowledges that in heterogeneous environments, service descriptions and requests may not always be consistent and more sophisticated techniques may be required to deal with the problem. This approach might become more common in the emerging environment of the Semantic Web and Web services.

Nevertheless, since IMPACT does not provide a white pages service, it excludes the possibility that an agent may have prior knowledge of which agent it wants to contact but not the contact address of that agent. Furthermore, it makes it difficult to monitor exactly which agents are registered in a multiagent system. Zeus and JADE consider this a vital function and require that all agents register with the white pages service. JACK seems to assume that in most cases agents will have prior knowledge of which agents they need to contact and may not even require a white pages service. RETSINA is the most flexible toolkit in this respect, since it provides both white pages and yellow pages services, but does not require that either is available to bootstrap the system since infrastructure services can be dynamically discovered.

Agent communication languages are clearly supported by all the systems (Zeus, JADE, JACK, and living markets with FIPA, and RETSINA with KQML). IMPACT supports message exchange between agents but does not define a specific agent communication language. The benefits of a standardized communication language, such as FIPA ACL, are obvious in open environments but are not as clear in more specialized domains in which a simpler approach may provide the required functionality.

Some form of ontology support is available in all the systems, with Zeus, JADE, and JACK providing a more open approach in which support is provided but specific ontologies are considered to be an application domain issue. RETSINA provides support for large, generic ontologies that can cover a wide range of domains. IMPACT allows for ontologies to *develop* as new agents enter the system by enabling developers to relate the new concepts introduced to existing ones. Again, IMPACT's approach may indicate that this is a possible path for large-scale heterogeneous systems where consistency is difficult to achieve. Nevertheless, the process may become unwieldy if too many new concepts are introduced, and relationships between them must be made by developers, who may not be best equipped to judge which relationships are the most appropriate. Note that the development of technologies for the Semantic Web, such as the OWL standard (discussed in Chapter 5) and supporting tools, will have a significant impact on agent toolkits. Agent developers should be able to take advantage of these more sophisticated tools for creating and reasoning about ontologies,[9] and redirect their energies towards improving other aspects of the toolkits.

Finally, although all the systems concerned can claim to support multiagent systems in heterogeneous environments, the claim for support for *open* heterogeneous systems is much harder to maintain. Open heterogeneous systems require standardization, such as that provided by FIPA, but at the same time need to acknowledge that flexible infrastructure support like RETSINA's is vital, and systems for dealing with inconsistencies such as IMPACT's will play a very important role.

3.10.3 Agent-Building Software

All the toolkits, with the exception of JADE, provide some agent-building software, with JACK and living markets being the most refined, a clear reflection of their commercial background. It could be argued that what is required is a development environment like those provided by JACK or living markets, combined with the infrastructural services provided by the other toolkits. Although agent technologies have progressed significantly, research projects cannot expend the resources required to develop sophisticated development environments. This is clearly an issue that must be dealt with through the takeup and support of such technologies by industry.

Another important issue in relation to agent-building software is the methodology used to develop a system. A refined agent development environment could also act as a guide through a methodology for agent-based development. JACK, Zeus, and living markets all allow for these through different routes. However, as with infrastructure issues, there are as yet no clearly agreed common methodologies.

3.10.4 Management Services

All of the systems provide some sort of management, but this is clearly an area that still requires development, and the way to proceed is not clear. Zeus adopts an approach whereby each agent is interrogated about its actions by specialized agents to provide a visualization of the whole system. This method is clearly costly. RETSINA provides support for visualization of the system through

9 Some examples are Protégé (http://protege.stanford.edu/) for ontology creation and editing, and RACER (http://www.cs.concordia.ca/~faculty/haarslev/racer/) for reasoning.

the Logger module, bypassing the usual agent communication channels. This is still expensive, but can be more effective than the Zeus approach. JADE allows monitoring of activity by interrogating containers about the agents operating within them. Finally, JACK provides a comprehensive approach for visualization that is integrated with the development environment. However, it is unclear how these methods scale, and how large-scale open agent systems could be managed by these means.

3.11 CONCLUSIONS

Toolkits for agent-based system development have reached a good level of maturity. There are now numerous examples of their application in a wide range of domains, and they have helped in solving real problems for real organizations. The review of toolkits in this chapter has shown that there are a variety of approaches to the problem, proof both of the complexity of the services that such toolkits attempt to offer and of the richness of the agent paradigm.

In order for an application developer to choose a toolkit, close attention must be paid to the application domain *and* the existing expertise within the organization that will develop the application. A toolkit that makes use of a complex agent architecture or advanced planning techniques can be too complicated for a wide range of applications. Furthermore, if there is no expertise that is able to appropriately take advantage of techniques made available by the toolkit, there is little point in attempting to use it for developing applications.

Agent toolkits are now adopting existing middleware technologies (like RETSINA) and attempting to integrate with the current computing environments in real organizations (like living markets). Such progress will make it even easier for agent toolkits to penetrate further into mainstream development. In turn, this will help feed back into making the toolkits more robust and extending them to deal better with issues that have not been addressed sufficiently so far, such as sophisticated security mechanisms, a better understanding of scalability issues, and adaptive policies for managing agent systems as distributed enterprise systems can be managed [52, 53].

References

[1] Lomuscio, A. R., M. Wooldridge, and N. Jennings, "A Classification Scheme for Negotiation in Electronic Commerce," *International Journal of Group Decision and Negotiation*, Vol. 12, No. 1, 2003, pp. 31–56.

[2] Ashri, R., I. Rahwan, and M. Luck, "Architectures for Negotiating Agents," *Multi-Agent Systems and Applications III*, V. Marik, J. Muller, and M. Pechoucek, (eds.), Volume 2691 of *LNCS*. Springer, 2003, pp. 136–146.

[3] Pynadath, D. V., and M. Tambe, "The Communicative Multiagent Team Decision Problem: Analyzing Teamwork Theories and Models," *Journal of Artificial Intelligence and Research*, Vol. 16, 2002, pp. 389–423.

[4] Rodriguez-Aguilar, J. A., and C. Sierra, "Enabling Open Agent Institutions," *Socially Intelligent Agents: Creating Relationships with Computers and Robots*, K. Dautenhahn, et al., (eds.), Boston, MA: Kluwer, 2002.

[5] Ferber, J., and O. Gutknecht, "A Meta-Model for the Analysis of Organisations in Multi-Agent Systems," *Proceedings of the Third International Conference on Multi-Agent Systems*, 1998, pp. 128–135.

[6] Zambonelli, F., N. Jennings, and M. Wooldridge, "Organisational Rules as an Abstraction for the Analysis and Design of Multi-Agent Systems," *International Journal of Software Engineering and Knowledge Engineering*, Vol. 11, No. 3, 2001, pp. 303–328.

[7] Bradshaw, J. M., et al., "Agents for the Masses," *IEEE Intelligent Systems*, Vol. 14, No. 2, 1999, pp. 53–63.

[8] Winikoff, M., L. Padgham, and J. Harland, "Simplifying the Development of Intelligent Agents," *AI2001: Advances in Artificial Intelligence, 14th Australian Workshop on Distributed AI*, 2001, pp. 557–568.

[9] Ashri, R., M. Luck, and M. d'Inverno, "Infrastructure Support for Agent-Based Development," *Foundations and Applications of Multi-Agent Systems*, M. d'Inverno et al., (eds.), Volume 2403 of *LNCS*, New York: Springer, 2002, pp. 73–88.

[10] Decker, K., K. Sycara, and M. Williamson, "Middle-Agents for the Internet," *Proceedings of the 15th Joint Conference on Artificial Intelligence*, San Mateo, CA: Morgan Kaufmann, 1997, pp. 578–583.

[11] O'Brien, P., and M. Wiegand, "Agents of Change in Business Process Management," *Software Agents and Soft Computing: Towards Enhancing Machine Intelligence*, H. S. Nwana and N. Azarmi, (eds.), Volume 1197 of *LNAI*, New York: Springer, 1997, pp. 132–145.

[12] Titmuss, R., I. Crabtree, and C. Winter, "Agents, Mobility and Multimedia Information," *Software Agents and Soft Computing: Towards Enhancing Machine Intelligence*, H. S. Nwana and N. Azarmi, (eds.), Volume 1197 of *LNAI*, New York: Springer, 1997, pp. 146–159.

[13] Nwana, H., et al., "ZEUS: A Tool-Kit for Building Distributed Multi-Agent Systems," *Applied Artificial Intelligence*, Vol. 13, No. 1, 1999, pp. 129–186.

[14] Smith, R., "The Contract Net Protocol: High-Level Communication and Control in a Distributed Problem Solver," *IEEE Transactions on Computers*, Vol. 29, No. 12, 1980.

[15] Sycara, K., et al., "The RETSINA MAS Infrastructure," *Autonomous Agents and Multi-Agent Systems*, Vol. 7, Nos. 1–2, 2003, pp. 129–186.

[16] Fellbaum, C., *WordNet: An Electronic Lexical Database*, Cambridge, MA: MIT Press, 1998.

[17] Sycara, K.,et al., "LARKS: Dynamic Matchmaking Among Heterogeneous Software Agents in Cyberspace," *Autonomous Agents and Multi-Agent Systems*, Vol. 5, No. 2, 2002, pp. 173–203.

[18] Subrahmanian, V., et al., *Heterogeneous Agent Systems*, Cambridge, MA: MIT Press, 2000.

[19] Eiter, T., V. Subrahmanian, and T. Rogers, "Heterogeneous Active Agents, III: Polynomially Implementable Agents," *Artificial Intelligence*, Vol. 117, No. 1, 2000, pp. 107–167.

[20] Eiter, T. and V. Subrahmanian, "Heterogeneous Active Agents, II: Algorithms and Complexity," *Artificial Intelligence*, Vol. 108, No. 1–2, 1999, pp. 257–307.

[21] Eiter, T., V. Subrahmanian, and G. Pick, "Heterogeneous Active Agents, I: Semantics," *Artificial Intelligence*, Vol. 108, Nos. 1–2, 1999, pp. 179–255.

[22] Bellifemine, F., A. Poggi, and G. Rimassa, "Developing Multi-Agent Systems with JADE," *Intelligent Agents VII: Agent Theories, Architectures, and Languages*, C. Castelfranchi and Y. Lesperance, (eds.), Volume 1986 of *LNCS*, New York: Springer, 2000, pp. 89–103.

[23] He, M., N. Jennings, and H. Leung, "On Agent-Mediated Electronic Commerce," *IEEE Transactions on Knowledge and Data Engineering*, Vol. 15, No. 4, 2003.

[24] Loach, S. A. D., and M. Wood, "Developing Multiagent Systems with agentTool," *Intelligent Agents VII: Agent Theories, Architectures, and Languages*, C. Castelfranchi and Y. Lesperance, (eds.), Volume 1986 of *LNCS*, New York: Springer, 2001, pp. 46–60.

[25] Loach, S. A. D., E. T. Matson, and Y. Li, "Multiagent Systems Engineering," *The International Journal of Software Engineering and Knowledge Engineering*, Vol. 11, No. 3, 2001.

[26] Collier, R., et al., "Beyond Prototyping in the Factory of Agents," *Multi-Agent Systems and Applications III*, V. Marik, J. Muller, and M. Pechoucek, (eds.), Volume 2691 of *LNCS*, New York: Springer, 2003, pp. 383–393.

[27] Boloni, L., et al., "The Bond Agent System and Applications," *Agent Systems, Mobile Agents, and Applications*, D. Kotz and F. Mattern, (eds.), Volume 1882 of *LNCS*, New York: Springer, 2000, pp. 99–112.

[28] Boloni, L., and D. C. Marinescu, "An Object-Oriented Framework for Building Collaborative Network Agents," *Intelligent Systems and Interfaces*, A. Kandle, et al., (eds.), Boston, MA: Kluwer, 2000, pp. 31–64.

[29] Boloni, L., and D. C. Marinescu, "Agent Surgery: The Case for Mutable Agents," *Parallel and Distributed Processing, 15 IPDPS 2000 Workshops*, J. D. P. Rolim, (ed.), Volume 1800 of *LNCS*, New York: Springer, 2000, pp. 578–585.

[30] Graham, J., and K. Decker, "Towards a Distributed Environment-Centered Agent Framework," *Intelligent Agents VI: Agent Theories, Architectures, and Languages*, N. Jennings and Y. Lesperance, (eds.), Volume 1757 of *LNCS*, New York: Springer, 1999, pp. 290–304.

[31] Wagner, T., et al., "The Struggle for Reuse: Pros and Cons of Generalization in TAEMS and Its Impact on Technology Transition," *Proceedings of the ISCA 12th International Conference on Intelligent and Adaptive Systems and Software Engineering (IASSE-2003)*, 2003, pp. 290–304.

[32] Graham, J., "Real-Time Scheduling in Distributed Multi-Agent Systems," Ph.D. thesis, University of Delaware, 2001.

[33] Martin, D. L., A. J. Cheyer, and D. B. Moran, "The Open Agent Architecture: A Framework for Building Distributed Software Systems," *Applied Artificial Intelligence*, Vol. 13, Nos. 1–2, 1999, pp. 91–128.

[34] Barber, K. et al., "Sensible Agents: An Implemented Multi-Agent System and Testbed," *Proceedings of the Fifth International Conference on Autonomous Agents*, New York: ACM Press, 2001, pp. 92–99.

[35] Moreau, L., et al., "SoFAR: An Agent Framework for Distributed Information Management," *Intelligent Agent Software Engineering*, Idea Group Publishing, 2003, pp. 49–67.

[36] Cruischank, D., L. Moreau, and D. de Roure, "Architectural Design of a Multi-Agent System for Handling Metadata Streams," *Proceedings of the 5th ACM International Conference on Autonomous Agents*, New York: ACM Press, 2001, pp. 505–512.

[37] Gray, R., et al., "D'Agents: Security in a Multiple-Language, Mobile Agent System," *Mobile Agents and Security*, G. Vigna, (ed.), Volume 1419 of *LNCS*, New York: Springer, 1998, pp. 154–187.

[38] Lange, D., and M. Oshima, *Programming and Deploying Java Mobile Agents with Aglets*, Reading, MA: Addison-Wesley, 1998.

[39] Baumann, J., et al., "MOLE: A Mobile Agent System," *Software — Practice and Experience*, Vol. 32, No. 6, 2002, pp. 575–603.

[40] Bellavista, P., A. Corradi, and C. Stefanelli, "A Secure and Open Mobile Agent Programming Environment," *Proceedings of the Fourth International Symposium on Autonomous Decentralized Systems*, New York: IEEE Computer Society Press, 1999, pp. 238–245.

[41] Claessens, J., B. Preneel, and J. Vandewall, "How Can Mobile Agents Do Secure Electronic Transactions on Untrusted Hosts? A Survey of the Security Issues and the Current Solutions," *ACM Transactions on Internet Technology*, Vol. 3, No. 1, 2003, pp. 28–48.

[42] Kun, Y., G. Xin, and L. Dayou, "Security in Mobile Agent Systems: Problems and Approaches," *ACM SIGOPS Operating Systems Review*, Vol. 34, No. 1, 2000, pp. 21–28.

[43] Tschudin, C. F., "Mobile Agent Security," in *Intelligent Information Agents*, M. Klusch, (ed.), New York: Springer, 1999, pp. 431–446.

[44] Lange, D. B., and M. Oshima, "Seven Good Reasons for Mobile Agents," *Communications of the ACM*, Vol. 42, No. 3, 1999, pp. 88–89.

[45] Gray, R. S., et al., "Mobile Agents: Motivations and State of the Art," in *Handbook of Agent Technology*, J. Bradshaw, (ed.), Menlo Park, CA: AAAI/MIT Press, 2001.

[46] Samaras, G., and C. Panayiotou, "Personalised Portals for the Wireless User Based on Mobile Agents," *Proceedings of the Second International Workshop on Mobile Commerce*, New York: ACM Press, 2002, pp. 70–74.

[47] Liu, C. F., and C. N. Chen, "A Sliding-Agent-Group Communication Model for Constructing a Robust Roaming Environment over Internet," *Mobile Networks and Applications*, Vol. 8, No. 1, 2003, pp. 61–74.

[48] Chaib-draa, N., and F. Dignum, "Trends in Agent Communication Language," *Computational Intelligence*, Vol. 2, No. 5, 2002, pp. 89–101.

[49] Reed, C., T. Norman, and N. R. Jennings, "Negotiating the Semantics of Agent Communication Languages," *Computational Intelligence*, Vol. 18, No. 2, 2002, pp. 229–252.

[50] Mayfield, J., Y. Labrou, and T. Finin, "Evaluation of KQML as an Agent Communication Language," *Intelligent Agents II: Agent Theories, Architectures, and Languages*, M. Wooldridge, J. Muller, and M. Tambe, (eds.), Volume 1037 of *LNCS*, New York: Springer, 1995, pp. 347–360.

[51] Bryson, J., and L. A. Stein, "Architectures and Idioms: Making Progress in Agent Design," *Intelligent Agents VII: Agent Theories, Architectures, and Languages*, C. Castelfranchi and Y. Lesperance, (eds.), Volume 1986 of *LNCS*, New York: Springer, 2000, pp. 73–88.

[52] Sloman, M., "Policy Driven Management for Distributed Systems," *Network and Systems Management*, Vol. 2, No. 4, 1994, pp. 333–360.

[53] Sloman, M., and E. Lupu, "Policy Specification for Programmable Networks," *Active Networks, First International Working Conference, IWAN*, S. Covaci, (ed.), Volume 1653 of *LNCS*, New York: Springer, 1999, pp. 73–84.

Chapter 4

Methodologies and Modeling Languages

Bernhard Bauer, University of Augsburg, Germany
Jörg Müller, Siemens AG, Germany

4.1 INTRODUCTION

Software engineering techniques are a key prerequisite of running successful software projects. Without a sufficient approach and adequate tools to support the development of software systems, it is virtually impossible to cope with the complexity of commercial software development processes. This tendency will increase over the years to come, and appropriate software engineering methods will continually be in high demand. A *software methodology* is typically characterized by a *modeling language* (used for the description of models, and for defining the elements of the model together with a specific syntax or notation, and associated semantics) and a *software process* (defining the development activities, the interrelationships among the activities, and the ways in which the different activities are performed). In particular, the software process defines phases for process and project management as well as quality assurance. Each activity results in one or more deliverables, such as specification documents, analysis models, designs, code, testing specifications, testing reports, performance evaluation reports, and so on, serving as input for subsequent activities.

The three key phases that one is likely to find in any software engineering process are those of analysis, design, and implementation. In a strict waterfall model, these are the only phases; more recent software development process models employ a "round-trip engineering" approach, and provide an iteration of smaller granularity cycles in which models developed in earlier phases can be refined and adapted in later phases.

Agent technology enables the realization of complex software systems characterized by situation awareness and intelligent behavior, a high degree of distribution, and mobility support. Agent technology has the potential to play a key role in enabling intelligent applications and services by improving automation of routine processes, and supporting nomadic users with proactive and intelligent assistance based on principles of adaptation and self-organization. Hence, agent technology can open the way to new application domains while supporting the integration of existing and new software, and make the development process for such applications easier and more flexible. However, deploying agent technology successfully in industrial applications requires industrial-quality software methods and explicit engineering tools.

A considerable number of agent-oriented methodologies and tools are available today, and the agent community is facing the problem of identifying a common vocabulary to support them. There is considerable interest in the agent R&D community in methods and tools for analyzing and designing complex agent-based software systems, including various approaches to formal specification (see [1] for a survey). Since 1996, agent-based software engineering has been in the focus of the ATAL workshop series; it also was the main topic of the 1999 MAAMAW workshop [2]. In particular, since 2000, the Agent-Oriented Software Engineering Workshop (AOSE) has become the major forum for research carried out on these topics, including new methodologies such as Tropos [3], Prometheus,[1] and MESSAGE.[2]

Various researchers have developed methodologies for agent design, touching on representational mechanisms, such as the Gaia methodology [4], or the extensive program under way at the Free University of Amsterdam on compositional methodologies for requirements [5], design [6], and verification [7]. In [8, 9], Kinny et al. propose a modeling technique for BDI agents. The close relationship between design mechanisms employed for agent-based systems and those used for object-oriented systems is identified by numerous authors (see, for example, [10]).

Having been the subject of intensive research activity for more than a decade, agent technology has still not met with broad acceptance in industrial settings (despite some encouraging success stories). We believe that three characteristics of industrial development have so far prevented wider adoption of agent technology:

1. The scope of industrial projects is much larger than typical research efforts.
2. The skills of developers are focused on established technologies, as opposed to leading-edge methods and programming languages.
3. The use of advanced technologies is not part of the success criteria of a project.

In order to establish a solid grounding for leveraging the usage of agent technologies in industrial applications, we recognize that accepted methods for industrial development must depend on widely standardized representations of artifacts supporting all phases of the software life cycle. In particular, these standardized representations are needed by tool developers to provide commercial-quality tools that mainstream software engineering departments need for industrial agent systems development.

Currently, most industrial methodologies are based on the Object Management Group's (OMG) Unified Modeling Language (UML) accompanied by process frameworks such as the Rational Unified Process (RUP; see [11] for details). The Model-Driven Architecture (MDA[3]) from the OMG allows a cascade of code generation from high-level (platform-independent) models via platform-dependent

1 http://www.cs.rmit.edu.au/agents/SAC/methodology.shtml
2 http://www.eurescom.de/public/projects/P900-series/p907
3 http://www.omg.org/mda

models to directly executable code (see, for example, the tool offered by Kennedy Carter[4]). Another approach for agile software engineering that has also been receiving active coverage is Extreme Programming [12].

In this chapter, we provide a detailed survey of methodologies for agent-based engineering of software systems. We start with a classification of the different approaches with respect to their formal basis, their goals, and their completeness. Subsequently, we review two popular classes of approaches to the software engineering of agent-based systems: knowledge engineering approaches and agent-oriented approaches. This is followed by overviews of approaches adapting object-oriented techniques to agent-based development, including both methodologies and modeling notations. The chapter closes with a discussion of open issues and future research opportunities. (Note that in this chapter, we assume that the reader already has some familiarity with standard object-oriented concepts and techniques, particularly UML.)

4.2 A CLASSIFICATION OF EXISTING METHODOLOGIES AND NOTATIONS

Most early approaches supporting the software engineering of agent-based systems were inspired by the knowledge engineering community. We are now witnessing a renaissance of these approaches, notably CommonKADS, when faced with the problem of managing large ontologies in the context of Semantic Web applications (discussed in more detail in Chapter 5). Agent-oriented approaches, prominently represented by Gaia (described in Section 4.4.1), focus directly on the properties of agent-based systems and try to define a methodology to cope with all aspects of agents. A relatively new tendency is to base methodologies and modeling languages on object-oriented techniques, like UML, and to build the agent-specific extensions on top of these object-oriented approaches. These three approaches, knowledge engineering, agent-oriented, and object-oriented, are reflected in the structure of this chapter. However, before going into further detail of the different methodologies and notations, we introduce a classification schema, with the aim of structuring the field. We propose the following dimensions for our schema:

- *Scope* (methodology, process, or modeling language): Is the approach a methodology consisting of a process and a modeling language; is only the process part of a software engineering approach defined such as the RUP; or is only a modeling language available like UML?
- *Basis*: Which software technology has the strongest influence on the approach (for example, a pure agent-oriented approach, formal specification techniques, object-orientation, or knowledge engineering)?
- *Phases*: In which phases of the software process is the methodology, process, or modeling language applicable (for example, early requirements, analysis, design, or implementation)?

4 http://www.kc.com/MDA/xuml.html

- *Syntax and semantics*: What is the approach regarding syntax and semantics; is there an underlying formal model, like in model-theoretic descriptions; or do we have an informal description, such as for the dynamic aspects of UML?
- *Application areas*: Is the approach domain-specific (for example, Internet agents), or is it a general-purpose approach?
- *Agency support*: What aspects specific to agent-based systems are supported (such as goals, intentions, interactions)?

A summary of existing methodologies compared against these criteria is shown in Table 4.1.

4.3 KNOWLEDGE ENGINEERING APPROACHES

Most early approaches supporting the software engineering of agent-based systems were inspired by the knowledge engineering community. The three most influential methodologies inspired by this strand of research are CommonKADS [13], CoMoMAS [14], and MAS-CommonKADS [15].

Knowledge engineers need tools and methods to design good knowledge-based systems (KBS), but these rely on the knowledge engineer's abilities. The CommonKADS methodology was developed to support knowledge engineers in modeling expert knowledge and developing design specifications in textual or diagrammatic form. Thus, CommonKADS is a knowledge engineering methodology as well as a knowledge management framework. Two extensions to CommonKADS have been developed that take agent-specific aspects into account: CoMoMAS and MAS-CommonKADS. In the following, we only discuss Common-KADS and MAS-CommonKADS; for CoMoMAS, we refer to [14].

MAS-CommonKADS [15] adds various extensions to CommonKADS: protocol engineering techniques (namely software development life cycle and MSC96 [16]); object-oriented techniques (OMT [17, 18] and OOSE); and enhanced support for additional phases within the software life cycle.

As shown in Figure 4.1, the CommonKADS methodology is described by components arranged at three layers: the context layer, the concept layer, and the artifact layer.

- *Organization model* describes the organizational context in which the knowledge-based system will work. In particular, it identifies the various stakeholders of the organization, namely *knowledge providers*, being experts in a specific domain; *knowledge users*, needing the knowledge to do their work successfully; and *knowledge decision makers*, influencing the work of the others (the knowledge providers and users) by making decisions. The organization model is described by organizational aspects about the function, involved departments (structure), business processes, power, quality, accessibility in time or space, authority, needed knowledge, and used resources of an organization. In addition, business processes have to be broken down into tasks (see the task model).
- *Task model* describes the tasks representing a goal-oriented activity, adding value to the organization, and executed in the organizational environment. The task model is represented as a set of tasks with a structure imposed on it. A task is described by well-defined input and output, defining

Table 4.1
Classification of Existing Methodologies

Approach	Scope	Basis	Phases	Syntax-Semantics	Application Area	Agency Support
Common KADS CoMoKADS MAS-CommonKADS	Methodology	KM	Analysis and design; CommonKADS: impl.	Syntax and semantics to some extent	Knowledge-centered applications	Organization tasks, agents, knowledge, interaction
Gaia ROADMAP	Methodology	AO	Analysis and high-level design (Gaia)	Syntax and semantics to some extent	Coarse-grained computational systems	Roles, agents, knowledge, interaction, services, acquaintance
SODA	Mainly process	AO society centered	Analysis and design	Some syntax	Open systems	Roles, agents, resources, societies, interaction
Kinny et al.	Methodology	OO and BDI agents	Analysis and design	Syntax and semantics to some extent	BDI agents	Agents, interaction, belief, goals, plans
MESSAGE	Methodology	OO and RUP	Mainly analysis	Syntax and semantics to some extent	Coarse-grained computational systems	Organizations, goals, tasks, agents, roles, knowledge, interaction
Tropos	Methodology	OO and BDI	Analysis, design, and implementation	Syntax and semantics to some extent	BDI agents	Actor, goal, plan, resource, capability, interaction
Prometheus	Methodology	OO and BDI	Analysis, design, and implementation	Syntax and semantics to some extent	BDI agents	Goals, beliefs, plans, events, agents, interaction, capabilities
MaSE	Methodology	OO and RUP	Analysis, design, and implementation	Syntax and semantics to some extent	Heterogeneous MAS	Goals, roles, interaction, agents
PASSI	Methodology	OO and RUP	Analysis, design, and implementation	Syntax and semantics to some extent	Mainly robotics	Societies, agents, roles, knowledge

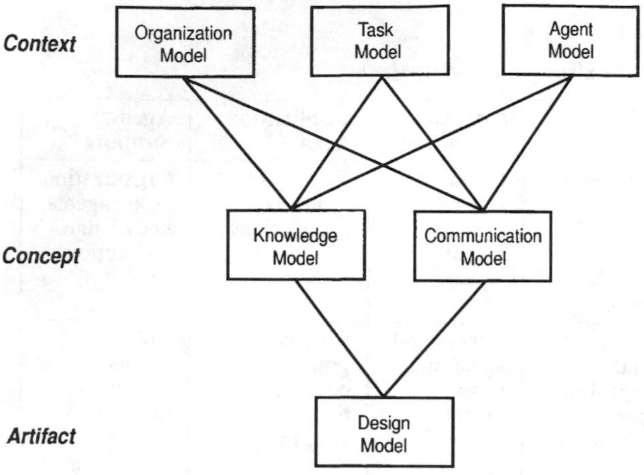

Figure 4.1 CommonKADS layers and components.

the goal of the task, control, features, environmental constraints such as quality or performance criteria, and its required capabilities, like knowledge or specific competencies. In particular, tasks are performed by agents. An information modeling view consists of the functional view (for example, the information flow), the static information structure view (for example, the structure of objects and their associations), and the control view (defining the ordering of the subtasks).

- *Agent model* describes all relevant properties like various roles, competencies, and reasoning capabilities of agents able to achieve tasks of the task model. It mainly provides a different viewpoint on information already available in other models. An agent is any actor performing some task, such as a database, an expert system, a user, or any software system. The agent model is described with the attributes: *name*, *type* (human, agent, and software system), *subclass-of* (to define inheritance), *position*, and *groups* (the groups to which an agent belongs). In addition, MAS-CommonKADS adds to this model the following components: *services*, describing specific facilities offered to other agents; *goals*, being the objectives of an agent; *reasoning capabilities* stating the requirements on the agent imposed by the task assignment; *general capabilities* such as its skills (including sensors and effectors) and agent (communication) languages; and *constraints* such as norms, preferences, and permissions of the agent.
- *Knowledge model* or *Expertise model* describes the capabilities of an agent with a bias towards knowledge-intensive problem-solving capabilities. The expertise model is divided into *domain knowledge* relevant for the application, *inference knowledge* being the basic reasoning knowledge, *task knowledge* being the goal and its decomposition into subgoals and subtasks, and *strategic knowledge*. The focus of CommonKADS lies in the definition of these models.

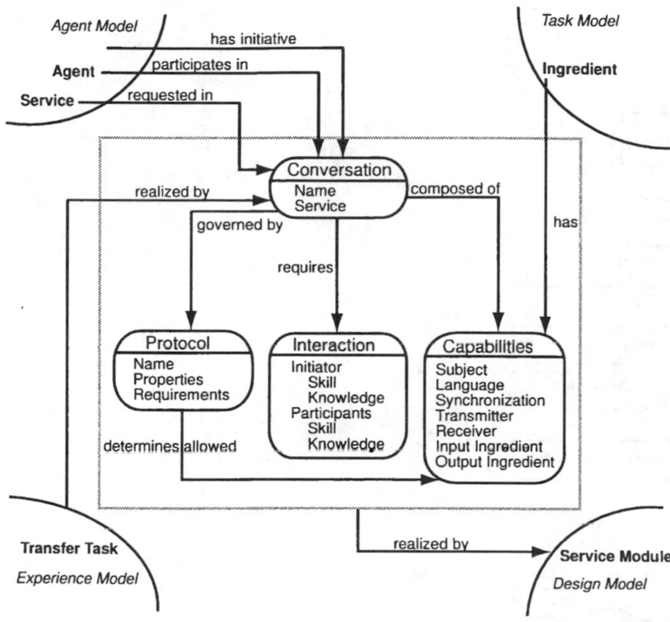

Figure 4.2 The CommonKADS coordination model. (*After:* [15].)

- *Communication model* describes—in an implementation-independent way—all the communication between agents in terms of transactions, transaction plans, initiatives, and capabilities needed in order to take part in a transaction. The main drawback of CommonKADS is the restricted communication model: due to its original aim, its focus is on the definition of human-computer interaction, and no support is provided for complex interaction between agents. As a consequence of this, MAS-CommonKADS adds an additional model, the *coordination model* (an example of which is shown in Figure 4.2), which applies different protocol techniques, as above, to extend the expressiveness of the specification method. The coordination model consists of conversations used to request a service or to request or update information; interactions defining simple interchange of messages; capabilities being the skills and knowledge of the agents involved in conversations; and protocols defining the set of rules for a conversation. The graphical notations used are, for example, message sequence charts [16] and communicating extended finite-state machines that support three types of events: message, external, and internal events, as shown in Figure 4.3.

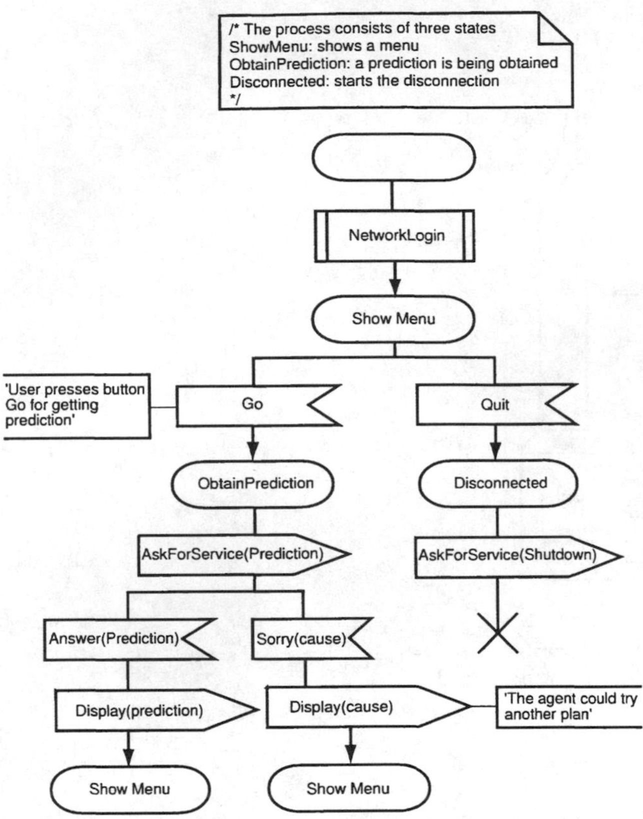

Figure 4.3 Extended finite-state machine in CommonKADS. (*After:* [15].)

- *Design model* describes the design of the system, its architecture, implementation platform, and software modules. Therefore a three-stage transformation process is suggested, consisting of *application design* describing the functional decomposition, object-oriented decomposition, and AI paradigms like constraint-based programming; *architectural design* defining a computational infrastructure capable of implementing the architecture; and *platform design* considering how the ideal knowledge representation and inference techniques should be implemented in the chosen software.

In addition, while the scope of CommonKADS covers the *analysis phase of software engineering*, MAS-CommonKADS extends support for the software engineering phases to the complete software life cycle, including the following (see [15]):

- *Conceptualization*: As in object-oriented analysis and design, MAS-CommonKADS starts with a use case centered approach to formalize the first description of the problem. The use cases also provide the basis for further testing.
- *Analysis*: The output of this phase is a detailed requirements specification obtained by *delimitation* to distinguish the agent-based system from the external nonagent system (resulting in a first version of the agent model and the coordination model); *decomposition* of the system based on the geographical, logical, and knowledge distribution; and *validation*, or correctness with respect to previous definitions and other models. The obtained models are the organization, task, agent, communication, cooperation, and expertise models.
- *Design*: This phase covers aspects such as *application design* through decomposition into submodules; *architecture design* through selection of a multiagent architecture and determining the infrastructure based on the applied network, used knowledge and the coordination; and *platform design*, addressing the needed software and hardware. The basis for this phase is mainly the expertise model and the task model.
- *Coding and testing*: This is performed on an individual agent basis.
- *Integration*: This relates to integration of the different individual agents and testing of the multiagent system.
- *Operation and maintenance*: This is as for any software system.

4.4 AGENT-ORIENTED APPROACHES

A perceived lack in the knowledge engineering software development methodologies was that they were not designed in the context of supporting the development of agent systems, and that as a result they had limited capability to support agent-specific functions, which could only partly be overcome by extensions such as those seen for MAS-CommonKADS. In this section, we review two main agent-oriented approaches, namely Gaia [4] with its extension, ROADMAP [19], and the SODA methodology [20].

4.4.1 Gaia and Its Extension ROADMAP

Gaia is a methodology for agent-oriented analysis and design supporting macro (societal) level as well as micro (agent) level aspects [4]. Gaia was designed to deal with coarse-grained computational systems, to maximize some global quality measure, and to handle heterogeneous agents independent of programming languages and agent architectures. It assumes static organization structures and agents that have static abilities and services, with fewer than 100 different agent types. ROADMAP extends Gaia by adding elements to deal with requirements analysis in more detail, by using use cases and to handle open systems environments. Moreover, it focuses more on the specification of interactions based on AUML (Agent UML, covered in Section 4.6) [21]. Here, we present a unified view of both methodologies.

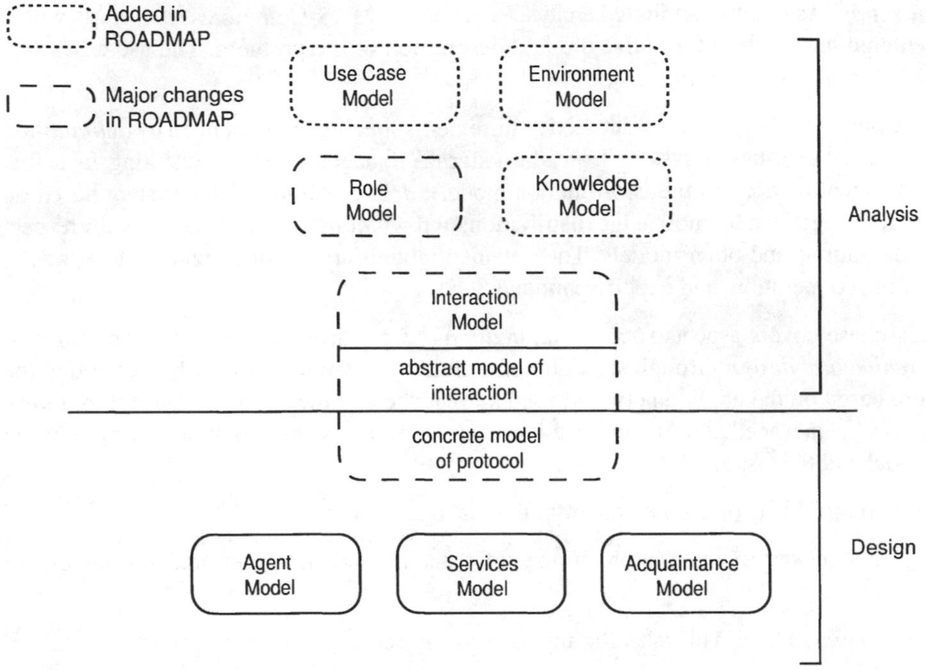

Figure 4.4 Models employed by Gaia and ROADMAP.

In Gaia, a system is developed from an organizational point of view, starting with an organizational model that is refined in subsequent development steps. It is intended to allow an analyst to progress systematically from a statement of requirements not formally described in the methodology (which in ROADMAP is mainly derived by applying use case models) to a design that is sufficiently detailed to be implemented directly, with the aim of obtaining detailed models from which the system can be constructed. The relevant models of Gaia and ROADMAP are shown in Figure 4.4.

In the analysis phase, Gaia defines the role and interaction models, whereas ROADMAP adds the use case, environment, and knowledge models. Gaia views an organization as a collection of roles standing in a certain relationship to one another, and taking part in systematic institutionalized patterns of interactions with other roles. These roles can subsequently be instantiated with actual individuals. ROADMAP starts—comparable to several object-oriented approaches—with a use case model from which it derives the environment, role, and knowledge models. The knowledge model is strongly related to the role model and the environment model. Both approaches deal with the definition of an interaction model, defining the conversation at a high level and at a low level. (ROADMAP allows designers, in addition, to apply the UML extension to sequence diagrams [21].)

In the design phase the agent model derived from roles is specified, as well as the services model and acquaintance model.

4.4.1.1 Analysis

In the analysis phase the following models are created, based on [4, 19].

- *Use case model* (only ROADMAP): Just as in the object-oriented (OO) world, ROADMAP suggests applying use cases to discover requirements in an effective and sufficient way. Similar to UML, the model includes a graphical representation of diagrams and specific text scenarios. However, the semantics of use cases is different from traditional OO approaches. In contrast to a traditional model that would assume a user to be interacting with the software system, the view taken is *imagined*, that a user interacts with a team of abstract ideal agents possessing the knowledge, ability, or mental states required to provide the best service.
- *Environment model* (only ROADMAP): The environment model, derived from the use case model, provides a holistic description of the system environment, since the ROADMAP approach targets complex open systems, usually embedded in highly dynamic and heterogeneous environments. The model is the knowledge foundation for any environmental changes during the system execution. It consists of a *tree hierarchy of zones* in the environment (for example, the Internet, a local computer, or the physical environment of a house) based on OO inheritance and aggregation and *zone schemas*, characterized by a textual description of the zones derived from the use cases and the *attributes*: *static objects* (any entity in the environment known to some agent, but with no interaction), *objects* (any entity an agent interacts with), *constraints*, *sources of uncertainty* (which have to be analyzed), and *assumptions* made about the zones.
- *Knowledge model* (only ROADMAP): The knowledge model, derived from the use case and environment model, provides a holistic description of the domain knowledge used in the system. It consists of a hierarchy of knowledge components and a description for each knowledge component, and thus identifies the knowledge required to deliver the agent behaviors in the appropriate zones for each use case. Knowledge components are assigned to roles and therefore connect the role model with the use case model and the environment.
- *Role model*: The role model identifies the key roles of the system. The roles typically correspond to individuals, departments, or organizations as in real life, and are characterized by four attributes, as follows:
  - *Responsibilities* define the functionality of an agent by giving the *liveness* properties (intuitively stating "something good happens") and *safety* properties such as invariants.
  - *Permissions* are defined in terms of rights, with information and knowledge resources that can be used by the role, and the resource limits within which the role executor must operate.
  - The *activities* of a role are some private actions a role can perform without interaction with other agents.

Table 4.2

Role Schemas and Names in Gaia

Role Schema	**Name of Role**
Description	*Protocols and activities in which the role plays a part*
Permissions	*Rights associated with the role*
Responsibilities	
Liveness	*Liveness properties*
Safety	*Safety properties*

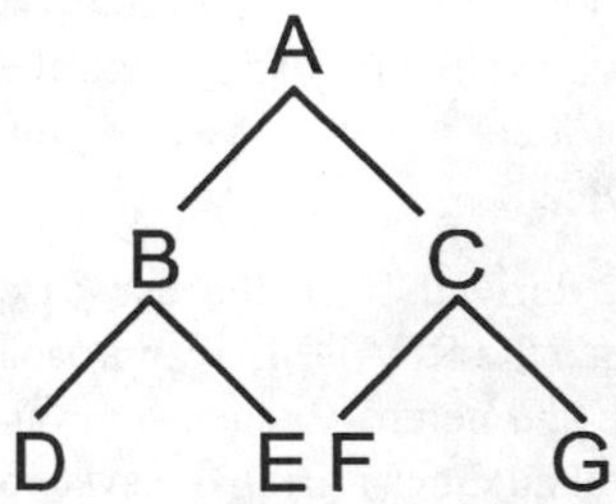

Figure 4.5 Role hierarchy in Gaia.

– Finally, *protocols* define the way that a role can interact with other roles, like the contract net (described in Chapter 2), in an abstract way.

In the design phase, the protocols are defined in more detail. Gaia's role model consists of a set of role schemata, one for each role in a system, as illustrated in Table 4.2. To this, ROADMAP adds a role hierarchy as shown in Figure 4.5. Here, the leaf nodes are atomic roles, representing characteristics of individual agents, whereas the other roles are composite roles, like A, B, and C, using aggregation. In ROADMAP, aggregation assumes a dynamic teamwork semantics; that is, the individual subroles are said to participate in the super-role, and each may own a thread of execution, a set of knowledge, and functionality. In addition, a composite role represents a localized organization or society of roles with attributes modeling social aspects (*subrole attribute*), like the organization structure, social goals, social tasks, or social laws. Moreover, the *knowledge attribute* represents local social knowledge. To extend and maintain open systems, ROADMAP allows changing the application architecture as well as the ability of individual agents during run time. This is obtained by allowing a role to have read, write, or create permissions on definitions of other roles.

- *Interaction model*: The interaction model was originally defined in Gaia for the definition of protocols. It describes the dependencies and relationships between various roles in a multiagent organization (providing a pattern of interaction). ROADMAP names this the *protocol model*, and defines in addition an *interaction model* based on AUML interaction diagrams. In our view, the latter belongs more to the design phase and therefore we discuss it in the next section. Gaia characterizes a protocol by the attribute's purpose (a brief textual description of the nature of the interaction, the *initiator* of the protocol, or the role or roles starting the conversation), the *responder* (or the role participating in the protocol), inputs and outputs (or the information used and supplied by the initiator and responder), as well as a brief textual description of any processing the protocol initiator performs during the course of the interaction (*processing*).

4.4.1.2 Design

In typical design processes such as those used in OO approaches, an abstract model of the analysis phase is transformed into a sufficiently concrete level that can easily be implemented. In contrast to this, the design phase in Gaia has the goal of developing a level of abstraction that is sufficiently specific to allow traditional design techniques to be used to implement the agents.

Both Gaia and ROADMAP define the *agent model*, *services model*, and *acquaintance model*. In addition, ROADMAP allows designers to refine the *interaction model*.

- *Interaction model*: The interaction model provides a detailed definition of the interaction between different roles or individual agents by applying AUML interaction diagrams, an extension of UML sequence diagrams, to model interaction diagrams such as the FIPA Contract Net Protocol. Note that since this work was done, a revised version has been developed in the context of FIPA.[5]

- *Agent model*: The agent model identifies the *agent types* that will make up the system, and can be thought of as a set of agent roles. The *agent instances* that will be instantiated from these types are documented by annotating agent types with, for example, n, $m..n$, or *, describing in the usual way the number of instances of an agent type. Based on efficiency aspects, an agent type implements a set of agent roles.

- *Services model*: The services model identifies the main services, defining the function of an agent as characterized by input, output, preconditions, and postconditions that are required to realize the agent's role. A service does not describe the implementation view of a specific function; instead it is derived from the list of protocols, activities, responsibilities, and liveness properties of a role. ROADMAP also takes the social and knowledge aspects of the previous models into account.

- *Acquaintance model*: The acquaintance model documents the lines of communication between the different agents. The purpose is to identify any potential communication bottlenecks that may cause problems at run time.

Examples of these models are shown in Tables 4.3, 4.4, and 4.5, loosely based on the example from [19]. The scenario assumes that the operation of a research lab is supported by an agent-based system. In Table 4.3, some roles are outlined such as *InformationExchange* for allowing agents to exchange papers and presentations between researchers and *OnlineDiscussion* for participating in

5 http://www.auml.org

Table 4.3

Partial Role Hierarchy

- System
  - InformationExchange
  - OnlineDiscussion
  - MeetingSupport
  - Admin
    - SysConfig // Software and hardware configuration
    - MobileDevMgt // Mobile device management
    - Profiles // Students, Researchers, Staff
    - Install // Install and update software
    - Location // For locating people in the lab
  - Security
    - PhysicalSecurity
    - Network_Computers
      - Virus_Worm_Protection
      - Intrusion_Detection
      - Server_Log_Analysis_and_Forensics
      - User_and_Program_Authentication
      - Content_Scanning
- Reliability
- Performance

online debates. In Table 4.4, an agent class implementing the *Admin* role is shown. Finally, Table 4.5 shows the Admin role activities and protocols.

4.4.2 SODA

Another agent-oriented software engineering methodology, mainly focusing on societies similar to Gaia's organizations, is SODA (societies in open and distributed agent spaces [20]). Like ROADMAP, it addresses some of the shortcomings of Gaia such as its inadequacies in dealing with open systems or self-interested agents. Moreover, SODA takes the agent environment into account and provides mechanisms for specific abstractions and procedures for the design of agent infrastructures. Based on the analysis and design of *agent societies* (exhibiting global behaviors not deducible from the behavior of individual agents) and *agent environments* (the space in which agents operate and interact, such as open, distributed, decentralized, heterogeneous, dynamic, and unpredictable environments), SODA provides support for modeling the *inter*agent aspects. However, *intra*agent aspects are *not* covered. Thus, SODA is not a complete methodology; rather, its goal is to define a coherent conceptual framework and a comprehensive software engineering procedure that accounts for the analysis and design of individual agents from a behavioral point of view, agent societies, and agent environments. Just like most of the methodologies considered here, SODA supports the analysis and design phase.

Table 4.4

Example of an Agent Class

Agent Class:	AdminAgent
Role Assigned:	Admin
Description:	Taking the role of Admin and providing services for protocols and activities of Admin
Services:	QueryConfigSvc **implements** Admin.SetConfig
	SetConfigSvc **implements** Admin.SetConfig
	QueryProfileSvc **implements** Admin.QueryProfile
	UpdateProfileSvc **implements** Admin.UpdateProfile
	QueryLocationSvc **implements** Admin.QueryLocation
	WaitSvc **implements** Admin.Wait

Table 4.5

Role Description

Role Name:		Admin
Description:		General administration of a researcher's system
Subroles:		SysConfig, MobileDevMgt, Profiles, Install and Location
Knowledge:		Software and hardware types, versions and settings
		User Profile, and Location regulations
Permission:		Changes all software and hardware settings
		Changes all Profiles
		Changes all Location info
		Changes System* // reflection
Responsibilities:		
Liveness:		
Admin	=	$(\text{Work} \mid \text{Wait})^{W}$
Work	=	$\text{QueryConfig}^{*} \parallel \text{SetConfig}^{*} \parallel \text{QueryProfile}^{*} \parallel$
		$\text{UpdateProfile}^{*} \parallel \text{QueryLocation}^{*}$
		involves sysConfig, deviceMgt, profiles, install and location
Safety:		Consistent (software and hardware settings)
		Consistent (profiles)
		Consistent (location info)
Protocols:		QueryConfig **involves** SysConfig.QueryConfig & DevMgt.SetConfig
		QueryProfile **involves** Profiles.QueryProfile
		UpdateProfile **involves** Profiles.UpdateProfile
		QueryLocation **involves** SysConfig.QueryConfig
Activities:		Wait

4.4.2.1 Analysis

During the analysis phase in SODA, the application domain is studied and modeled, the available computational resources and the technological constraints are listed, and the fundamental application goals and targets are identified. The result of the analysis phase is typically expressed in terms of high-level abstractions and relationships, providing designers with a formal or semiformal description of the intended overall application structure and organization. The SODA analysis phase delivers three models [20]:

- *Role model*: The application goals are modeled in terms of the tasks to be achieved, which are associated with *roles* and *groups*. *Tasks* are expressed in terms of the responsibilities they involve, the competencies they require, and the resources they depend upon. Responsibilities are expressed in terms of the states of the world that should result from task accomplishment, while tasks are classified as either individual or social. Typically, social tasks are those that require a number of different competencies and access to several different resources, whereas individual tasks are more likely to require well-delimited competence and limited resources. Each individual task is associated with an individual role, which is defined in terms of its individual task, its permissions to access resources, and the corresponding interaction protocol. Analogously, social tasks are assigned to groups. A group is defined in terms of its social tasks, its permissions to access the resources, the participating social roles, and the corresponding interaction rule. A social role describes the role played by an individual within a group, and may either coincide with an already defined (individual) role, or be defined *ex novo*, in the same form as an individual role, by specifying an individual task as a subtask of one assigned to a group to which the individual belongs.
- *Resource model*: The application environment is modeled in terms of the *services* available, which are associated with abstract *resources*. A resource is defined in terms of the service it provides, its access modes, the permissions granted to roles and groups to exploit its service, and the corresponding interaction protocol. If a task assigned to a role or a group requires a given service, the access modes are determined and expressed in terms of the granted *permission* to access the resource in charge of that service. Such a permission is then associated with that role or group.
- *Interaction model*: The interaction involving roles, groups, and resources is modeled in terms of *interaction protocols*, expressed as *information* required and provided by roles and resources in order to accomplish its individual tasks, and *interaction rules*, governing interaction among social roles and resources so as to make the group accomplish its social task.

4.4.2.2 Design

Design in SODA is concerned with the representation of the abstract models resulting from the analysis phase in terms of the design abstractions provided by the methodology. The result of the design phase is typically expressed in terms of abstractions that can be mapped one-to-one onto the actual components of the deployed system.

- *Agent model*: An *agent class* is defined as a set of (one or more) individual and social roles. As a result, an agent class is characterized by the tasks, the set of permissions, and the interaction protocols associated with its roles. Agent classes can be further characterized in terms of other features: their *cardinality* (the number of agents of that class), their *location* (with respect to the topological model defined in this phase—either fixed for static agents, or variable for mobile agents), and their *source* (from inside or outside the system, given the assumption of openness). Since SODA only deals with *inter*agent aspects (the observable behavior of an agent), the *intra*-agent aspects are not covered in SODA, and can be based on results of other methodologies.

- *Society model*: Each group is mapped onto a *society of agents*. An agent society is first characterized by the social tasks, the set of the permissions, the participating social roles, and the interaction rules associated with its groups. The main issue in the society model is how to design interaction rules so as to make societies accomplish their social tasks. Since this deals with managing agent interaction, the problem of achieving the desired social behavior by means of suitable social rules is basically a *coordination* issue. As a result, societies in SODA are designed around *coordination media*: the abstractions provided by coordination models for the coordination of multicomponent *systems*. Thus, the first task in the design of agent societies is the choice of the most fit coordination model, the one providing the abstractions that are expressive enough to model the society interaction rules. In this way, a society is designed around coordination media embodying the interaction rules of its groups in terms of *coordination rules*. The behavior of suitably designed coordination media, along with the behavior of the agents playing social roles and interacting through such media, causes an agent society to pursue its social tasks as a whole. This allows societies of agents to be designed as first-class entities.

- *Environment model*: Resources are mapped onto *infrastructure classes*. An infrastructure class is first characterized by the services, the access modes, the permissions granted to roles and groups, and the interaction protocols associated with its resources. Infrastructure classes can be further characterized in terms of other features: their cardinality (the number of infrastructure components belonging to that class), their location (with respect to topological abstractions), their *owner* (which may or may not be the same as the owner of the agent system, given the assumption of decentralized control). The design of the components belonging to an infrastructure class may follow the most appropriate methodology for that class; since SODA does not specifically address these issues, components like databases, expert systems, or security facilities can all be developed according to the most suitable specific methodology. What is determined by SODA is the outcome of this phase, the services to be provided by each infrastructure component, and the interfaces resulting from its associated interaction protocols. Finally, SODA assumes that a topological model of the agent environment is provided by the designer but does not provide for topological abstractions on its own, since any system or any application domain may call for different approaches to the problem.

4.4.3 Comparison

Both agent-oriented methodologies presented in this section deal with analysis as well as the design phase, resulting in a design specification that can either be directly mapped onto an underlying system (ROADMAP, SODA) or to which state-of-the-art technologies can be applied to refine the models to obtain a well-designed model of the system (Gaia).

The role model of SODA is similar to the role model of Gaia and ROADMAP, since both associate different functionality with an agent satisfying a role, but with different ways of deriving them. Interactions are covered in all three approaches, with the difference that SODA adds interaction rules among groups within a society, whereas Gaia and ROADMAP deal with interaction between agents of specific roles. The motivation behind the resource model and the environment model of ROADMAP is similar, but its expression is based on different views on the environments. The use case model and knowledge model of ROADMAP seem to be necessary models to ensure that the requirements are well-defined, and to cope with the information (knowledge) available and used in the system. The SODA agent model deals with similar aspects to the Gaia and ROADMAP role and agent model with some smaller differences; in particular, the different aspects are totally shifted to the design phase in SODA.

4.5 METHODOLOGICAL EXTENSIONS TO OBJECT-ORIENTED APPROACHES

A good procedure (if not the only viable one) for the successful industrial deployment of agent technology is to present the new technology as an incremental extension of known and trusted methods, and to provide powerful engineering tools that support industry-accepted methods of technology deployment. Accepted methods of industrial software development depend on standard representations for artifacts to support the analysis, specification, and design of agent software.

At present, agent-oriented software engineering still lacks the availability of suitable software processes and tools, yet the Unified Modeling Language (UML) is gaining wide acceptance for the representation of engineering artifacts using the object-oriented paradigm. Viewing agents as the next step beyond objects leads several authors (see, for example, [21] for a discussion of this topic) to explore extensions to UML, and idioms within UML, to accommodate the distinctive requirements of agents as well as defining software methodologies based on object-oriented approaches. In general, building methods and tools for agent-oriented software development on top of their object-oriented counterparts seems appropriate, as it lends itself to smoother migration between these different technology generations and, at the same time, improves accessibility of agent-based methods and tools to the object-oriented developer community which, as of today, prevails in industry.

In this section, we more closely examine agent methodologies that directly extend object-oriented approaches, while in the following section we consider UML notations and extensions available for the specification of agent-based systems. Since most of the notations use graphical representations of software artifacts, we use examples taken from the original research papers, but provide only little explanation for reasons of brevity.

4.5.1 Agent Modeling Techniques for Systems of BDI Agents

One of the first methodologies for the development of BDI agents based on OO technologies was presented in [8, 9, 22]. The agent methodology distinguishes between the *external viewpoint*—the system is decomposed into agents, modeled as complex objects characterized by their purpose, their responsibilities, the services they perform, the information they require and maintain, and their external interactions—and the *internal viewpoint*—the elements required by a particular agent architecture (an agent's beliefs, goals, and plans) must be modeled for each agent.

The methodology for the *external aspects* consists of four major steps (as described in [9]):

1. Identify the roles of the application domain, and identify the lifetime of each role; elaborate an agent class hierarchy. The initial definition of agent classes should be quite abstract, not assuming any particular granularity of agency.
2. For each role, identify its associated responsibilities and the services provided and used to fulfill those responsibilities. As well as services provided to and by other agents upon request, services may include interaction with the external environment or human users. Conversely, a responsibility may induce a requirement that an agent be notified of conditions detected by other agents or users. Decompose agent classes to the service level.
3. For each service, identify the interactions associated with the provision of the service, the performatives (speech acts) required for those interactions, and their information content. Identify events and conditions to be noticed, actions to be performed, and other information requirements. Determine the control relationships between agents. At this point, the internal modeling of each agent class can be performed.
4. Refine the agent hierarchy. Where there is commonality of information or services between agent classes, consider introducing a new agent class that can be specialized by existing agent classes to encapsulate common aspects. Compose agent classes, via inheritance or aggregation, guided by commonality of lifetime, information and interfaces, and similarity of services. Introduce concrete agent classes, taking into account implementation-dependent considerations of performance, communication costs and latencies, fault-tolerance requirements, and so on. Refine the control relationships. Finally, based on considerations of lifetime and multiplicity, introduce agent instances.

The methodology for *internal modeling* can be expressed as two steps, as shown in [9]:

1. Analyze the means of achieving the goals. For each goal, analyze the different contexts in which the goal must be achieved. For each of these contexts, decompose each goal into activities, represented by subgoals, and actions. Analyze the order and the conditions under which these activities and actions need to be performed, the way in which failure should be addressed, and generate a plan to achieve the goal. Repeat the analysis for subgoals.
2. Build the beliefs of the system. Analyze the various contexts, and the conditions that control the execution of activities and actions, and decompose them into component beliefs. Analyze the

input and output data requirements for each subgoal in a plan, and make sure that this information is available either as beliefs or as outputs from prior subgoals in the plan.

These steps are iterated as the models that capture the results of the analysis are progressively elaborated, revised, and refined. Refinement of the internal models feeds back to the external models; building the plans and beliefs of an agent class clarifies the information requirements of services, particularly with respect to monitoring and notification. Analyzing interaction scenarios, which can be derived from the plans, may also lead to the redefinition of services. For each of these views different models are described, based on [8, 9].

External Viewpoint

The external view is characterized by two models that are largely independent of the underlying BDI architecture.

- The *agent model* describes the hierarchical relationship among different abstract and concrete agent classes (*agent class model*), and identifies the agent instances that may exist within the system, their multiplicity, and the time at which they come into existence (*agent instance model*).
- An *agent class model* is similar to a UML class diagram denoting both abstract and concrete (instantiable) agent classes. Abstract classes are distinguished by some kind of stereotype. Inheritance and aggregation are defined in a similar way to UML. Other associations between agent classes are not allowed. Agent classes may have attributes but not operations. Attributes may not be arbitrary user-named data items, but are restricted to a set of predefined reserved attributes. For example, each class may have associated belief, goal, and plan models, specified by the attributes, beliefs, goals, and plans. Other attributes of an agent class include its belief-state-set and goal-state-set, which determine possible initial mental states. Particular elements of these sets may then be specified as the default initial mental state for the agent class, via the initial-belief-state and initial-goal-state attributes. Multiple inheritance is permitted. As usual, inheritance denotes an *is-a* relationship, and aggregation denotes a *has-a* relationship, but in the context of an agent model these relationships have a special semantics. Agents inherit and may refine the belief, goal, and plan models of their superclasses. Note that it is, for example, the set of plans that is refined, rather than the individual plans. Aggregation denotes the incorporation within an agent of subagents that do not have access to each other's beliefs, goals, and plans.
- An *agent instance model* is an instance diagram that defines both the static agent set instantiated at compile-time (marked by some kind of stereotype) and the dynamic agent set instantiated at run-time. In contrast to UML class and object diagrams, an agent instance is linked to a concrete agent class by an instantiation edge, whereas in UML instances are underlined. Static instances must be named, but the naming of dynamic instances may be deferred until their instantiation. A multiplicity instantiation is supported. The initial mental state of an agent instance may be specified by the *initial-belief-state* and *initial-goal-state* attributes whose values are particular elements of the belief and goal state sets of the agent class. If not specified, the defaults are

the values associated with the agent class. For dynamic agent instances, these attributes may be overridden at the time the agent is created.

- The *interaction model* describes the responsibilities of an agent class, the services it provides, associated interactions, and control relationships between agent classes. This includes the syntax and semantics of messages used for interagent communication, and for communication between agents and other system components, such as user interfaces.

Internal Viewpoint

BDI agents are viewed as having certain mental attitudes, *beliefs*, *desires*, and *intentions*, which represent, respectively, their informational, motivational, and deliberative states. These aspects are captured, for each agent class, by the following models:

- The *belief model* describes the information about the environment and the internal state that an agent of that class may hold, and the actions it may perform. The possible beliefs of an agent and their properties, such as whether or not they may change over time, are described by a *belief set*. In addition, one or more *belief states*—particular instances of the belief set—may be defined and used to specify an agent's initial mental state. The belief set is specified by a set of object diagrams that define the domain of the beliefs of an agent class. A belief state is a set of instance diagrams that define a particular instance of the belief set. Formally, it is defined by set of typed predicates whose arguments are terms over a universe of predefined and user-defined function symbols. The classes and instances defined therein correspond, in many cases, to real entities in the application domain but, unlike an object model, the definitions do not define the behaviors of these entities, since they represent an agent's *beliefs* about those entities. A class in a belief set diagram serves to define the type signatures of attributes of an object, functions that may be applied to the object, and other predicates that apply to the object, including actions, which have a special role in plans. Attributes, which define binary predicates, are specified in the usual way.

- The *goal model* describes the goals that an agent may possibly adopt, and the events to which it can respond. It consists of a *goal set* that specifies the goal and event domain and one or more *goal states*—sets of ground goals—used to specify an agent's initial mental state. Formally, a goal set is a set of goal formula signatures. Each such formula consists of a modal goal operator applied to a predicate from the belief set. The modal goal operators are: *achieve* (denoted by !) representing a goal of achievement, *verify* (denoted by ?) representing a goal of verification, and *test* (denoted by $) representing a goal of determination. Goal formulas occur within activities in the bodies of plans and within their activation events.

- The *plan model* describes the plans that an agent may possibly employ to achieve its goals. It consists of a *plan set*, which describes the properties and control structure of *individual plans*. Plans are modeled similarly to simple UML state chart diagrams, which can be directly executed, showing how an agent should behave to achieve a goal or respond to an event. In contrast to UML, there are several differences: activities may be subgoals, denoted by formulas from the agent's goal set; conditions are predicates from the agent's belief set; actions include those defined in the

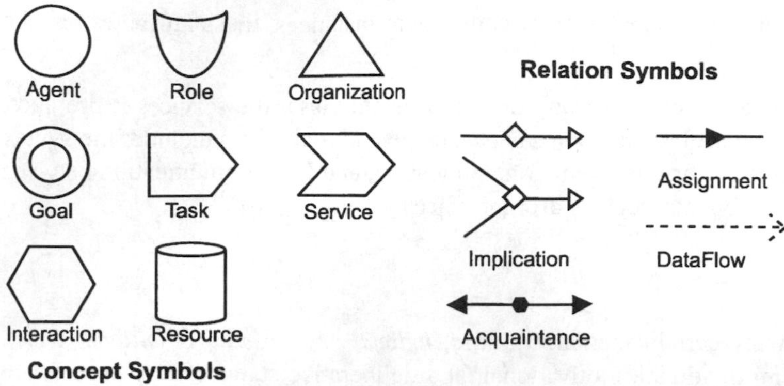

Figure 4.6 Concept symbols and relation symbols in MESSAGE.

belief set, and built-in actions. The latter include *assert* and *retract*, which update the belief state of the agent.

4.5.2 MESSAGE

MESSAGE (methodology for engineering systems of software agents) [23] is a methodology that builds upon best practice methods in current software engineering such as UML for the analysis and design of agent-based systems. It consists of (1) applicability guidelines; (2) a modeling notation that extends UML by agent-related concepts (inspired, for example, by Gaia); and (3) a process for analysis and design of agent systems based on RUP. The MESSAGE modeling notation extends UML notation by key agent-related concepts. We describe the notation used in MESSAGE based on the example presented in [23]. For details of the example, refer to this paper. The concept and relation symbols used are shown in Figure 4.6.

The main focus of MESSAGE is on the phase of analysis of agent-based systems. For this purpose, MESSAGE presents five analysis models, which analysts can use to capture different aspects of an agent-based system. The models are described in terms of sets of interrelated concepts. The five models are as follows:

- *Organization model*: The organization model captures the overall structure and behavior of a group of agents, and the external organization working together to reach common goals. In particular, it represents the responsibilities and authorities with respect to entities such as processes, information, and resources, and the structure of the organization in terms of suborganizations such as departments, divisions, and sections, expressed through power relationships (for example, superior-subordinate relationships). Moreover, it provides the *social view* characterizing the overall behavior of the group, while the agent model covers the *individual view* dealing with

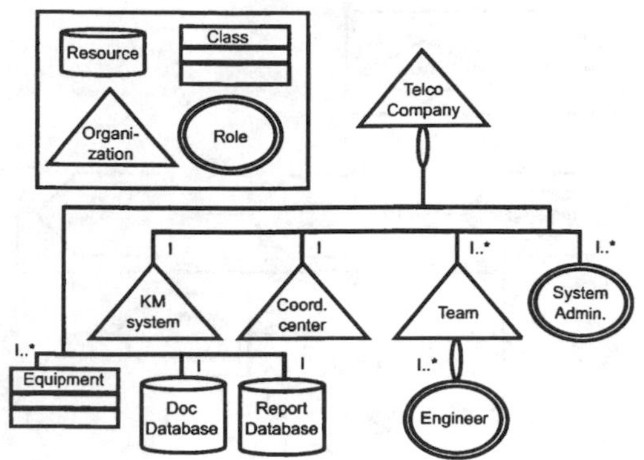

Figure 4.7 Examples of organization diagrams: structural relationships.

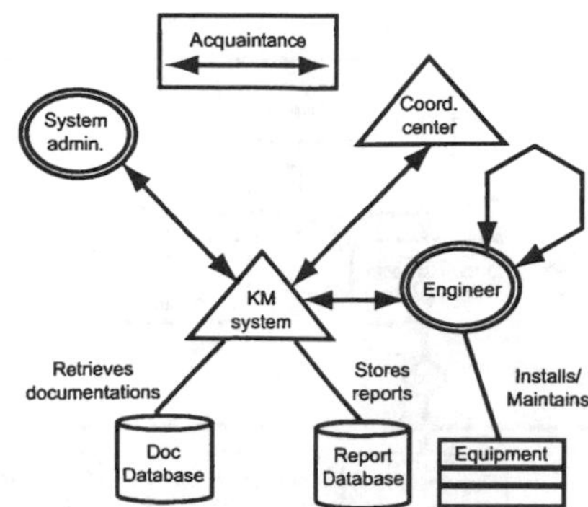

Figure 4.8 Examples of organization diagrams: acquaintance relationships (analysis phase 0 and 1).

the behavior of agents to achieve common or social goals. It offers software designers a useful abstraction for understanding the overall structure of the multiagent system, the agents themselves, the resources involved, the role of each agent, their responsibilities, and those tasks that are achieved individually and those achieved through cooperation. Different types of organization diagrams are available in MESSAGE to support the graphical representation of social concepts (see Figures 4.7 and 4.8).

- *Goal/task model*: The goal/task model defines the goals of the composite system (the agent system and its environment) and their decomposition into subgoals. It also covers the responsibility of agents for their commitments, the performance of tasks and actions by agents, the goals the tasks satisfy and the decomposition of tasks into subtasks, as well as describing tasks involved in an organizational workflow. It captures what the agent system and constituent agents do in terms of the goals that they work to attain and the tasks they must accomplish. Finally, the model also captures the way that goals and tasks of the system as a whole are related to goals and tasks assigned to specific agents and the dependencies among them.

  Goals and tasks both have attributes of type situation, such that they can be linked by logical dependencies to form graphs that show, for example, decomposition of high-level goals into subgoals, and how tasks can be performed to achieve goals. UML activity diagrams are applied for presentation purposes. Goals describe the desired states of the system and its environment, whereas tasks describe state transitions that are needed to satisfy agent goal commitments. Such state transitions are specified as precondition and postcondition attribute pairs. Actions are atomic tasks that can be performed by agents to satisfy their goal commitments. Task inputs are model elements (adapted from UML defining elements composing models) that are processed in the task, while task outputs are updates of the input model elements plus any new model element produced by the task. The desired states of a model element are specified by attributes called invariants, which are conditions that should always be true. Examples of goals and tasks are shown in Figures 4.9 and 4.10.

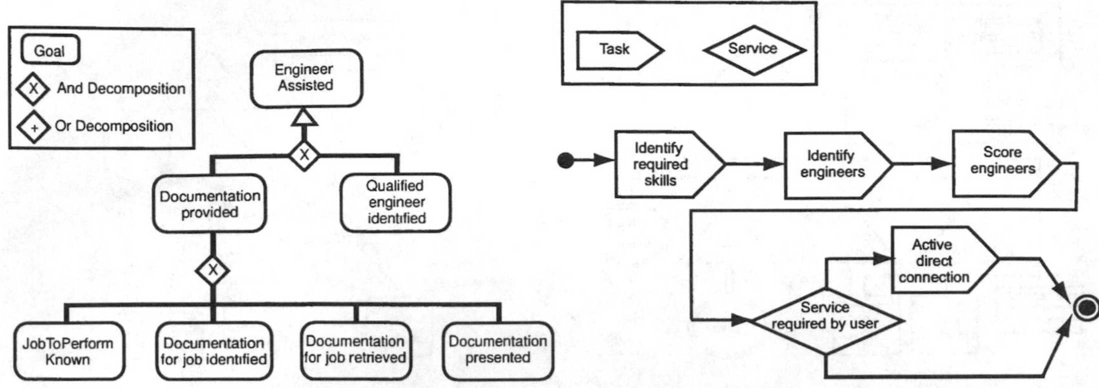

Figure 4.9 Example of a goal implication diagram.

Figure 4.10 Example of a workflow diagram.

- *Agent/role model*: The agent model consists of a set of individual agents and roles. The relationship between a role and an agent is defined analogously to that between an interface and an object class: a role describes the external characteristics of an agent in a particular context. An agent may be capable of playing several roles, and multiple agents may be able to play the same role. Roles can also be used as indirect references to agents. One aspect of the agent model is that it gathers together information specific to an individual agent or role, including its relationships to other entities. In particular, it contains a detailed and comprehensive description of each individual agent, providing an internal view that includes the agent's goals and the services (or the functional capability) they provide. This contrasts with the external perspective provided by the organization model. For each agent or role, the agent model uses schemata supported by diagrams to define its characteristics, such as the goals it is responsible for, the events it needs to sense, the resources it controls, the tasks it knows how to perform, *behavior rules*, and so on. An example of an agent model is illustrated in Figure 4.11.
- *Domain (information) model*: The domain model functions as a repository of relevant information about the problem domain. The conceptualization of the specific domain is assumed to be a mixture of *object-oriented* (by which all entities in the domain are classified in classes, and each class groups all entities with a common structure) and *relational* (by which a number of relations describe the mutual relationships between the entities belonging to the different classes). Thus, the domain model defines the *domain-specific classes* agents deal with, and describes the structure of each class in terms of a number of (possibly zero) attributes with values that can belong to primitive types or that can be instances of other domain-specific classes. In addition, *domain-specific relations*, holding among the instances of the domain-specific classes, are captured. Class diagrams are used for this model, as illustrated in Figure 4.12.
- *Interaction model*: The interaction model is concerned with capturing the way in which agents (or roles) exchange information with each another (as well as with their environment). The

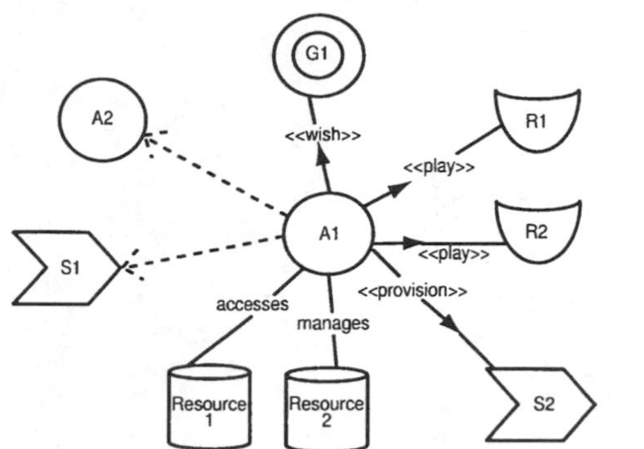

Figure 4.11 Example of agent diagram.

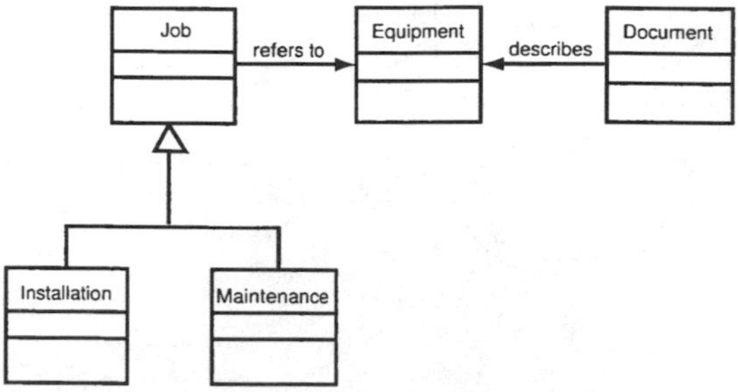

Figure 4.12 Example of domain model as UML class diagrams.

content of the messages within an interaction may be described in the domain model. Interactions are specified from both a high-level perspective (based on the interaction protocols from the Gaia methodology, described in Section 4.4.1) and a low-level perspective (based on the UML interaction protocols, described in Section 4.6.1). For each interaction among agents and roles, the model shows the initiator, the collaborators, the motivator (which, generally, is a goal for which the initiator is responsible), the relevant information supplied or achieved by each participant, the events that trigger the interaction, other relevant effects of the interaction (such as an agent becoming responsible for a new goal). Larger chains of interaction across the system (corresponding, for example, to use cases) can also be considered, such as delegation or workflows. An example of interaction is shown in Figure 4.13 and later in Section 4.6.1 on agent interaction diagrams.

4.5.3 Tropos

Tropos[6] [3, 24] is another good example of an agent-oriented software development methodology that is based on object-oriented techniques. In particular, Tropos relies on UML and offers processes for the application of UML mainly for the development of BDI agents and the agent platform JACK [25]. Some elements of UML (like class, sequence, activity, and interaction diagrams) are also adopted for modeling object and process perspectives. Tropos also uses the concepts of i*,[7] such as actors (where actors can be agents, positions, or roles), as well as social dependencies among actors (including goals, soft goals, tasks, and resource dependencies), which are embedded in a modeling framework that also supports generalization, aggregation, classification, and the notion of contexts [26]. Thus, Tropos was developed around two key features. First, the notions of agents, goals, plans, and various other knowledge-level concepts are provided as fundamental primitives used uniformly throughout the software development process. Second, a crucial role is assigned to requirements analysis and

6 http://www.cs.toronto.edu/km/tropos
7 http://www.cs.toronto.edu/km/istar

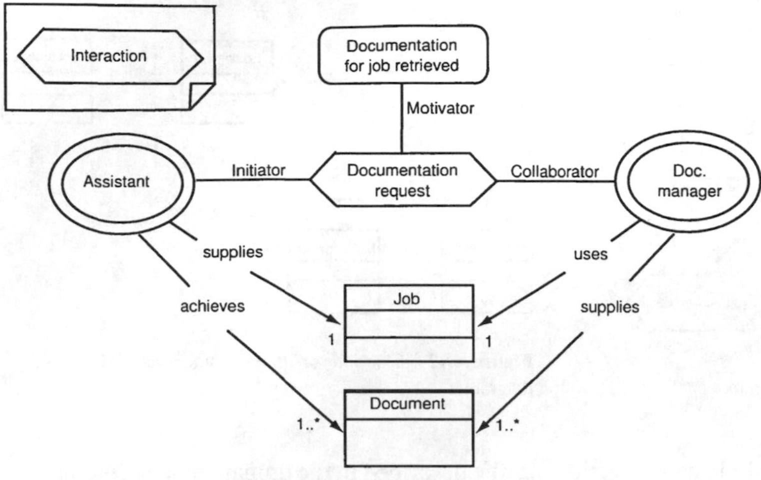

Figure 4.13 Example of a MESSAGE interaction.

specification when the system-to-be is analyzed with respect to its intended environment using a phase model, as follows:

- *Early requirements*: Identify relevant stakeholders (represented as actors), along with their respective objectives (represented as goals).
- *Late requirements*: Introduce the system to be developed as an actor, describing the dependencies to other actors and indicating the obligations of the system towards its environment.
- *Architectural design*: Introduce more system actors with assigned subgoals or subtasks of the goals and tasks assigned to the system.
- *Detailed design*: Define system actors in detail, including communication and coordination protocols.
- *Implementation*: Transform specifications into a skeleton for the implementation, mapping from the Tropos constructs to those of an agent programming platform.

The Tropos specification uses the notation illustrated in Figure 4.14, and also makes use of the types of models described here [3]:

- *Actor and dependency model*: Actor and dependency models, graphically represented through actor diagrams, result from the analysis of social and system actors, as well as from their goals and dependencies for goal achievement, as shown in Figure 4.15. An actor has strategic goals and intentionality, and represents a physical agent (such as a person) or a software agent, as well as

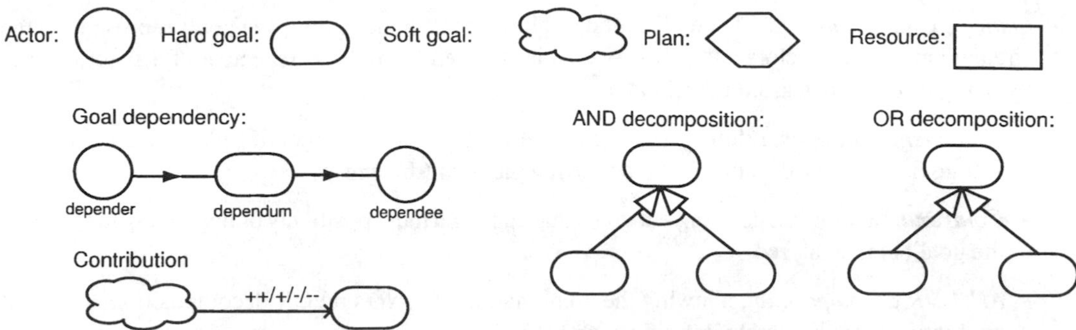

Figure 4.14 Examples of Tropos notation.

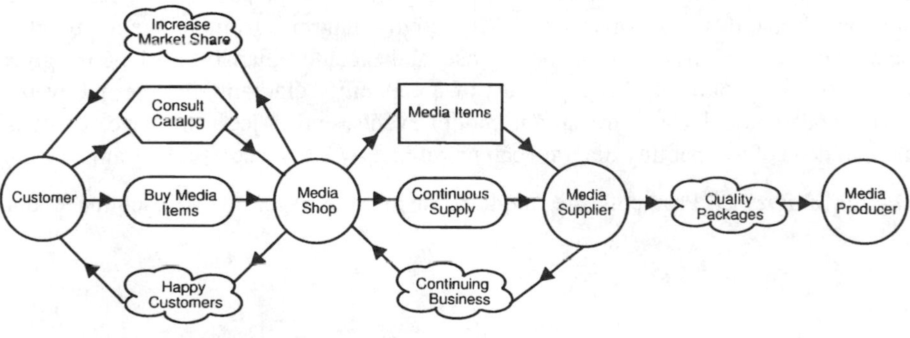

Figure 4.15 Actor diagram in Tropos. (*After:* [26].)

a role (which is an abstract characterization of the behavior of an actor within some specialized context) or a *position* (or a set of roles, typically played by one agent). An agent can occupy a position, while a position is said to cover a role. Actor models are extended during the late requirements phase by adding the system as another actor, along with its interdependencies with social actors. Actor models at the architectural design level provide a more detailed account of the system-to-be actor and its internal structure. This structure is specified in terms of subsystem actors, interconnected through data and control flows that are modeled as dependencies. A dependency between two actors indicates that one actor depends on another in order to attain some goal, execute some plan, or deliver a resource. By depending on other actors, an actor is able to achieve goals that it would otherwise be unable to achieve on its own, or not as easily, or not as well.

- *Goal and plan models*: Goal and plan models allow the designer to analyze goals representing the strategic interests of actors and plans. A goal is satisfied from the perspective of a specific actor by using three basic reasoning techniques:
  - *Means-ends analysis*, refining a goal into subgoals in order to identify plans, resources, and soft goals that provide a means for achieving the goal (the *end*);
  - *Contribution analysis*, pointing out goals that can contribute positively or negatively in reaching the goal being analyzed;
  - *AND/OR decomposition*, allowing the combination of AND and OR decompositions of a root goal into subgoals, thereby refining a goal structure.

  Two kinds of goals are distinguished, namely hard goals and soft goals, the latter having no clear-cut definition or criteria as to whether they are satisfied. Goal models are first developed during early requirements using the initially identified actors and their goals.
- *Capability diagram*: A capability, modeled either textually (for example, as a list of capabilities for each actor) or as capability diagrams using UML activity diagrams from an agent's point of view, represents the ability of an actor to define, choose, and execute a plan to fulfill a goal, given a particular operating environment. Starting states of a capability diagram are external events, whereas activity nodes model plans, transitions model events, and objects are used to model beliefs. Each plan node of a capability diagram can be refined by UML activity diagrams.
- *Agent interaction diagrams*: Protocols are modeled using the Agent UML sequence diagrams [21].

4.5.4 Prometheus

Like Tropos, Prometheus [27] is an iterative methodology covering the complete software engineering process and aiming at the development of intelligent agents (in particular BDI agents) using goals, beliefs, plans, and events, resulting in a specification that can be implemented with JACK [25]. The Prometheus methodology covers three phases, namely those of system specification, architectural design, and detailed design. Figure 4.16 illustrates the Prometheus process [27].

In the following, we describe the three phases of the Prometheus methodology [27]. More details can be found at the Prometheus Web site.[8]

- *System specification*: The system specification focuses on identifying the basic functions of the system, along with inputs (percepts), outputs (actions), and their processing (for example, how percepts are to be handled and any important shared data sources to model the system's interaction with respect to its changing and dynamic environment). To understand the purpose of a system, use case scenarios, borrowed from object-orientation with a slightly enhanced structure, give a more holistic view than mere analysis of the system functions in isolation.

8 http://www.cs.rmit.edu.au/agents/SAC/methodology.shtml

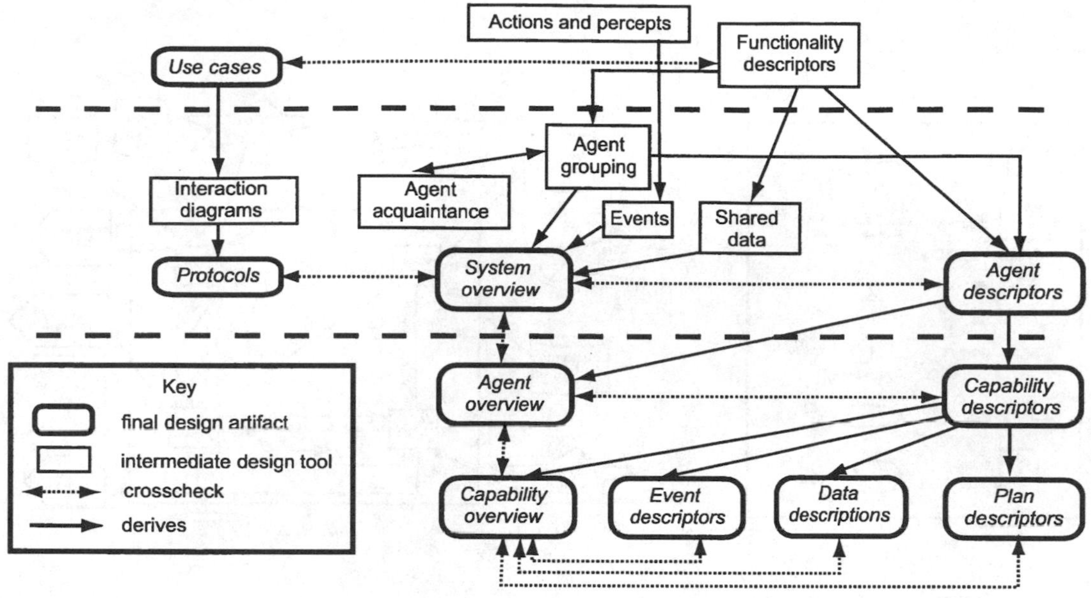

Figure 4.16 Prometheus process overview.

- *Architectural design*: The architectural design phase subsequent to system specification determines which agents the system will contain and how they will interact. The major decision to be made during the architectural design is which agents should exist within the system. The key design artifacts used in this phase are the *system overview diagram* tying together agents, events and shared data objects, *agent descriptions*, and the *interaction protocols* (based on Agent UML sequence diagrams [21]) fully specifying the interaction between agents. Agent messages are also identified, forming the interface between agents. Data objects are specified using traditional object-oriented techniques. Using the examples from [28], the diagrams are as illustrated in Figure 4.17.

- *Detailed design*: The detailed design phase describes the internals of each agent and the way in which it will achieve its tasks within the overall system. The focus is on defining capabilities (modules within the agent), internal events, plans, and detailed data structures. The outcomes from this phase are *agent overview diagrams* (see Figure 4.18) providing the agent's top-level capabilities, *capability diagrams* (see Figure 4.19), detailed *plan descriptors*, and *data descriptions*. Capabilities can be nested within other capabilities so that the model supports an arbitrary number of layers in the detailed design in order to achieve an understandable complexity at each level. They are refined until all capabilities are defined in terms of other capabilities, or (eventually) in terms of events, data, and plans.

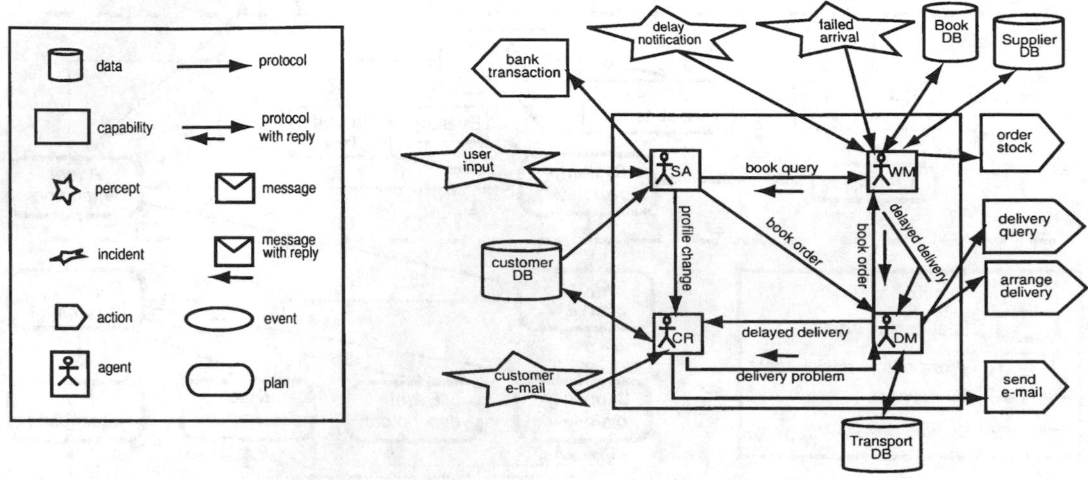

Figure 4.17 Example of system overview diagram.

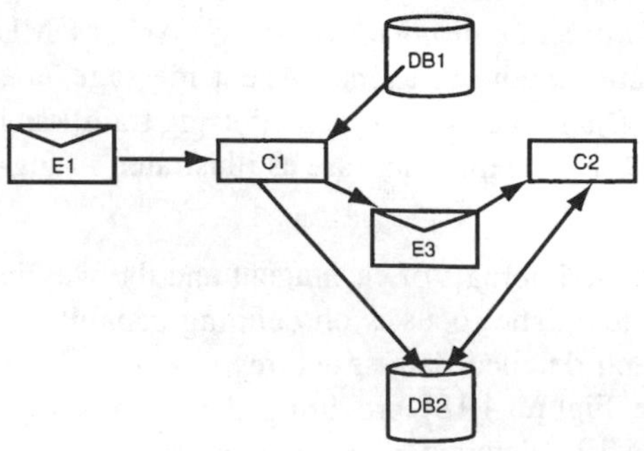

Figure 4.18 Example of agent overview diagram.

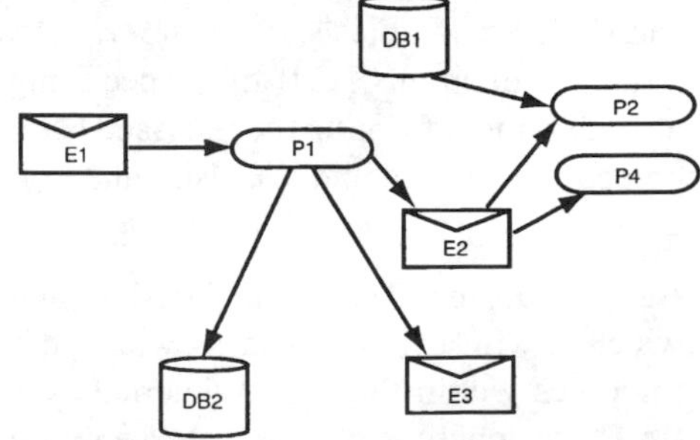

Figure 4.19 Example of capability overview diagram. (*After:* [28].)

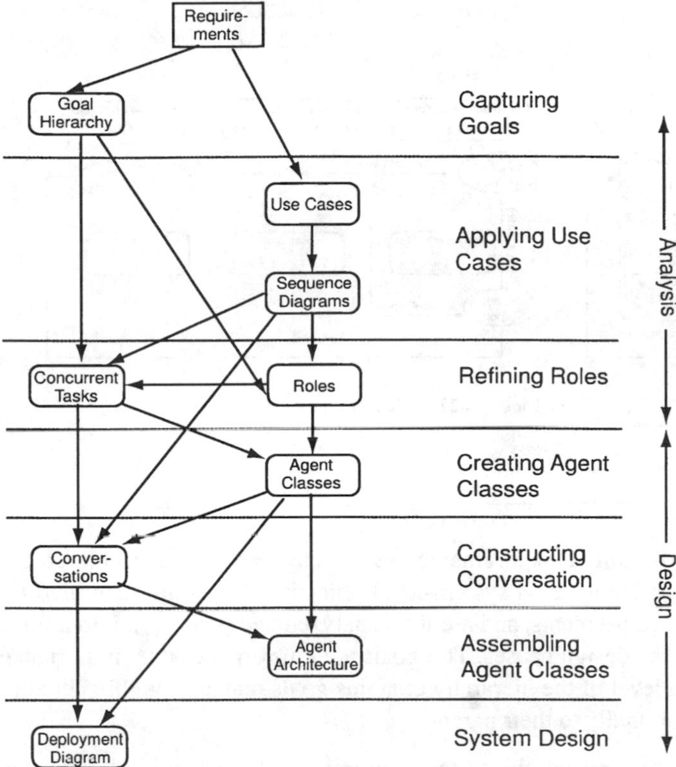

Figure 4.20 MaSE software engineering process. (*After:* [30].)

4.5.5 MaSE

Multiagent systems engineering (MaSE) has been developed to support the complete software development life cycle from problem description to realization. It offers an environment for analyzing, designing, and developing heterogeneous multiagent systems independent of any particular multiagent system architecture, agent architecture, programming language, or message-passing system. It takes an initial system specification, and produces a set of formal design documents in a graphical style. In particular, MaSE offers the ability to track changes throughout the different phases of the process. We base the presentation in this section on [29], but for details we refer the reader to [30, 31]. The complete software engineering process is depicted in Figure 4.20.

The MaSE methodology is heavily based on UML and RUP. The software development process is focused on analysis and design, with the different models to be covered as follows:

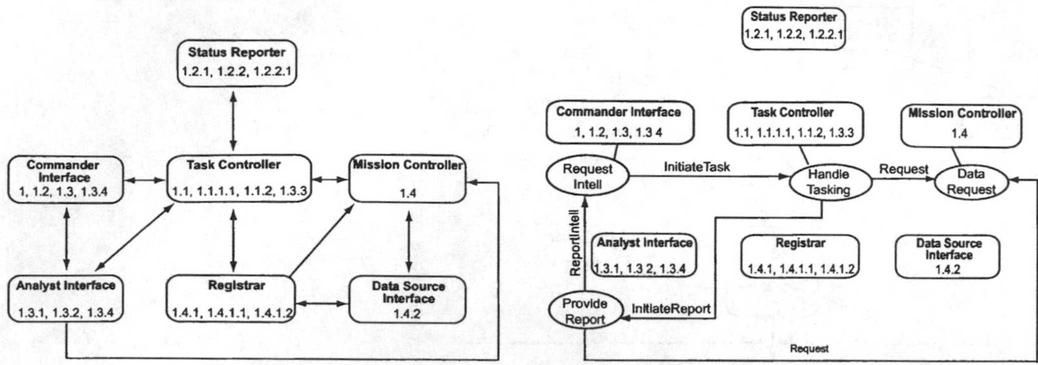

Figure 4.21 Traditional role model.

Figure 4.22 MaSE role model.

- *Capturing goals*: In this phase, the initial requirements are transformed into a structured set of system goals, which are always defined as a system-level objective. Goals are identified by distilling the essence of the set of requirements, and are then analyzed and structured into a form that can be passed on and used in the design phases. The goals are thus organized by importance in a goal hierarchy diagram. Each level of the hierarchy contains goals that are roughly equal in scope, and all subgoals relate functionally to their parent.
- *Applying use cases*: Use cases are drawn from the system requirements as in any UML analysis. Subsequently, sequence diagrams are applied to determine the minimum set of messages that must be passed between roles. Typically, at least one sequence diagram is derived from a use case.
- *Refining roles*: The roles and concurrent tasks are assigned from the goal hierarchy diagram and the sequence diagrams. A role in MaSE is an abstract description of an entity's expected function, and encapsulates the system goals for which the entity is responsible. MaSE allows a traditional role model and a methodology-specific role model including information on interactions between role tasks, as shown in Figures 4.21 and 4.22. Interactions are represented by the ellipses, while the numbering below role names indicates which goals are associated with each role.
- *Creating agent classes*: The agent classes are identified from component roles. The result of this phase is an agent class diagram depicting agent classes and the conversations between them.
- *Constructing conversations*: A MaSE conversation defines a coordination protocol between two agents. Specifically, a conversation consists of two communication class diagrams, one each for the initiator and responder. A communication class diagram is a pair of finite-state machines that define the conversation states of the two participant agent classes.
- *Assembling agent classes*: The internals of agent classes are created based on the underlying architecture of the agents, such as BDI agents, reactive agents, and so on.

- *System design*: System design takes the agent classes and instantiates them as actual agents. It uses a deployment diagram to show the numbers, types, and locations of agents within a system.

4.5.6 PASSI

PASSI (process for agent societies specification and implementation)[9] [32] is an agent-oriented iterative requirement-to-code methodology for the design of multiagent systems mainly driven by experiments in robotics. The methodology integrates design models and concepts from both object-oriented software engineering and artificial intelligence approaches. PASSI is supported by a Rational Rose plug-in to provide a dedicated design environment. In particular, automatic code generation for the models is partly supported, and one focus of the work lies in patterns and code reuse. The review in this section is based on [32]. The models and phases of the PASSI methodology are shown in Figure 4.23.

The PASSI methodology consists of five models (system requirements, agent society, agent implementation, code model, and deployment model) which include several distinct phases as described below.

- *System requirements model*: The system requirements model is obtained in different phases: The *domain description* phase results in a set of use case diagrams in which scenarios are detailed using sequence diagrams. Based on use cases, the next phase of *agent identification* defines packages in which the functionality of each agent is grouped, and activity diagrams for the task specification of the agent concerned. That is, in contrast to most agent-oriented methodologies, agents are identified based on their functionality and not on their roles. The *role identification* phase is a functional or behavioral description of the agents as well as a representation of its relationships to other agents, described by a set of sequence diagrams. Roles are viewed as in traditional object-oriented approaches. One activity diagram is drawn for each agent in the *task specification* phase, where each diagram is divided into two segments, one dealing with the tasks of an agent and one with the tasks of the interacting agent.
- *Agent society model*: The agent society model is also derived in several phases. The *ontology description* describes the agent society or organization from an ontological point of view. Thus, two diagrams are introduced, the *domain ontology description* and the *communication ontology description*, usually presented using class diagrams and XML Schemas for textual representation. The *role description* phase models the life of the agents in terms of their roles, so that social or organizational roles and behavioral roles are represented by class diagrams in which roles are classes grouped in packages representing the agents. In particular, role changes can be defined. Roles are obtained by composing several tasks (based on the functionality of an agent).
- *Agent implementation model*: Agent implementation covers the *agent structure definition* and the *agent behavior description* phases. The former describes the *multiagent level* represented by classes where attributes are the knowledge of the agent, methods are the tasks of an agent, and relationships between agents define the communication between them. The latter phase

9 http://mozart.csai.unipa.it/passi

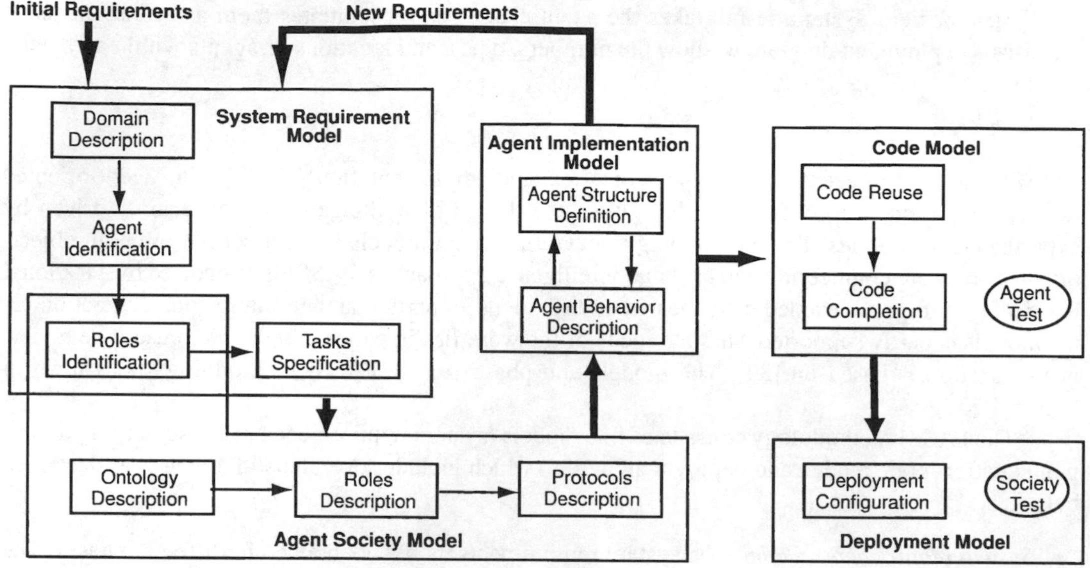

Figure 4.23 Models and phases of the PASSI methodology.

describes the *single-agent level*, which defines a single class diagram for each agent, describing the complete structure of an agent with its attributes and methods. In particular, the methods needed to register the agent, and for each task of the agent, are represented as a class.

- *Code model*: Based on the FIPA standard architecture (see Chapter 5), standard code pieces are available for reuse and therefore automatic code generation from the models is partly supported.
- *Deployment model*: UML deployment diagrams are extended to define the deployment of the agents and, in particular, to specify the behavior of mobile agents.

4.5.7 Comparison

The six methodologies reviewed in this section all reflect the view of an agent as an autonomous entity that attempts to reach its goals in a dynamic environment. All these approaches assume an explicit (symbolic) mental model of the agent including notions such as knowledge or beliefs, goals, roles, and some sort of means to achieve goals (such as intentions or plans). In this respect, there are minor variations in the concepts that are supported by the different approaches and in the terminology. For example, the concept of a plan in the BDI model corresponds to that of a task in MESSAGE. Also, there is a common distinction between some sort of micromodel describing the agent, and a macromodel describing the multiagent system (or, more accurately, the agent's model of the multiagent system). In different methodologies, this is covered by the concepts of an external model in BDI, organizational and interaction models in MESSAGE, capability and agent interaction diagrams in Tropos, or acquaintance models in Prometheus. Differences in this respect are fairly minor.

The main criteria that allow us to compare (and differentiate between) the different approaches discussed in this section are:

- Their degree of coverage of the software development process;
- The quality of the tools provided and compatibility with software development standards.

In this respect, the BDI methodology described in Section 4.5.1 is the first and oldest attempt to provide development support for BDI agents. It is based on the proprietary dMARS model and does not provide any standard-compatible tools. What makes this approach unique is the fact that the authors were the first to recognize the importance of agent technology as a software engineering paradigm and the need to provide developers with support in designing agent-based software. MESSAGE focuses on the analysis and early design phase, while extending UML and providing a design and analysis process based on RUP, which makes the methodology more easily accessible for software engineers with an object-oriented mindset. The differentiating factor of the Tropos methodology is that it provides extensive support for the requirements analysis and, in particular, the early requirements analysis, which is beyond the scope of most other approaches. Like MESSAGE, Tropos relies on UML and provides some extensions to UML. Prometheus provides a wide process coverage ranging from analysis to detailed design. In particular, it allows designers to specify, for example, interaction diagrams using Agent UML, which may turn out to be advantageous if Agent UML becomes the predominant UML extension for implementing agent-based systems. The MaSE methodology focuses on the phases of analysis and design. Being based on UML and RUP, MaSE provides interesting practical features such as the ability to track changes made throughout the different phases of the process. Finally, the interesting aspect of the PASSI methodology is that it provides a dedicated design environment via a Rational Rose plug-in, as well as support for automated code generation, patterns and code reuse. As a possible limitation, PASSI has been driven by work on robotics applications, which may impose some constraints on its suitability for other domains.

To conclude, none of the more recent methodologies is definitely better than the other. Also none of them has yet reached commercial status, so using them to develop agent-based software may require some patience and goodwill from the software designer. On the other hand, they support the design of agent-based, proactive, open systems at a level of abstraction that greatly extends that of state-of-the-art object-oriented methodologies. In the end, the quality of tool support may be the main factor for choosing between them.

4.6 MODELING NOTATIONS BASED ON UML: AGENT UML

The UML modeling notation has been applied by many for the modeling of different aspects of agent-based software systems. While some approaches (such as [33, 34]) use plain UML 1.4 as a

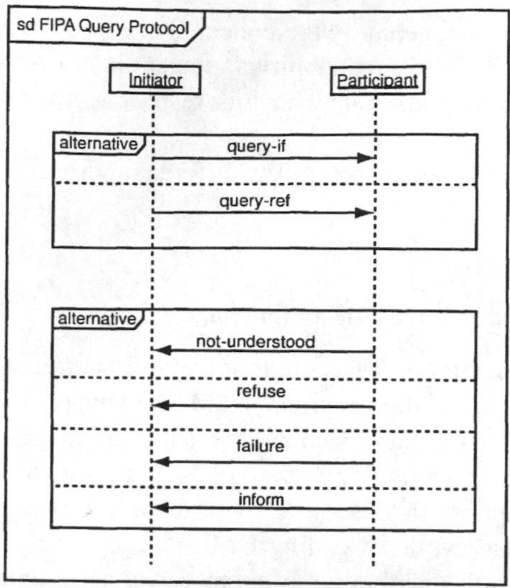

Figure 4.24 FIPA Query Protocol.

base notation for agent-based software development, there is a shared understanding that UML as presented in version 1.4 is not sufficient for modeling agent-based systems [21]. The forthcoming UML 2 standard will address some current limitations, and some parts of a UML extension for agent-based systems will be taken into consideration in UML 2. Consequently, in what follows, we only present those extensions of UML 1.4 for which, to our knowledge, no updated version based on UML 2 is available. The notion of Agent UML will be used, summarizing any extensions of UML to agents. UML (extensions) can be used to define interaction protocols, roles, societies, agent classes, ontologies, and plans. In the following, we show how these specific aspects of a multiagent system are modeled using UML.

4.6.1 Interaction Protocols

One of the first extensions to UML, in particular sequence diagrams, was proposed in [21, 35]. This notation was also applied as a basis for the specification of FIPA interaction protocols. In the meantime, this description has been adapted to UML 2. An agent interaction protocol [36] can thus be represented as a sequence diagram, as shown in Figure 4.24.

The figure defines a sequence diagram (the FIPA Query Protocol in the example) for a specific protocol between two individual agents (individuals are indicated by underlining the agent names, Initiator and Participant). Alternatively, such a protocol can start with a *query-if* or a *query-ref* (depicted by the alternative box) and the Participant can answer with either a *not-understood, refuse,*

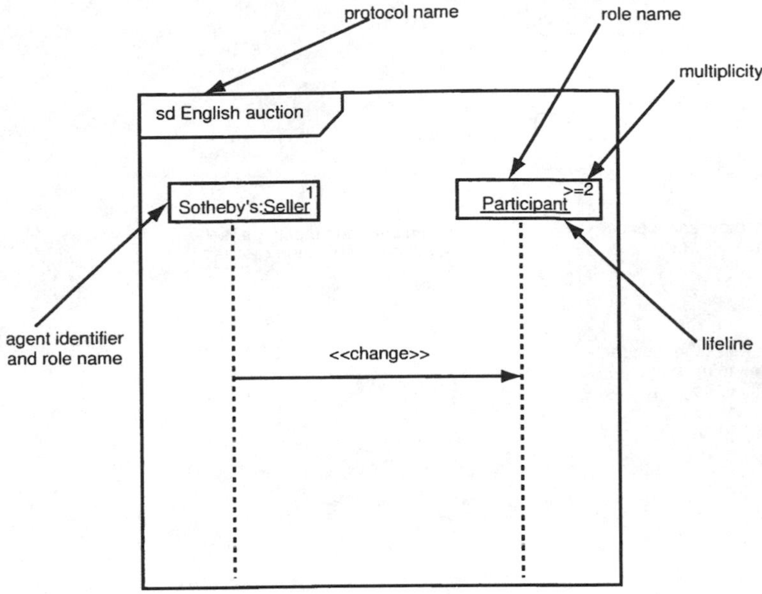

Figure 4.25 Detailed view of interaction protocol definitions.

failure, or *inform*. The vertical lifeline (dotted line) defines the lifetime of the agents, which can explicitly be stopped by an x. Role changes are marked by the stereotype <<change>>. Details are shown in Figure 4.25. Messages can be sent between agents, but also within an agent as shown in Figure 4.26.

This extension distinguishes between asynchronous and synchronous messages, takes blocking, nonblocking, and time constraints into consideration, and allows the definition of templates (interaction diagrams with formal parameters), which can then be instantiated in different contexts, like a generic FIPA contract net protocol. It applies UML 2 concepts such as Alternative, Option, Break, Parallel, Weak Sequencing, Strict Sequencing, Negative, Critical Region, Ignore/Consider, Assertion, and Loop.

In addition, however, UML 2 demands the definition of further diagram types:

- The *interaction overview diagram* is a diagram that depicts interactions through a variant of activity diagrams in a way that promotes overview of the control flow. It focuses on the overview of the flow of control, in which each node can be an interaction diagram.
- The *communication diagram* (formerly called collaboration diagram) focuses on object relationships in which the message passing is central. The sequencing of messages is given through

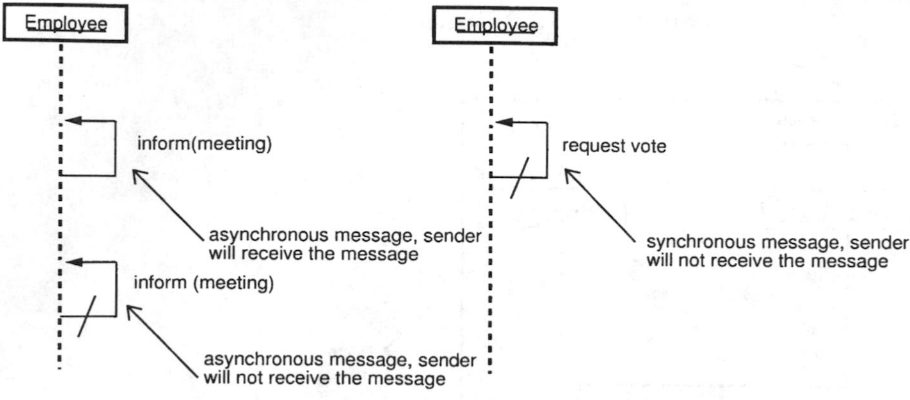

Figure 4.26 Messages within an agent.

a sequence numbering scheme. Sequence diagrams and collaboration diagrams express similar information, but show it in different ways.

- The *timing diagram* is an interaction diagram that shows the change in state or condition of a lifeline (representing a classifier instance or classifier role) over linear time. The most common usage is to show the change in state of an object over time in response to accepted events or stimuli.

4.6.2 Social Structures

We have seen in the above methodologies that the modeling of roles, groups, and societies are important aspects that must be taken into consideration during the specification of agent-based systems. We have already noticed how different approaches deal with these aspects in different ways, in particular in the context of using UML.

In this section we take a closer look at an approach suggested by Parunak and Odell [37]. Based on the emphasis on the correspondence between multiagent systems and social systems, they combine several organizational models for agents, including AALAADIN, dependency theory, interaction protocols, and holonic modeling, in a general theoretical framework, and show how UML can be applied and extended to capture constructions in that framework.

Parunak and Odell's model is based on the following artifacts:

- *Roles:* It is assumed that the same role can appear in multiple groups if they embody the same pattern of dependencies and interactions. If an agent in a group holds multiple roles concurrently, it may sometimes be useful to define a higher-level role that is composed of some of those more elementary roles.

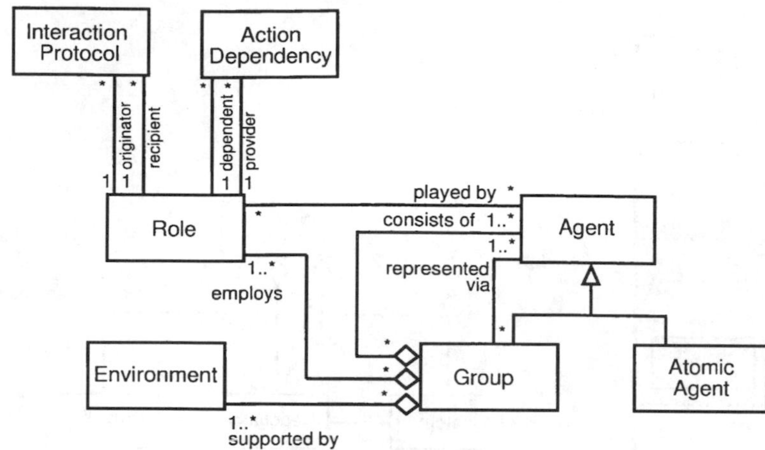

Figure 4.27 Conceptual model of Parunak and Odell's approach.

- *Environments:* Environments are not only passive communications frameworks with everything of interest relegated to them, but actively provide three information processing functions: They *fuse* information from different agents passing over the same location at different times; they *distribute* information from one location to nearby locations; and they provide *truth maintenance* by forgetting information that is not continually refreshed, thereby getting rid of obsolete information.
- *Groups:* Groups represent social units that are sets of agents associated by a common interest, purpose, or task. Groups can be created for three different reasons:
  1. To achieve more efficient or secure interaction between a set of agents (*intragroup associations*).
  2. To take advantage of the synergies between a set of agents, resulting in an entity (the group) that is able to realize products, services, or processes that no individual alone would be capable of (through *group synergies*).
  3. To establish a group of agents that interacts with other agents or groups in a coherent way, for example, to represent a shared position on a subject (*intergroup associations*).

The conceptual model of Parunak and Odell's approach is illustrated in Figure 4.27.

In [38], the authors provide some examples for modeling social agent environments, namely a terrorist organization and its relationship to a weapons cartel. Groups are modeled by class diagrams and swimlanes, as shown in Figures 4.28 and 4.29, denoting that the Terrorist Organization involves two roles, Operative and Ringleader, where the Ringleader agent coordinates Operative agents. The

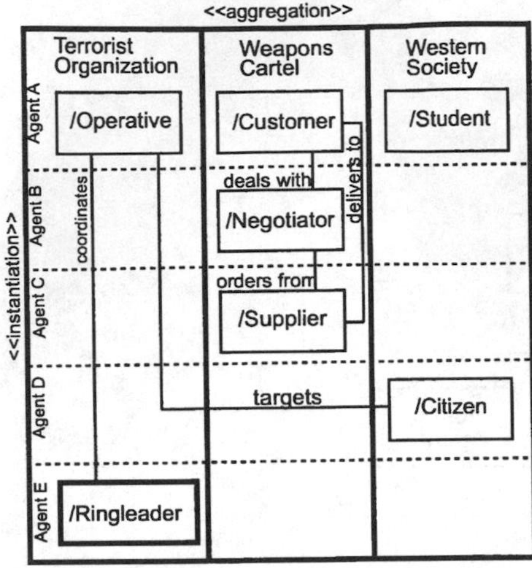

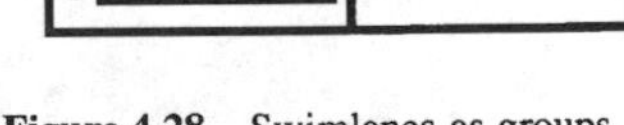

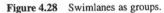

Figure 4.28 Swimlanes as groups.

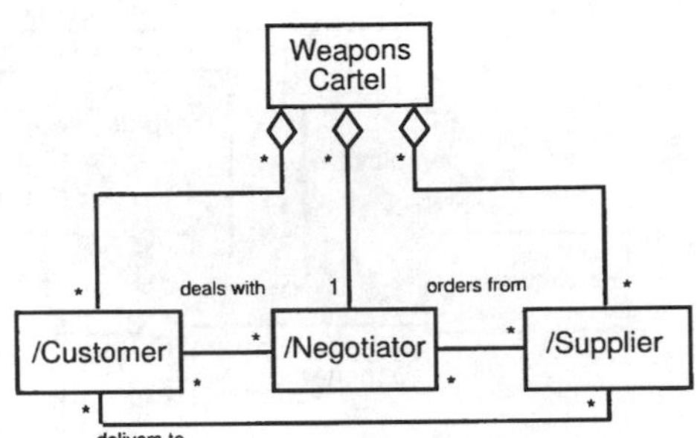

Figure 4.29 Class diagrams define roles.

second swimlane is based on agent instances; for example, agent A plays the roles of Operative, Customer, and Student.

Sequence diagrams are used to show roles as patterns of interactions, class diagrams model the kinds of entities that exist in a system along with their relationships, and sequence diagrams model the interactions that may occur among these entities. Figure 4.30 depicts the permitted interactions that may occur among Customer, Negotiator, and Supplier agents for a weapons procurement negotiation. Figure 4.31 shows an activity graph modeling groups of agents as individual agents. In this way, the kinds of dependencies are expressed that are best represented at a group level.

4.6.3 Agent Classes

To our knowledge, basing agent classes on UML class diagrams has so far only been considered by [39, 40]. The latter is currently being revisited within FIPA, and an updated version was scheduled to be available by the end of 2003. As described by [40], a distinction is made between an *agent class*, defining a blueprint for, and the type of, an individual agent, and between *individual agents* (being instances of an agent class). An agent class diagram shown in Figure 4.32 specifies agent classes.

Bauer [40] states that usual UML notation with stereotypes can be used to define such an agent class, but for readability reasons, the notation of Figure 4.32 was introduced.

- *Agent class descriptions and roles*: As we have seen, agents can satisfy distinguished roles in most of the methodologies. The general form of describing agent roles in Agent UML [35] is

$$\underline{instance - 1...instance - n/role - 1...role - m : class}$$

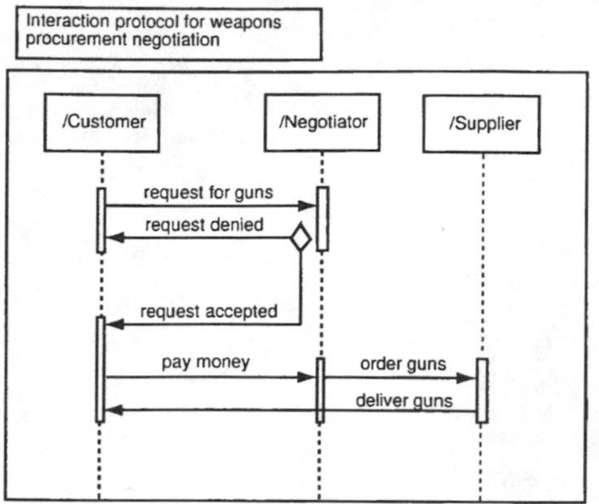

Figure 4.30 Sequence diagram depicting an interaction protocol.

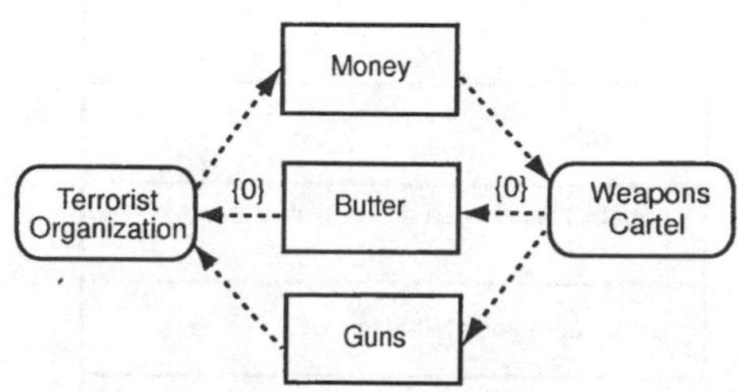

Figure 4.31 An object-flow activity graph specifying roles as patterns of activities.

denoting a distinguished set of agent instances, with $instance - 1, \ldots, instance - n$ satisfying the agent roles, $role - 1, \ldots, role - m$, with $n, m \geq 0$ and the class it belongs to. Instances, roles, or the class can be omitted, and for classes the role description is not underlined.

- *State description*: A state description is similar to a field description in class diagrams with the difference that a distinguished class *wff* (for *well-formed formula*) for all kinds of logical descriptions of the state is introduced, independent of the underlying logic. This extension allows the definition of, for example, BDI agents. Beyond the extension of the type for the fields, visibility and a persistency attribute can be added (denoted by the stereotype <<persistent>>) to allow the user agent to be stopped and restarted later in a new session. Optionally, the fields can be initialized with some values. In the case of BDI semantics, three instance variables can be defined, named *beliefs*, *desires*, and *intentions* of type *wff*, and describing the beliefs, desires, and intentions of a BDI agent. These fields can be initialized with the initial state of a BDI agent. The semantics state that the *wff* holds for the beliefs, desires, and intentions of the agent. In a pure goal-oriented semantics, two instance variables of type *wff* can be defined, named *permanent-goals* and *actual-goals*, holding the formula for the permanent and actual goals. Usual UML fields can be defined for the specification of a plain object-oriented agent (an agent implemented on top of, for example, a Java-based agent platform). However, in different design stages, different kinds of agents can be appropriate; at a conceptual level, BDI agents can be implemented by a Java-based agent platform, so that refinement steps from BDI agents to Java agents are performed during the agent development.
- *Actions*: Proactive behavior is defined in two ways, using proactive actions and proactive agent state charts (the latter of which is considered later). Thus, two kinds of actions can be specified for an agent: proactive actions (denoted by the stereotype <<pro-active>>) are triggered by the agent itself if the precondition of the action evaluates to true. *Reactive* actions (denoted by

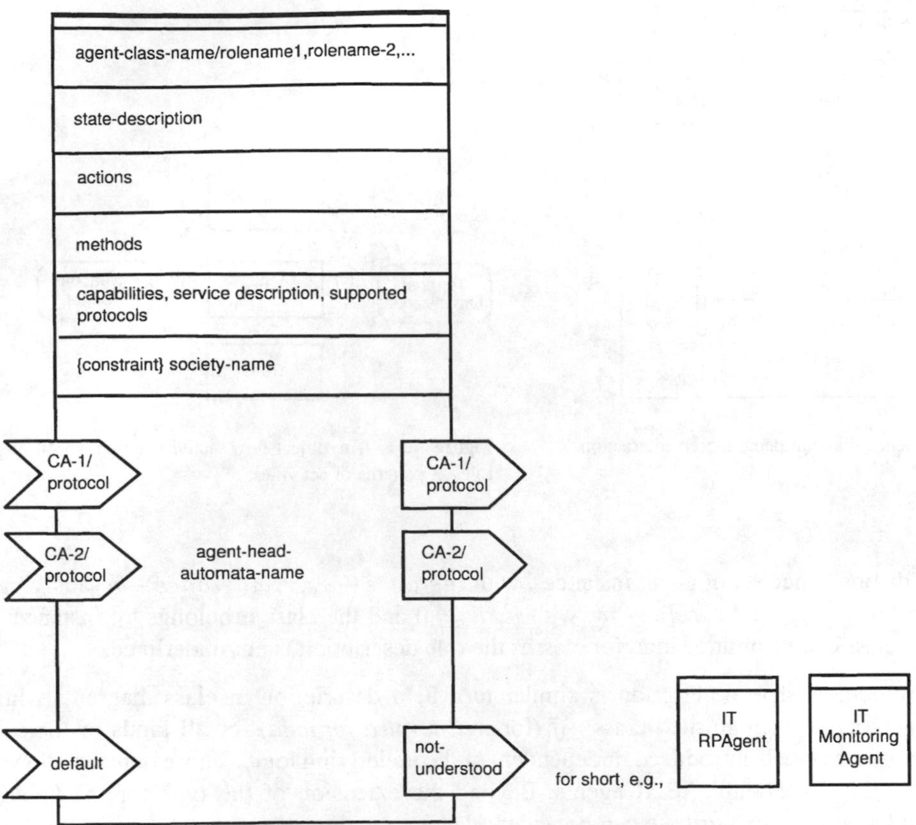

Figure 4.32 Agent class diagram and its abbreviations.

the stereotype <<re-active>>) are triggered by another agent (on receiving a message from that other agent). The description of an agent's actions consists of the action signature with visibility attribute, the action name, and a list of parameters with associated types. Preconditions, postconditions, effects, and invariants, as in UML, define the semantics of an action.

- *Methods*: Methods are defined as in UML, eventually with preconditions, postconditions, effects, and invariants.
- *Capabilities*: The capabilities of an agent can be defined either in an informal way or using class diagrams; for example, defining FIPA-service descriptions.
- *Sending and receiving of communicative acts*: The sending and receiving of communicative acts characterize the main interface of an agent to its environment. By communicative act (CA), the

Figure 4.33 Incoming and outgoing messages.

type of the message as well as the other information, like sender, receiver, or content in FIPA-ACL messages, is covered. It is assumed that classes and objects represent the information about communicative acts. The incoming messages and outgoing messages are drawn as shown in Figure 4.33. Then, the received or sent communicative act can either be a class or a concrete instance. The notation *CA-1 / protocol* is used if the communicative act of class *CA-1* is received in the context of an interaction protocol. In the case of an instance of a communicative act, the notation *CA-1 / protocol* is applied. As an alternative notation, *protocol[CA-1]* and *protocol[CA-1]* can be used. The context / *protocol* can be omitted if the communicative act is interpreted independent of some protocol. In order to react to all kinds of received communicative acts, we use a distinguished communicative act *default* matching any incoming communicative act. The *not-understood* CA is sent if an incoming CA cannot be interpreted.

- *Matching of communicative acts*: A received communicative act has to be matched against the incoming communicative acts of an agent to trigger the corresponding behavior of the agent. The matching of the communicative acts depends on their ordering, from top to bottom, to deal with the case that more than one communicative act of the agent matches an incoming message. The simplest case is the default case, by which *default* matches everything and *not-understood* is the answer to messages not understood by an agent. Since instances of communicative acts are matched as well as classes of communicative acts, free variables can occur within an instantiated communicative act. This matching is formally defined in [40].

4.6.4 Representing Ontologies by Using UML

As we have already mentioned, for example, with PASSI, several research approaches, such as [41] and [42], are dealing with the definition of ontologies using UML class diagrams, not only from the agent community but also from the Semantic Web community [32, 43].

Bergenti et al. [41] take a pragmatic view of an ontology definition by applying UML class diagrams as shown in Figure 4.34, defining the entities and relating them to specific agents. Cranefield et al. use UML to define agent communication languages (ACL) and content languages, like an object-oriented implementation of the FIPA ACL or FIPA SL [42] (as in Figure 4.35). They also apply UML to ontology definition in [44]. In [45], an extension of UML is defined to cover DAML, with Table 4.6 showing the high-level mapping between UML and DAML (described in more detail in Chapter 5). The correspondence relations between UML extensions and DAML are summarized in Table 4.7.

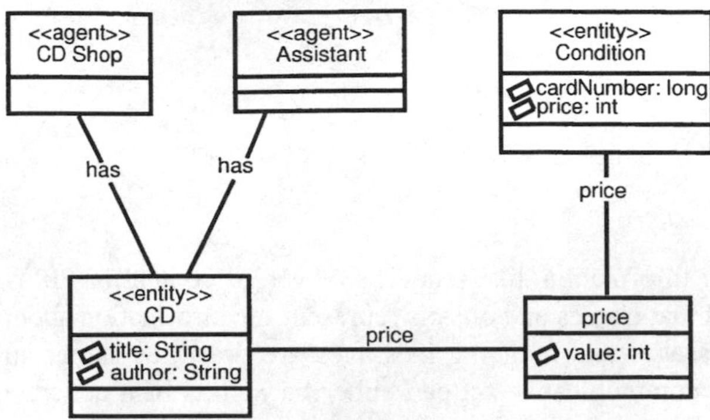

Figure 4.34 UML-based ontology definition.

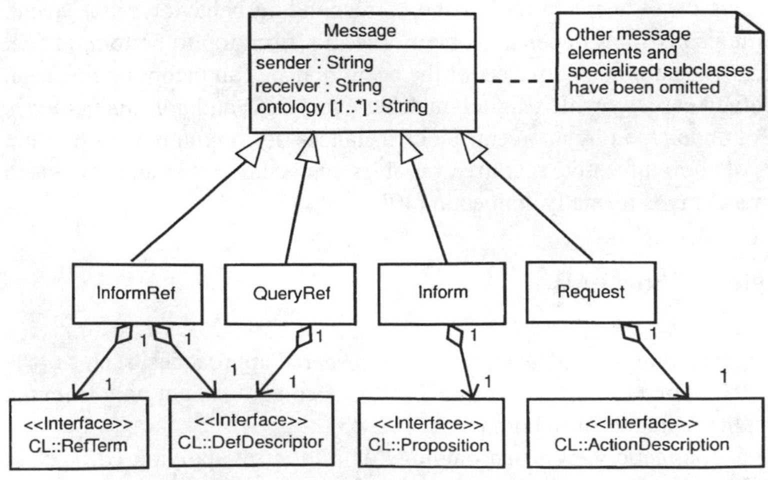

Figure 4.35 Excerpt of object-oriented design of FIPA ACL/SL.

Table 4.6
Comparison Between DAML and UML

DAML Concept	Similar UML Concepts
Ontology	Package
Class As sets (disjoint, union)	Class Difficult to represent
Hierarchy	Class generalization aspects
Property	Aspects of attributes, associations, and classes
Hierarchy	None for attributes, limited generalization for associations, class generalization relations
Restriction	Constrains association ends, including multiplicity and roles. Implicitly as class containing the attribute.
Data types Instances and values	Data types Object instances and attribute values

Source: [45].

4.6.5 UML Representation for Goals and Plans

Goals and plans are described by state charts or activity diagrams in several methodologies (see above). Huget [36], uses UML 2 activity diagrams for the description of goals and plans. Here, we present his example of a goal diagram corresponding to the interaction between the customer and the order acquisition (illustrated in Figure 4.36).

The goal diagram expresses the following. The Customer first performs the action, *Order Item*. This ordered item is received by the Order Acquisition. The Order Acquisition checks if the ordered item is on catalog (through the action, *Browse Catalog*). If the ordered item is off catalog, then the next action is on A.[10] This characteristic only changes how the item is produced and priced. If the ordered item is in the catalog, the Order Acquisition checks the price and the delay (action *Verify price and delay*). If the proposal made by the customer cannot be processed for this delay and price, then the Order Acquisition goes to E. After several actions, the Order Acquisition comes back to B to make a counterproposal that may or may not be accepted by the customer. If the customer accepts the counteroffer, the next action is to write an invoice (action *Write invoice*). If the customer does not accept, it can make another proposal in the same way as above. Finally, after writing the invoice, the customer has two choices: either accepting the order (action *Buy item*) or canceling the order (action *Cancel order*).

To conclude, the use of UML as a representation for goals and plans has several advantages, including the possibility of using commercial tools (such as Rational Rose plug-in), easier accessibility

10 There exists only one matching for a letter: one encircled letter A with incoming arrow on this figure and one encircled letter A with outgoing arrow defined elsewhere.

Table 4.7
Mapping of DAML and UML Extensions

UML	DAML
class	Class
instanceOf	type
type of ModelElement	type
attribute	ObjectProperty or Datatype Property
binary association	ObjectProperty
generalization	subClassOf
<<subPropertyOf'>> stereotyped dependency between 2 associations	subPropertyOf
generalization between stereotyped classes	subPropertyOf
note	comment
name	label
"seeAlso" tagged value on a class and association	seeAlso
"isDefinedBy" tagged value on a class and association	isDefinedBy
class containing the attribute	"subClassOf" a property restriction
source class of an association	"subClassOf" a property restriction
attribute type	"toClass" on a property restriction
target class of an association	"toClass" on a property restriction
<<equivalentTo>> stereotyped dependency	equivalentTo
<<sameClassAs>> stereotyped dependency between two classes	sameClassAs
<<samePropertyAs>> stereotyped dependency between two associations	samePropertyAs
<<Ontology>> stereotyped package	Ontology
"versionInfo" tagged value on a package	versionInfo
import (dependency stereotype)	imports
multiplicity	cardinality
multiplicity range Y..Z	Y = minCardinality, Z = maxCardinality
association target with end multiplicity = 0..1 or 1	UniqueProperty
association source with end multiplicity = 0..1 or 1	UnambiguousProperty
<<inverseOf>> stereotyped dependency between two associations	inverseOf
<<TransitiveProperty>> stereotype of an association	TransitiveProperty

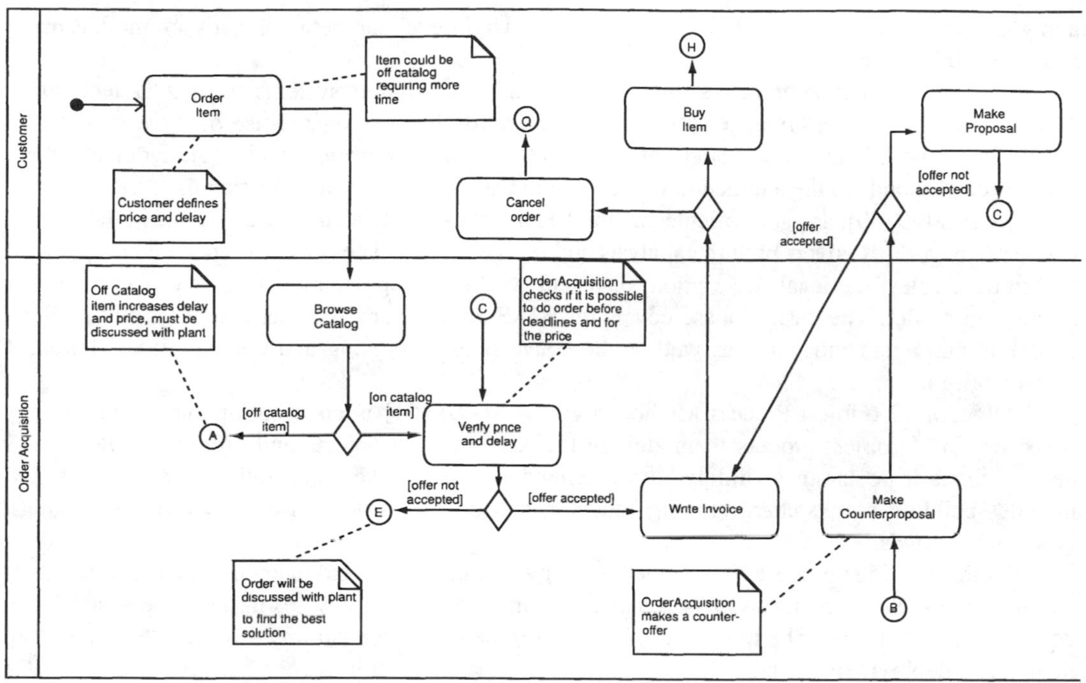

Figure 4.36 Supply chain management scenario as activity diagram. (*After:* [36].)

for software designers with an object-oriented mindset, as well as the possibility of defining mappings to and from other representations.

4.7 MISCELLANEOUS APPROACHES

In the literature, there are many other methodologies based on different software techniques. The purpose of this section is to provide the reader with a brief overview and links to some of these approaches.

ADELFE (Atelier pour le developpement de logiciels à fonctionnaliteé emergente) [46, 47] is a methodology mainly based on the Rational Unified Process and UML extensions for agents. The aim is to allow the specification of systems coping with unpredictable events that occur in the environment, and to select the appropriate action under these unpredictable events. Flake, Geiger, and Küster [48] present a UML-based approach for the specification of agent-based systems, and BDI agents in particular. They extend use case diagrams and class diagrams by the notions of agents and goals, using new actor symbols and stereotypes. High-level and detailed plans are models using restricted UML state charts.

One of the first approaches towards modeling agent-based systems using OO techniques was that described by Burmeister [10]. Here, the approach relies on the use of three models: an *organization model*, an *agent model* based on BDI, and a *cooperation model* (the latter of which roughly corresponds to the interaction model seen in Gaia, as described in Section 4.4.1).

MASB [49, 50], an agent-oriented method, is mainly influenced by research done in the field of cooperative work. It covers both the analysis and design phases. The former is specified by scenario description, role functional description, data and world conceptual modeling, and a system-user interaction model. The design phase covers the MAS architecture and scenario description, object modeling and agent modeling, as well as the conversation modeling and the overall validation of system design.

OPM/MAS (Object-Process Methodology for MAS) [51] is an agent-oriented methodology based on OPM (object-process methodology [52]), combining objects and processes. OPM/MAS deals with static declarative building blocks defined as objects, like organizations and societies, and includes building blocks characterizing behavior, and dynamics defined as processes, like agents, tasks, or messages.

Bush et al. [53] propose Styx, a methodology guiding the development of collaborative agent-based systems. Styx applies use case maps describing potential processes through the system, and domain concepts to describe the world of discourse, the role responsibility model, role relationship model, and deployment model.

Kendall et al. [54] present an agent-based methodology based on object-oriented methodologies and enterprise modeling methodologies, IDEF (integration definition for function modeling), as well as CIMOSA (computer integrated manufacturing open system architecture) for enterprise modeling.

Other types of methodologies include formal approaches, such as Cassiopeia [55], DESIRE [56, 57], the SMART agent framework for representing and reasoning about agents in Z [58, 59], and CAMLE [60] to mention only a few. Knublauch also presented an agent approach based on Extreme Programming in [61]. Further methodologies and approaches are discussed in [1, 62].

In [63], Wagner presents a UML profile for an agent-oriented modeling approach called an agent-object-relationship modeling language (AORML). AORML can be viewed as an extension of UML covering (among other things) *interaction frame diagrams* describing the action event classes and commitment/claim classes determining the possible interactions between two agent types (or instances), *interaction sequence diagrams* depicting prototypical instances of interaction processes, and *interaction pattern diagrams* for representing general interaction patterns.

4.8 SUMMARY AND CONCLUDING REMARKS

In this chapter, we have surveyed a number of important research contributions in the area of methodologies and notations for the development of agent-based systems. Three main roots can be identified, starting first with approaches based on knowledge engineering principles. While the strength of these approaches lies in their ability to represent the entities and relationships relevant for a domain from a knowledge-level perspective, they lack support for specific agent-related constructs. The recognition of these limitations has led to the emergence of purely agent-oriented approaches that provide rich support for modeling artifacts such as goals, intentions, and organizations. A problem with these approaches was that their underlying conceptual models were proprietary and difficult to understand for industrial software developers without an education in agent technology. At the same time, no industrial-strength tools were available to alleviate some of the complexity for developers. As a consequence, purely agent-oriented software methodologies did not easily migrate to industrial applicability. In response, a number of methodologies were developed that extended state-of-the-art object-oriented approaches, such as UML and RUP, and built agent-oriented features into and on top of these object-oriented models. While this introduces a number of trade-offs, in particular regarding the natural design of agent-based systems, the main advantage of these approaches is that they fit more easily into the object-oriented paradigm and that high-quality tools can be developed by extending existing object-oriented tools. It appears that while objects and agents are clearly different notions (see, for example, the discussion in [64]), agent-oriented software engineering can greatly benefit from OO technologies and approaches. In particular, agent-oriented approaches are also suitable for areas in which object-oriented modeling has shortcomings. Here, the abstractions inherent in agent-oriented software engineering can help to overcome the limitations of the object-oriented approach.

Summarizing the different approaches, we distill the following necessary aspects to be covered by a methodology covering major areas of agent-based systems.

4.8.1 Analysis

The analysis must deal with the following aspects:

- *Use cases*: Taken from object-oriented software development, use case scenarios are a suitable method to derive the functional requirements of a system.
- *Environment model*: In [37], Odell et al. consider several aspects of environment modeling ranging from physical environments to agent communication, and how these considerations could be embedded into the FIPA architecture.
- *Domain/ontology model*: This model defines the ontologies of the domain and relates them to other existing ontologies using, for example, UML and Semantic Web representation languages.
- *Role model*: This model describes the roles in a domain, on the one hand in the traditional object-oriented sense (actor-role relationship), and on the other defining roles characterizing social relationships within an agent-based system.
- *Goal/task model*: This model defines the objectives of an agent in terms of soft and hard goals, and should also support means-ends analysis (as in Tropos). Moreover, the notion of tasks and plans should be provided to support the description of agent behavior at a high level of abstraction.
- *Interaction model*: This model defines the regime of interaction and collaboration among entities and groups of entities, at a level that abstracts away from specific interaction protocols.

- *Organization/society model*: This model defines to a reasonable extent the real-world society and organization, and hence the social context within which agents in an agent-based system act and interact.
- *Business process models*: The notion of business processes is key for corporate business applications. Business processes describe the means and the ends of business interactions. For agents to support corporate applications, it is important to be able to access executable definitions of business processes, to reason about the semantics of goal-directed business processes,[11] and to relate business processes to the organizational model, the interaction model, and the task model.

4.8.2 Design

- *Interaction protocol model*: This model defines the interaction between different agent classes, agent instances, and roles at the level of interaction protocols, such as the contract net.
- *Internal agent model*: This model deals in particular with goals, beliefs, and plans of agent classes, how they are defined and which underlying architecture is used.
- *Agent model*: This model describes the behavior of agents and agent groups: how different agent collaborate independent of their implementation. The interaction model defines the concrete interaction of the agents, whereas the internal agent model defines the internal behavior of an agent in terms of, for example, BDI, and the agent model defines the behavior of an agent as seen by other agents.
- *Service/capability model*: This defines the services and capabilities of agents, mostly using service description languages and mechanisms such as UDDI or DAML-S.
- *Acquaintance model*: This model provides agents with models of other agents' beliefs, capabilities, and intentions. It can be used to determine suitable partners for collaboration or to predict other behavior, for example, in a coordination task.
- *Deployment/agent instance model*: This model describes which agent instances exist, migration of agents, and the dynamic creation of agents.

4.8.3 Conclusions

It appears that one single methodological approach does not fit all purposes. This is particularly true given the breadth of domains for agent technology, and the diversity of the underlying agent and multi-agent architectures. How to deal with this situation is an open question. One possible approach that might allow us to cope with the different requirements of different application developers could be the introduction of a meta-methodology that supports the various types of models described above and

11 http://www.agentissoftware.com

provides adequate mappings. An example of such an approach currently being pursued in the object-oriented world is the SPEM[12] initiative currently in discussion at the OMG, allowing the construction of different methodologies on top of an existing meta-methodology.

An important prerequisite to bringing agent technology to market successfully is the availability of expressive and usable development tools, to enable software engineers to construct methodologies, define the various models listed above, and to achieve automatic model transformation as far as possible, for example based on the model-driven architecture (MDA).[13] Finally, it appears that (independent of the methodology used) the question of how agent-based approaches can be embedded and migrated into mainstream IT infrastructures and solutions is another key factor to determine which elements of the current work on agent-oriented software engineering will be successful in real-world software engineering environments. The interested reader should consult [65] for a detailed discussion of some of the issues that are related to interoperability and migration of agent-based software.

Acknowledgments

We would like to thank Michael Luck for the invitation to contribute a chapter on agent methodologies in this book. Moreover, we want to thank all the people involved within FIPA TCs dealing with methodologies and notation for preparing an excellent collection of state-of-the-art papers on the AUML Web site, `http://www.auml.org`.

References

[1] Iglesias, C., M. Garrijo, and J. Gonzalez, "A Survey of Agent-Oriented Methodologies," *Proceedings of the 5th International Workshop on Intelligent Agents V: Agent Theories, Architectures, and Languages (ATAL-98)*, J. Müller, M. P. Singh, and A. S. Rao, (eds.), Volume 1555 of *LNCS*, New York: Springer, 1999, pp. 317–330.

[2] Garijo, F., and M. Boman, (eds.), *Multi-Agent System Engineering (MAAMAW'99)*, Volume 1647 of *LNCS*, New York: Springer, 1999.

[3] Giunchiglia, F., J. Mylopoulos, and A. Perini, "The TROPOS Software Development Methodology: Processes, Models and Diagrams," *Proceedings of the First International Joint Conference on Autonomous Agents and Multi Agent Systems AAMAS'02*, C. Castelfranchi and W. Johnson, (eds.), New York: ACM Press, 2002, pp. 35–36.

[4] Wooldridge, M., N. Jennings, and D. Kinny, "The Gaia Methodology for Agent-Oriented Analysis and Design," *Autonomous Agents and Multi-Agent Systems*, Vol. 3, No. 3, 2000, pp. 285–312.

[5] Herlea, D. E., et al., "Specification of Behavioural Requirements Within Compositional Multi-Agent System Design," *Proceedings of the 9th European Workshop on Modelling Autonomous Agents in a Multi-Agent World: Multi-Agent System Engineering (MAAMAW'99)*, F. J. Garijo, and M. Boman, (eds.), Volume 1647 of *LNCS*, New York: Springer, 1999, pp. 8–27.

[6] Brazier, F. M. T., C. M. Jonker, and J. Treur, "Principles of Compositional Multi-Agent System Development," *Proceedings of the 15th IFIP World Computer Congress, WCC'98, Conference on Information Technology and Knowledge Systems, IT&KNOWS'98*, J. Cuena, (ed.), 1998, pp. 347–360.

12 http://www.omg.org/technology/documents/formal/spem.htm

13 http://www.cs.rmit.edu.au/agents/SAC/methodology.shtml

[7] Jonker, C. M., and J. Treur, "Compositional Verification of Multi-Agent Systems: A Formal Analysis of Pro-Activeness and Reactiveness," *Proceedings of the International Workshop on Compositionality, COMPOS'97*, W. P. de Roever, H. Langmaack, and A. Pnueli, (eds.), Volume 1536 of *LNCS*, New York: Springer, 1997, pp. 350–380.

[8] Kinny, D., and M. Georgeff, "Modelling and Design of Multi-Agent Systems," *Intelligent Agents III: Proceedings of the Third International Workshop on Agent Theories, Architectures, and Languages (ATAL-96)*, J. Müller, M. Wooldridge, and N. R. Jennings, (eds.), Volume 1193 of *LNCS*, New York: Springer, 1996, pp. 1–20.

[9] Kinny, D., M. Georgeff, and A. Rao, "A Methodology and Modelling Technique for Systems of BDI Agents," *Agents Breaking Away: Proceedings of the Seventh European Workshop on Modelling Autonomous Agents in a Multi-Agent World*, Y. Demazeau and J.-P. Müller, (eds.), Volume 1038 of *LNCS*, New York: Springer, 1996, pp. 56–71.

[10] Burmeister, B., "Models and Methodology for Agent-Oriented Analysis and Design," *Working Notes of the KI'96 Workshop on Agent-Oriented Programming and Distributed Systems*, K. Fischer, (ed.), DFKI, 1996.

[11] Jacobson, I., G. Booch, and J. Rumbaugh, *The Unified Software Development Process*, Reading, MA: Addison-Wesley, 1998.

[12] Beck, K., *Extreme Programming Explained*, Reading, MA: Addison-Wesley, 1999.

[13] Schreiber, A. T., et al., "CommonKADS: A Comprehensive Methodology for KBS Development," *IEEE Expert*, Vol. 9, No. 3, 1994, pp. 28–37.

[14] Glaser, N., "Contribution to Knowledge Modelling in a Multi-Agent Framework (the CoMoMAS Approach)," Ph.D. thesis, Université Henri Poincaré, Nancy I, 1996.

[15] Iglesias, C., et al., "A Methodological Proposal for Multiagent Systems Development Extending CommonKADS," *Proceedings of the Tenth Knowledge Acquisition Workshop*, Banff, Canada, 1996.

[16] Rudolph, E., P. Graubmann, and J. Grabowski, "Tutorial on Message Sequence Charts," *Computer Networks and ISDN Systems*, Vol. 28, No. 12, 1996, pp. 1629–1641.

[17] Rumbaugh, J., "OMT: The Development Process," *JOOP Journal of Object Oriented Programming*, Vol. 8, No. 2, 1995, pp. 8–16.

[18] Rumbaugh, J., "OMT: The Dynamic Model," *JOOP Journal of Object Oriented Programming*, Vol. 7, No. 9, 1995, pp. 6–12.

[19] Juan, T., A. R. Pearce, and L. Sterling, "ROADMAP: Extending the Gaia Methodology for Complex Open Systems," *Proceedings of the First International Joint Conference on Autonomous Agents and Multi Agent Systems AAMAS'02*, C. Castelfranchi and W. Johnson, (eds.), New York: ACM Press, 2002, pp. 3–10.

[20] Omicini, A., "SODA: Societies and Infrastructures in the Analysis and Design of Agent-Based Systems," *Agent-Oriented Software Engineering*, Volume 1957 of *LNCS*, P. Ciancarini and M. Wooldridge, (eds.), New York: Springer, 2001, pp. 185–193.

[21] Bauer, B., J. Muller, and J. Odell, "Agent UML: A Formalism for Specifying Multiagent Software Systems," *International Journal on Software Engineering and Knowledge Engineering (IJSEKE)*, Vol. 11, No. 3, 2001, pp. 207–230.

[22] Kinny, D., M. P. Georgeff, and A. S. Rao, "A Methodology and Modelling Technique for Systems of BDI Agents," *Agents Breaking Away, 7th European Workshop on Modelling Autonomous Agents in a Multi-Agent World*, W. Van de Velde and J. W. Perram, (eds.), Volume 1038 of *LNCS*, New York: Springer, 1996, pp. 56–71.

[23] Caire, G., et al., "Agent Oriented Analysis Using MESSAGE/UML," *Agent-Oriented Software Engineering II*, M. Wooldridge, G. Wei, and P. Ciancarini, (eds.), Volume 2222 of *LNCS*, New York: Springer, 2001, pp. 119–135.

[24] Mylopoulos, J., M. Kolp, and J. Castro, " UML for Agent-Oriented Software Development: The Tropos Proposal," *UML 2001 — The Unified Modeling Language, Modeling Languages, Concepts, and Tools, 4th International Conference*, M. Gogolla and C. Kobryn, (eds.), Volume 2185 of *LNCS*, New York: Springer, 2001, pp. 422–441.

[25] Busetta, P., et al., *JACK Intelligent Agents — Components for Intelligent Agents in Java*, Technical Report tr9901, http://www.agent-software.com/.

[26] Castro, J., M. Kolp, and J. Mylopoulos, "Towards Requirements-Driven Information Systems Engineering: The TROPOS Project," *Information Systems*, Vol. 27, No. 6, 2002, pp. 365–389.

[27] Padgham, L., and M. Winikoff, "Prometheus: A Methodology for Developing Intelligent Agents," *Agent-Oriented Software Engineering III*, F. Giunchglia, J. Odell, and G. Weiß, (eds.), Volume 2585 of *LNCS*, New York: Springer, 2003, pp. 174–185.

[28] Cervenka, R., "Modeling Notation Source: Prometheus," http://www.auml.org/auml/documents/Prometheus030402.pdf, September 2003.

[29] Wood, M. F., and S. A. A. DeLoach, "An Overview of the Multiagent Systems Engineering Methodology," *Proceedings of the First International Workshop on Agent-Oriented Software Engineering*, P. Ciancarini and M. Wooldridge, (eds.), Volume 1957 of *LNCS*, New York: Springer, 2000, pp. 127–141.

[30] Wood, M. F., "Multiagent Systems Engineering: A Methodology for Analysis and Design of Multiagent Systems," M.Sc. thesis, AFIT/GCS/ENG/00M-26, School of Engineering, Air Force Institute of Technology (AU), Wright-Patterson AFB, OH, 2000.

[31] DeLoach, S. A., and M. F. Wood, *Multiagent Systems Engineering: The Analysis Phase*, Technical Report, Air Force Institute of Technology, AFIT/EN-TR-00-02, 2000.

[32] Cossentino, M., and C. Potts, "A Case Tool Supported Methodology for the Design of Multi-Agent Systems," *The 2002 International Conference on Software Engineering Research and Practice (SERP'02)*, 2002.

[33] Lind, J., *Iterative Software Engineering for Multiagent Systems: The MASSIVE Method*, Volume 1994 of *LNCS*, New York: Springer, 2001.

[34] Kühnel, R., *Agentenbasierte Software — Methode und Anwendungen*, Reading, MA: Addison-Wesley, 2000.

[35] Bauer, B., J. P. Muller, and J. Odell, "An Extension of UML by Protocols for Multiagent Interaction," *Proceedings of the Fourth International Conference on Multi-Agent Systems (ICMAS-00)*, E. H. Durfee, (ed.), IEEE Computer Society, 2000.

[36] Huget, M.-P., "FIPA-Modelling: Interaction Diagrams," http://www.auml.org/auml/documents/ID-03-07-02.pdf, September 2003.

[37] Odell, J. J., et al., "Modeling Agents and Their Environment," *Agent-Oriented Software Engineering III*, F. Giunchiglia, J. Odell, and G. Weiß, (eds.), Volume 2585 of *LNCS*, New York: Springer, 2002, pp. 16–31.

[38] Parunak, H. V. D., and J. Odell, "Representing Social Structures in UML," *Agent-Oriented Software Engineering II*, M. Wooldridge, G. Weiß, and P. Ciancarini, (eds.), Volume 2222 of *LNCS*, New York: Springer, 2001, pp. 1–16.

[39] Wagner, G., "The Agent-Object-Relationship Metamodel: Towards a Unified View of State and Behavior," *Information Systems*, Vol. 28, No. 5, 2003, pp. 475–504.

[40] Bauer, B., et al., "Agents and the UML: A Unified Notation for Agents and Multi-Agent Systems?" *Agent-Oriented Software Engineering II*, M. Wooldridge, G. Wei, and P. Ciancarini, (eds.), Volume 2222 of *LNCS*, New York: Springer, 2001, pp. 148–150.

[41] Bergenti, F., and A. Poggi, "A Development Toolkit to Realize Autonomous and Inter-Operable Agents," *Proceedings of the Fifth International Conference on Autonomous Agents*, New York: ACM Press, 2001, pp. 9–16.

[42] Cranefield, S., S. Haustein, and M. Purvis, "UML-Based Ontology Modelling for Software Agents," *Proceedings of the Workshop on Intelligent Information Integration, 16th International Joint Conference on Artificial Intelligence*, 1999.

[43] Chang, W. W., "A Discussion of the Relationship Between RDF-Schema and UML," http://www.w3.org/TR/1998/NOTE-rdf-uml-19980804/, September 2003.

[44] Cranefield, S., and M. Purvis, "Generating Ontology-Specific Content Languages," *Proceedings of the Workshop on Ontologies in Agent Systems, 5th International Conference on Autonomous Agents*, 2001, pp. 29–35.

[45] Baclawski, K., et al., "Extending UML to Support Ontology Engineering for the Semantic Web," *UML 2001 — The Unified Modeling Language, Modeling Languages, Concepts, and Tools, 4th International Conference*, M. Gogolla and C. Kobryn, (eds.), Volume 2185 of *LNCS*, New York: Springer, 2001, pp. 342–360.

[46] Bernon, C., et al., "ADELFE: A Methodology for Adaptive Multi-Agent Systems Engineering," *Engineering Societies in the Agents World III, Third International Workshop, ESAW 2002*, P. Petta, R. Tolksdorf, and F. Zambonelli, (eds.), Volume 2577 of *LNCS*, New York: Springer, 2002, pp. 156–169.

[47] Bernon, C., et al., "The Adelfe Methodology for an Intranet System Design," *AOIS '02, Agent-Oriented Information Systems, Proceedings of the Fourth International Bi-Conference Workshop on Agent-Oriented Information Systems (AOIS-2002 at CAiSE*02)*, P. Giorgini et al., (eds.), Volume 57 of *CEUR Workshop Proceedings*, 2002.

[48] Flake, S., C. Geiger, and J. M. Küster, "Towards UML-Based Analysis and Design of Multi-Agent Systems," *International NAISO Symposium on Information Science Innovations in Engineering of Natural and Artificial Intelligent Systems*, 2001.

[49] Moulin, B., and L. Cloutier, "Collaborative Work Based on Multiagent Architectures: A Methodological Perspective," *Soft Computing: Fuzzy Logic, Neural Networks and Distributed Artificial Intelligence*, F. Aminzadeh and M. Jamshidi, (eds.), Upper Saddle River, NJ: Prentice Hall, 1994, pp. 261–296.

[50] Moulin, B., and M. Brassard, "A Scenario-Based Design Method and an Environment for the Development of Multiagent Systems," *Distributed Artificial Intelligence Architecture and Modelling: Proceedings of the First Australian Workshop on Distributed Artificial Intelligence*, C. Zhang and D. Lukose, (eds.), Volume 1087 of *LNCS*, New York: Springer, 1996, pp. 216–231.

[51] Sturm, A., D. Dori, and O. Shehory, "Single-Model Method for Specifying Multi-Agent Systems," *The Second International Joint Conference on Autonomous Agents & Multiagent Systems*, New York: ACM Press, 2003, pp. 121–128.

[52] Dori, D., *Object-Process Methodology: A Holistic System Paradigm*, New York: Springer, 2002.

[53] Bush, G., S. Cranefield, and M. Purvis, "The STYX Agent Methodology," *Information Science Discussion Papers Series*, University of Otago, 2001.

[54] Kendall, E. A., M. T. Malkoun, and C. Jiang, "A Methodology for Developing Agent Based Systems," *Distributed Artificial Intelligence Architecture and Modelling: Proceedings of the First Australian Workshop on Distributed Artificial Intelligence*, C. Zhang and D. Lukose, (eds.), Volume 1087 of *LNCS*, New York: Springer, 1996, pp. 85–99.

[55] Coolinot, A., A. Drougol, and P. Benhamou, "Agent Oriented Design of a Soccer Robot Team," *Proceedings on the Second International Conference on Multi-Agent Systems (ICMAS-96),* V. Lesser, (ed.), Menlo Park, CA: AAAI Press, 1996, pp. 41–47.

[56] Brazier, F., et al., "Formal Specification of Multi-Agent Systems: A Real-World Case," *Proceedings of the First International Conference on Multi-Agent Systems*, Menlo Park, CA: AAAI/MIT Press, 1995, pp. 25–32.

[57] Dunin-Keplicz, B., and J. Treur, "Compositional Formal Specification of Multi-Agent Systems," *Intelligent Agents: Theories, Architectures, and Languages*, M. Wooldridge and N. R. Jennings, (eds.), Volume 890 of *LNCS*, New York: Springer, 1995, pp. 102–117.

[58] Luck, M., and M. d'Inverno, "A Formal Framework for Agency and Autonomy," *Proceedings of the First International Conference on Multi-Agent Systems*, Menlo Park, CA: AAAI/MIT Press, 1995, pp. 254–260.

[59] Luck, M., N. Griffiths, and M. d'Inverno, "From Agent Theory to Agent Construction: A Case Study," *Intelligent Agents III: Proceedings of the Third International Workshop on Agent Theories, Architectures, and Languages*, J. P. Müller, M. Wooldridge, and N. Jennings, (eds.), Volume 1193 of *LNCS*, New York: Springer, 1997, pp. 49–63.

[60] Zhu, H., "A Formal Specification of Evolutionary Software Agents," *ICFEM'2002: Proceedings of the IEEE International Conference on Formal Engineering Methods,* C. George and H. Miao, (eds.), New York: Springer, 2002, pp. 249–261.

[61] Knublauch, H., "Constraining Autonomy Through Norms," *Proceedings of the First International Joint Conference on Autonomous Agents and Multi Agent Systems AAMAS'02,* C. Castelfranchi and W. Johnson, (eds.), New York: ACM Press, 2002, pp. 704–711.

[62] Wooldridge, M., and P. Ciancarini, "Agent-Oriented Software Engineering: The State of the Art," *Agent-Oriented Software Engineering, First International Workshop, AOSE 2000,* M. Wooldridge and P. Ciancarini, (eds.), Volume 1957 of *LNCS*, New York: Springer, 2001, pp. 1–28.

[63] Wagner, G., "A UML Profile for External Agent-Object-Relationship (AOR) Models," *Agent-Oriented Software Engineering III*, F. Giunchiglia, J. Odell, and G. Weiß, (eds.), Volume 2585 of *LNCS*, New York: Springer, 2002, pp. 138–149.

[64] Wooldridge, M. J., *An Introduction to Multiagent Systems*, New York: Wiley, 2002.

[65] Müller, J. P., and B. Bauer, "Agent-Oriented Software Technologies: Flaws and Remedies," *Agent-Oriented Software Engineering III*, F. Giunchiglia, J. Odell, and G. Weiß, (eds.), Volume 2585 of *LNCS*, New York: Springer, 2003, pp. 210–227.

Chapter 5

Standards for Agent Development

Steven Willmott, Ulises Cortés, and David Cabanillas
Universitat Politiécnica de Catalunya, Spain

5.1 INTRODUCTION

Standardization of agent technologies has been in progress in various organizations since the mid-1990s and was often the subject of significant debate, particularly on whether work in such an active research area could in fact be standardized at all. Five years later there have certainly been significant successes as well as areas where standardization has progressed less than had been hoped.

Standardization has progressed most slowly on the more theoretical higher-level aspects of agent technology such as formal communication semantics and notions of autonomy, and there are still a wide range of approaches being discussed. On the positive side, however, the various standardization activities have had an undeniable impact on the visibility of agent technologies and resulted in standards convergence on many pragmatic development issues (interoperability, low-level messaging, domain models, toolkits, and APIs), all of which are essential for wider use.

Through these activities, standards-based agent technology today provides a good basis for many of the engineering aspects related to agent systems even if some of the higher-level issues remain unresolved. From an agent development perspective, relevant standards can be divided into two groups:

- Dedicated agent standards: Standardization efforts specifically targeting agent technologies.
- Agent-enabling standards: Other standard technologies that are increasingly making it easier to develop agents, integrate them with other systems, and apply agent technology.

This chapter introduces the major technologies falling into each of the categories—the Foundation for Intelligent Physical Agents (FIPA) Agent Standard, the Knowledge Query Manipulation Language (KQML), and mobile agent standards for the first, and activities such as Knowledge Interchange

Format (KIF), Web services, the Semantic Web, and Grid computing for the second. Sections 5.6 and 5.7 provide overviews of standards-related tools and applications of standards, respectively.

The notion of "standard" used in the chapter is deliberately broad, including de jure approaches (such as FIPA), de facto standards (as could occur in the mobile agents domain, for example), and references to standard technologies from other domains that could be useful for agent development. The objective of the chapter is also not to recommend one technology over another but to describe the agent standards landscape and provide sufficient pointers for readers to make up their own minds on which approaches to pursue.

There is also significant other work on agents and standards, which this chapter aims to complement. These include [1] which introduces the FIPA standard, [2] which describes the need for agent communication standards in mobile agent systems, and finally, [3] which describes some of the initial aims and challenges behind FIPA.

5.2 FOUNDATION FOR INTELLIGENT PHYSICAL AGENTS STANDARDS

FIPA[1] is a nonprofit organization founded in 1996 to promote interoperability between heterogeneous software agents and agent-based systems. FIPA is widely recognized as the major standards body in the area of agent-based computing, and develops standards in areas such as Agent Communication Languages (ACLs), Interaction Protocols (IPs), content languages, agent management, and message infrastructures. The FIPA standards cover many of the main areas of agent development as shown in Figure 5.1, and each of the areas shown is covered in one of the following sections.

FIPA standards have been used in a wide range of research projects including large-scale activities such as the ACTS FACTS project[2] and Agentcities.[3] To date, there are nearly 20 implementations of the current generation of specifications, many of them open source and with significant user communities.

In late 2000, FIPA adopted a new process for development of its standards (moving through draft, experimental, and final standard levels of development) and the consortium recently voted to approve the first full set of specifications to the final standards status after extensive comment periods. These new standard level documents were ratified in November 2002, finalizing and formalizing the experimental level specifications which preceded them.

It is expected that implementations will begin to adopt the new standards as part of their new development cycle; hence, this description is based on the new standards set, although almost always the description should be relevant to the previous generation.

1 http://www.fipa.org
2 http://www.labs.bt.com/profsoc/facts
3 http://www.agentcities.org

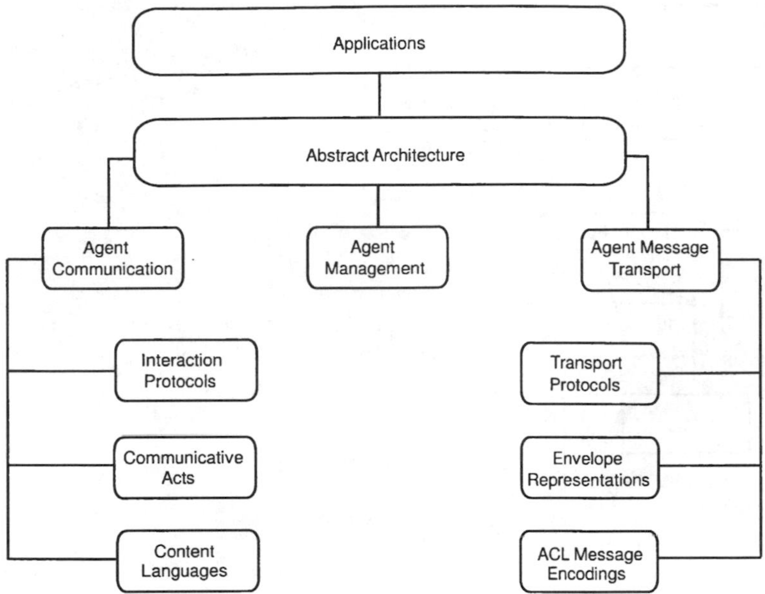

Figure 5.1 Overview of FIPA agent standards, each area being defined by one or more specifications.

5.2.1 FIPA Abstract Architecture

The FIPA Abstract Architecture Specification (FIPA00001)[4] acts as an overall description of the FIPA standard set. In particular, it defines core notions such as agents, services for agents, and the elements necessary to enable agents to handle multiple message transport systems, agent languages, and other components.

The purpose of the network architecture is primarily to enable the reification of FIPA agent concepts into a number of target technology environments (concrete realizations), the more concrete FIPA specifications such as agent management (see following sections) being one of those target environments. The abstract architecture definitions then act as reference points for defining mappings between the different realizations as shown in Figure 5.2.

The abstract architecture specification is a useful document for orientation in the FIPA specification environment but in most cases is not essential for development of specific implementations (most implementations currently derive from agent management, agent communication, and other

4 Rather than listing all FIPA standards as full references, this section provides the unique identifier of the standard (the keyword "FIPA" followed by five digits); the associated document can be retrieved from the FIPA specification repository at http://www.fipa.org based on this identifier.

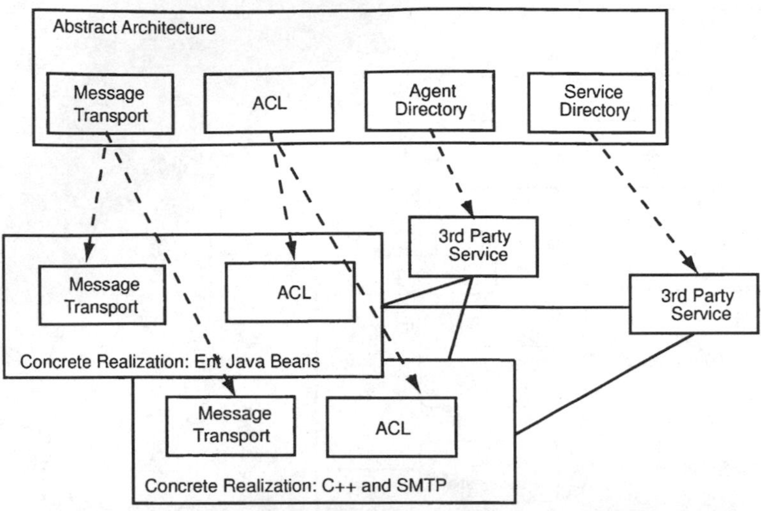

Figure 5.2 Abstract architecture mappings to different concrete realizations with shared services for some architectural elements. (*After:* FIPA00001 [4].)

concrete level specifications—everything below the abstract layer in Figure 5.2). There are currently two reifications of the architecture, as follows:

- The Java Agent Services API, designed to validate the abstract architecture (see Section 5.2.6).
- The FIPA2003 standard specification set, described in the following sections. These concrete-level specifications generally implement and specialize the abstract architecture, although there are some overlaps.

5.2.2 FIPA Agent Management

The FIPA Agent Management Specification (FIPA00023) defines the type of run-time environment that FIPA agents inhabit, the services that are expected to be available to them, and the management actions that can be carried out by or for them. The specification introduces the notion of an agent platform (Figure 5.3) as the key building block of such an environment. FIPA agent platforms include the following mandatory components:

- An agent run-time environment: defining the notion of agenthood used in FIPA and a life cycle for such systems. A platform can implement its run-time environment in almost any way, inside a single Java virtual machine, for example, or using a distributed object system to manage separate processes on many remote machines.

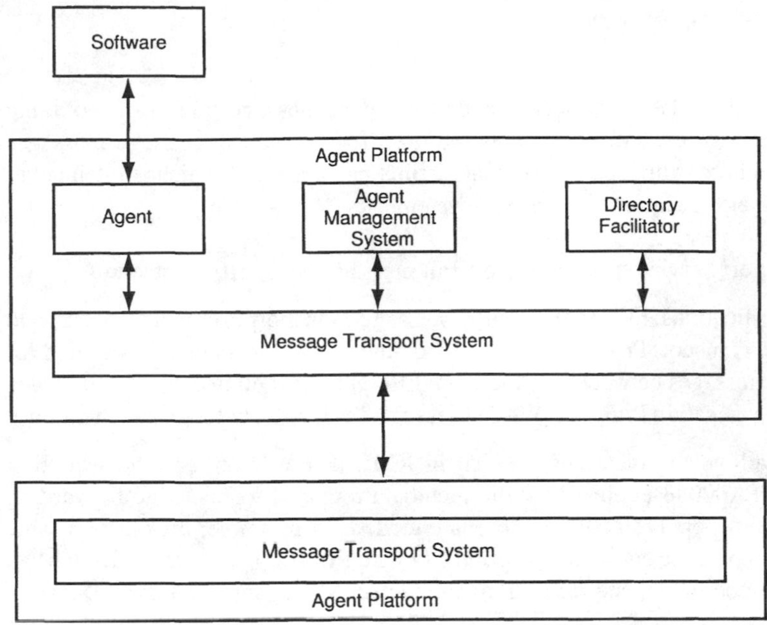

Figure 5.3 FIPA Agent Platform Reference Model. (*After:* FIPA00023 [5].)

- A directory facilitator (DF): acting as a yellow pages service for the agents on the platform, enabling them to advertise and discover service offerings. Provisions are also made for the federation of DFs between different agent platforms.
- An agent management system (AMS): acting as a white pages service (to allow agents registered on the platform to locate one another) and as the main authority on the platform controlling service and resource use (enforcing the agent life cycle).
- Message transport systems: communication services for on and off platform agent message exchange (see Section 5.2.3).

Each of these components is specified in detail in terms of functionality and interfaces (for the agent run time in terms of a life cycle) and is widely implemented in a range of FIPA agent platform implementations. (Note, however, that management of platform resources is currently not usually handled by the AMS in most platform implementations but by external user accessible interfaces.)

5.2.3 FIPA Agent Message Transport Service

One of the most detailed areas of FIPA specification is that of agent message transport, providing specifications of encodings, interfaces, and subsystems required for agents to exchange messages with one another. The standard here is divided into several distinct parts, each of which is intended to be a modular component of an agent platform's transport system:

- FIPA00067 Message Transport Service specifies the overall message transport architecture.
- Two transport protocol specifications, FIPA00075 (FIPA Message Transport Protocol for IIOP) and FIPA00084 (FIPA Message Transport Protocol for HTTP), define the low-level details required for the on-the-wire transfer of messages between interfaces on different agent platforms. (There is also an experimental Wireless Application Protocol (WAP) Message Transport Protocol specification.)
- Two message transport envelope specifications, the first in XML (FIPA00085) and the second in a bit-efficient encoding (FIPA00088), define how the metadata required for message forwarding over individual Message Transport Protocols (MTPs) is encoded. In principle, they are reusable across different MTPs, but in practice both are used primarily with FIPA00084, since the IIOP MTP already has a native CDR encoding defined for IIOP by the Object Management Group (OMG).
- Lastly, the message transport area also includes several ACL message representation specifications that define the precise syntax to be used when sending messages. There are currently three such encodings: FIPA00069, bit-efficient encoding, FIPA00070 S-expression "String" encoding (which is used by almost all current FIPA agent implementations), and the FIPA00071 XML encoding (implemented by a number of platforms).

These standards components fit together to enable message transport between agents in two different ways as shown in Figure 5.4. FIPA also allows for the possibility that agents simply interact in some arbitrary direct way (the third way shown in the diagram) but this need not be subject to any standardization. As shown in the figure, it is important to note that:

- FIPA defines the external transport interfaces of agent platforms (via the agent communication channel—ACC) in terms of the overall transport architecture, the MTPs, and the message envelopes.
- The resulting external interfaces can then be accessed by either ACCs (method 1 in the figure) or agents (method 2 in the figure) directly from other platforms or on the same platform.
- The internal interface an agent may have to its platform's messaging services is deliberately not defined, to provide flexibility for individual toolkit developers.

The objective, as with the abstract architecture, is to foster a modular approach to message transport that will enable different combinations of lower-level messaging technologies to be used to support agent message exchange.

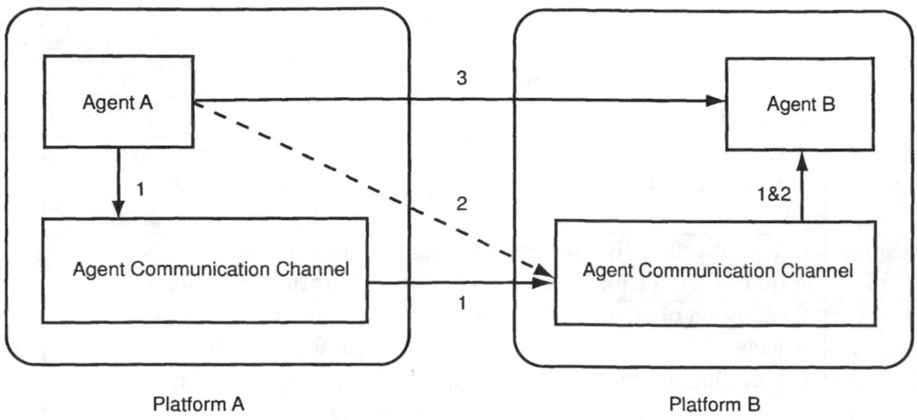

Figure 5.4 FIPA-defined transport mechanisms. (*After:* FIPA00067 [6].)

5.2.4 FIPA Agent Communication Standards

Arguably, one of the most important areas of FIPA standardization is that of agent-agent communication. While the message transport standards (described in the previous section) deal with how bits should be transported from one agent to another, it is much more difficult to define the precise meaning (or semantics) of these bits.

In recent years the views in the agent community as to what is necessary to enable such communication have converged to a great extent, and this is reflected in the FIPA standard. Although not defined explicitly anywhere in the standards set, the generic communication stack shown in Table 5.1 reflects the major components present in most architectures. Different parts of this generic model are defined by different FIPA specifications. These communication specifications are divided into the following four groups:

- The FIPA-ACL Message Structure Specification (FIPA00061) defines the framework for FIPA-ACL messages, the components that must be present, and how they must be interpreted.[5]
- A library of communicative acts or performatives (FIPA00037) defines formal and informal meanings (semantics) for a set of different communicative acts specified by FIPA. These specifications therefore define the range of message types available in FIPA systems.
- FIPA Protocols define a number of different interaction sequences (message sequences) for standard situations that may occur in agent systems. The protocols include simple examples such as a *request*

5 Note that this specification does not define a message syntax, but this is done by adopting one of the ACL representation specifications described in Section 5.2.3.

Table 5.1

Generic Communication Stack

Level	Description	Example
Conversation (Interaction Protocol)	A sequence of communicative acts related to a particular topic	A sequence of messages communicating about buying and eating an apple
Communicative Act	Communication (Expression of Agent Attitude) about a piece of content	Requesting somebody to perform the action of ...
Content Expression	Description of states of the world over objects	Expressing the action of eating an apple
Ontology	Description of objects in the domain	Meaning of "apple" and "eat"
Syntax	Representation of Content	HTML, JPG, SQL
Protocol	Data exchange protocol (ISO layer 7)	HTTP, GIIOP, SMTP
Transport	Physical transport and low-level transport protocols (ISO layers 1–6)	Optical Fiber, TCP-IP, and so on

sequence, and more complicated examples such as contract nets (introduced in Chapter 2) and experimental auction protocols.

- Content Language defines one content language for use in FIPA Messages. The language (FIPA-SL defined in FIPA00008) is also used in all agent management interactions and for formally defining the FIPA-ACL semantics. There are also three other experimental status languages: FIPA-KIF (based on ANSI KIF presented in Section 5.5.1), FIPA-RDF (capturing elements of FIPA-SL in W3C's Resource Description Framework representation), and FIPA-CCL (which allows the expression of choices and constraints).

Together, these specifications can be used to construct interactions between agents. Protocols are often used as the first building blocks, indicating which ACL messages (performatives) are needed. The ACL message structure, syntaxes, and definitions are then used to construct the messages, and FIPA-SL is used to express the message content as shown in Table 5.2. In the table, the object variable, `?x` is just defined as meeting the criteria for the predicate "is-car," which would need to be defined in the car ontology. The use of a `query-ref` performative indicates that the agent is asking about information related to a particular reference (in this case represented by the variable `?x`).

It is important to note that FIPA remains neutral on the ontology language to be used for expressing domain knowledge associated with a communication. Increasingly, however, FIPA platform implementations seem likely to support DAML-OIL or OWL as the ontology representations of choice (see Section 5.5.2 for a discussion of these ontology standards).

Table 5.2
FIPA Agent Message Example of a Query for Any Known Object Matching the Object Variable ?x

```
(query-ref
 :sender (agent-identifier :name i)
 :receiver (agent-identifier :name j)
 :ontology car
 :language FIPA-SL
 :content
   ``((any ?x (is-car ?x)))''
)
```

5.2.5 Applications

In addition to the main technology standards, FIPA also provides a number of specifications that support application development in specific domains. In particular, there are three specifications related to this, which have now been accepted to standard level:

- The FIPA Nomadic Application Support Specification (FIPA00014) defines methods and mechanisms for supporting deployment of FIPA-compliant systems in environments where connectivity is only intermittent, and permanent (or near permanent) connection to network resources cannot be guaranteed. The specification includes provisions for management of communication channels, management of directory entries, and negotiation of message transport characteristics.
- The FIPA Device Ontology Specification (FIPA00091) defines a standard nomenclature for specifying device characteristics used in mobile environments.
- A Quality of Service Ontology Specification (FIPA00094) defines a standard nomenclature for specifying quality of service characteristics used in mobile environments.

Each of these is the result of long-standing activity within FIPA to support the application of FIPA agents in mobile environments. There are also a number of informative, experimental application descriptions, described in Section 5.9.

5.2.6 Java Agent Services (JAS)

As part of the work on the FIPA abstract architecture, a number of FIPA member organizations, including Fujitsu Laboratories of America, Sun, and IBM, led the specification of a concrete instantiation of the abstract architecture in the form of a Java API. The resulting Java Agent Services project followed the Sun Microsystems Java Community Process (JCP) [7] to register the resulting API in the "javax.agent" namespace.

At the time of this writing, the API specification was in the final phase of the JCP review, and a reference implementation has been produced. More information on JAS can be found at http://www.java-agent.org.

5.2.7 Other FIPA Specifications

As well as the mainstream standards presented in the previous sections, there are a number of other specifications (past and present) within FIPA that have yielded useful results. These include the following:

- The FIPA Ontology Service Specification (FIPA00086) provides a useful model of functionality and interfaces for agent-based systems, providing ontological information. The model derives from the OKBC [8] definition.
- FIPA Application Specifications for individual application domains are still available with experimental status. Although they have not yet been updated to work with the latest generation of standards, the applications Personal Travel Assistant (FIPA00080), Audio-Visual Entertainment and Broadcasting (FIPA00081), Network Management and Provisioning (FIPA00082), and Personal Assistant (FIPA00083) are useful models, since they provide a snapshot of motivating scenarios for the use of standard agent technology.
- The FIPA Agent Management Support for Mobility (FIPA00005) provides a useful starting point for developers contemplating mobile agent systems development. However, as described earlier, FIPA is no longer active in the area of mobile agents.
- FIPA Domains and Policies Specification (FIPA00089) provides a high-level description of notions such as domain, policy, a range of use cases, and descriptions of architectural elements needed to implement them. Although still incomplete, the document is likely to undergo further development and already provides a useful introduction to the issues involved.

Since each of these is currently *deprecated*, or at least not in the main set of standards, they are generally not in active use. They may, however, prove a useful resource for developers working on specific problems in these areas. As with the mainstream specifications, these documents can be accessed on the FIPA Web site.[6]

5.2.8 FIPA Standards Index

Table 5.3 gives a concise list of the current standard level specifications matched to specification numbers.

6 http://www.fipa.org

Table 5.3

Index of FIPA Standard-Level Specifications

Identifier	Specification Title
FIPA00001	FIPA Abstract Architecture Specification
FIPA00008	FIPA SL Content Language Specification
FIPA00014	FIPA Nomadic Application Support Specification
FIPA00023	FIPA Agent Management Specification
FIPA00026	FIPA Request Interaction Protocol Specification
FIPA00027	FIPA Query Interaction Protocol Specification
FIPA00028	FIPA Request When Interaction Protocol Specification
FIPA00029	FIPA Contract Net Interaction Protocol Specification
FIPA00030	FIPA Iterated Contract Net Interaction Protocol Specification
FIPA00033	FIPA Brokering Interaction Protocol Specification
FIPA00034	FIPA Recruiting Interaction Protocol Specification
FIPA00035	FIPA Subscribe Interaction Protocol Specification
FIPA00036	FIPA Propose Interaction Protocol Specification
FIPA00037	FIPA Communicative Act Library Specification
FIPA00061	FIPA ACL Message Structure Specification
FIPA00067	FIPA Agent Message Transport Service Specification
FIPA00069	FIPA ACL Message Representation in Bit-Efficient Specification
FIPA00070	FIPA ACL Message Representation in String Specification
FIPA00071	FIPA ACL Message Representation in XML Specification
FIPA00075	FIPA Agent Message Transport Protocol for IIOP Specification
FIPA00084	FIPA Agent Message Transport Protocol for HTTP Specification
FIPA00085	FIPA Agent Message Transport Envelope Representation in XML Specification
FIPA00088	FIPA Agent Message Transport Envelope Representation in Bit Efficient Specification
FIPA00091	FIPA Device Ontology Specification
FIPA00094	FIPA Quality of Service Specification

See http://www.fipa.org for a current list.

Table 5.4

Example KQML Messages

`(ask-one :content (PRICE IBM ?price) :receiver stock-server :language LPROLOG :ontology NYSE-TICKS)`	Asking for a single stock price quote for a particular company.
`(subscribe :content (stream-all :content (PRICE IBM ?price)))`	Requesting future updates on all price changes for the same stock item—note the embedded message inside another message.

Source: [9].

5.3 KQML

KQML [9] was developed as part of the DARPA Knowledge Sharing Effort in the early 1990s and shares a common heritage with KIF (see Section 5.5.1).

The language specifications provide for syntax and semantics for exchanging information and knowledge. The language was originally designed to enable the construction of large-scale knowledge bases by enabling more flexible data exchange, but it was also rapidly adopted by agent researchers as a way for structuring message exchanges between their systems. As with FIPA-ACL, KQML is based on speech act theory and the notion of performatives (there are around 35 compared to FIPA's 20 or so) and uses very similar structures. Examples of what can be expressed in KQML are shown in Table 5.4. Several flavors of KQML emerged (such as Stanford's KQML+KIF "ACL" [10]) and a more formal semantics was added [11].

Given the similarities between FIPA-ACL and KQML, the main differentiating factor between them is perhaps that over the past 2 to 3 years there has been a general trend towards the greater adoption of FIPA-ACL, which now arguably has a greater number of available toolkits and active users, as well as being more uniform in use (there are few dialects in active use, whereas KQML has several).

There are some differences in the semantics of the two languages, however, and this would become an issue if the implemented agents began to actively use the modal logic levels of the languages (relating to belief, desire, intention, uncertainty, and so forth) for reasoning. There are also a number of toolkits based primarily on the KQML language (Stanford's JatLite[7] being one). A good selection of KQML resources can be found at http://www.cs.umbc.edu/kqml.

5.4 MOBILE AGENT STANDARDS

Mobile agents are software agents that can freeze execution (code, state, and data) at a particular run-time location (virtual or physical machine) and be transported through a computer network to another run-time location to continue their active operation in the new location.[8] The development of standards in this area is particularly challenging because of the following reasons:

- The range of systems sometimes described as mobile agents is very wide, from specially coded self-executing TCP-IP packets in *active networks* (see capsule systems in [12], for example), to mobile CORBA (OMG's Common Object Request Broker Architecture) objects such as in Voyager,[9] and more complex agents using toolkits such as Aglets.[10]
- The level of interoperability required is also very different from the message exchanges described in the previous sections—agents arriving at a particular location must be able to execute (code compatibility), access local resources (file handles, threads, and so forth), and be securely sandboxed to ensure agent and platform security.

Standardization is thus concerned more with the code level, and issues are more closely related to distributed object technologies such as CORBA than the FIPA standards. As described in [2], however, both levels together would be required to develop what might be regarded as a *complete* mobile agent system. The main standards efforts in the mobile agents area to date have been:

- The OMG Mobile Agent System Interoperability Facility (MASIF) Specification [13].
- The FIPA Agent Management Support for Mobility Specification (FIPA00005).

Both of these groups are now unfortunately relatively inactive and have not produced complete standards documents. However, results include reference models for mobility that may be useful as a basis for future standards.

Realistically, mobile agent systems to date still rely heavily on all participants using the same mobile agent toolkit (for example, Aglets, Grasshopper [14], or one of the many others available), creating single-vendor environments that cannot strictly be described as standards based. As mobile

7 http://java.stanford.edu

8 Note that there are several definitions. For example, not all mobile agent systems allow the capture of state. However, this description, we believe, captures the spirit of most mobile agent technologies.

9 http://www.recursionsw.com/products/voyager

10 http://aglets.sourceforge.net

agents establish themselves, however, it may be that one or more of these toolkits becomes sufficiently established to create a de facto standard in the area.

5.4.1 OMG MASIF

The MASIF standardization activity within OMG began life as a submission to a technology call by a number of organizations including General Magic, IBM, Crystaliz, and GMD Fokus. The resulting specification was completed in 1998 and can be found in full in [13]. The document provides specifications for three areas:

- Agent management deals with remotely creating agents, starting them and stopping them, as well as other life cycle functions.
- Agent tracking addresses the location of agents in a mobile agent environment including remote queries to directories of agents on different platforms.
- Agent transport provides methods for receiving and fetching agent class files between different platforms and subsequently making them available for agent management functions and execution.

The specifications for the first two elements are considered easy to implement, but the specification for the last is more complex. MASIF defines a reference terminology for mobile agent systems containing definitions for notions of agents, mobility, state, and, in particular, several notions of locality.

Place A place is a context in which an agent can execute, so a place is an execution environment.

Agency An agency is an agent system. An agency can have several places. An agent system represents a platform that can create, interpret, execute, and transfer agents.

Region A region is a group of agencies that belong to a single authority.

These definitions illustrate the difference between mobile and nonmobile agent systems—the notion that agents move from one run-time environment to another during their lifetime.

The technical specifications themselves are defined in terms of standard CORBA services (naming, life-cycle, externalization, and security services) available in many CORBA ORB (Object Request Broker—the main CORBA mechanism to refer remote procedure calls between systems) implementations. The standards are captured in two Interface Definition Language (IDL) interface definitions: MAFAgentSystem and MAFFinder. These interfaces must be implemented by mobile agent platforms in order to be considered compliant with the MASIF standard. They allow the specified remote operations implied by the standard to be carried out transparently, whatever the software platform the remote platform is actually using. More details on MASIF can be found in the OMG specification document [13] and a useful companion paper [15].

5.4.2 FIPA Agent Mobility Standard

The FIPA Agent Management Support for Mobility Specification (FIPA0005) formed part of the FIPA'98 specification set but was not developed further after 1999. The specification sought to

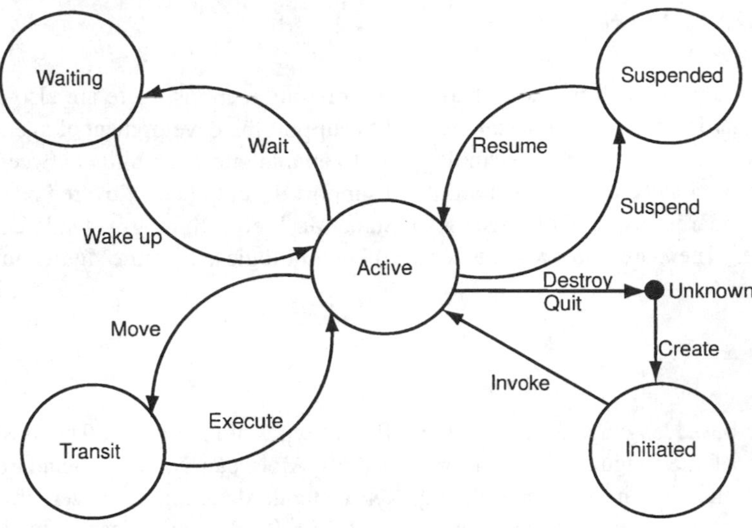

Figure 5.5 FIPA mobile agent life cycle. (*After:* FIPA00005 [16].)

determine the minimum provisions necessary to allow agents to take advantage of mobility and covered four main areas:

- Definition of terms related to mobility (notions of stationary agents, mobile agents, migration, and so forth);
- Minimal specifications of the management actions that would need to be supported by a FIPA platform to provide mobile agent functionality;
- An ontology specification for elements of an agent profile that described items such as agent data, code, and other associated information in a standard framework;
- A mobility life cycle, shown in Figure 5.5, and a number of different mobility protocols describing different modes of agent transfer between systems.

Lastly, there is a discussion on the necessary steps that would need to be taken to integrate with the OMG MASIF standard.

The FIPA mobile agent specifications were primarily intended as an extension to the standard set of FIPA specifications to cover mobility cases (or rather prevent them from being excluded). In practice they were not widely implemented or used—seemingly because they gave too little detail on the low-level mechanisms required for mobility, acting primarily to remove barriers to mobile agent platforms also implementing FIPA functionality.

5.5 AGENT-ENABLING STANDARDS

As well as the dedicated agent standards efforts described in the previous sections, there are also a host of standard or pseudostandard technologies that can be used to support the development of agent systems. Again, the key objective of many of these technologies is to enable interoperability between software systems and they are often accompanied by toolkits to support development. Covered here are the American National Standards Institute's (ANSI) KIF, Semantic Web (Ontology) standards, Web services, and Grid services. There are also several other useful technologies, the more significant of which are covered in Chapter 6.

5.5.1 KIF

KIF is a well-established logic-based language for expressing different types of knowledge. The most up-to-date "standard" version of the language is the proposed draft American National Standard (dpANS) NCITS.T2/98-004[11] that is currently undergoing ANSI standardization. However, this process may have stalled, and there are now renewed efforts on KIF-related standardization, with the two following being particularly notable:

- The Common Logic Standard Effort[12] has been submitted to ISO/IEC JTC1 SC32 as a new work item, and aims to use KIF as a basis for a new universal knowledge representation language.
- There is a new variant of KIF being used in the standardization of the IEEE Standard Upper Ontology.[13] So-called SUO KIF [17] may itself also subsequently become a candidate for standardization along with the SUO.

There are also several other extended versions of the language that have been adapted for different purposes, such as Ontolingua KIF used in Ontolingua Knowledge Tools [18] and FIPA-KIF [19] adapted as a FIPA specification.

The KIF language has a LISP-like syntax (a declarative syntax), and can be used to express arbitrary logical sentences, making it useful for a wide range of knowledge representation tasks including the expression of *metaknowledge* (hence the use in Ontolingua). Examples of the statements that can be made in KIF are shown in Table 5.5.

Although the ANSI standardization process is not complete, and there are a number of dialects available, KIF's flexibility and the renewed interest make it worth considering as a possible language for agent-systems development. It is particularly suited to projects that require some knowledge exchange but do not need the full stack of protocols, agent communication languages, and so on. The language has been used in a significant number of agent-related projects and there are a range of tools available (see Section 5.8.3) both for generating and parsing KIF expressions, and for reasoning about KIF knowledge bases.

11 http://logic.stanford.edu/kif/dpans.html
12 http://cl.tamu.edu
13 The IEEE Standard Upper Ontology Working Group, http://suo.ieee.org

Table 5.5
Example KIF Sentences

`(holds true (is-alive schrodinger-cat))`	Stating that Schrodinger's Cat is alive.
`(believes steve '(material moon stilton))`	Stating that Steve believes the Moon is made of Stilton (note the quote used to escape a second KIF sentence).

Source: [20].

5.5.2 The Semantic Web and Ontology Frameworks

The Semantic Web and other development efforts for ontology technologies have been the subject of intense research activity over the past 2 to 3 years. The core of this research is the development of common representations (languages) that can be used to express metaknowledge about data, applications, and other resources. In particular, the aim is to capture knowledge about the meaning of keywords, phrases, and statements in existing Web pages and (through activities such as DAML-S, considered in Section 5.6.1) in describing software services so they can be discovered in a networked environment.

In practice, ontology languages enable developers to express statements about facts such as relationships between different classes of objects (vegetables are a subclass of plants and also a subclass of edible things), and in the same way as a database schema, about the expected structure of data instances referring to different classes (that a car is expected to have a registration number, a color, a make, and so forth). Such languages also allow developers to express logical statements about the world ([21] and other KL-ONE derived systems, for example) such as "All wines from Chile are good."

From a standardization perspective, Figure 5.6 shows the progression of what has now become the mainstream of Semantic Web standards development. Starting with separate U.S. (DARPA Agent Markup Language, or DAML) and European (Ontology Inference Language, or OIL) efforts merging to the DAML-OIL activity, this has subsequently evolved to the Ontology Web Language (OWL) with the Web Ontology Working Group[14] at W3C. At the time of this writing, OWL had W3C *candidate recommendation* status and was very close to gaining W3C *proposed recommendation* status, which is the last step before being made a W3C *recommendation*. The majority of developers currently using DAML-OIL are converting their tools to OWL.

14 http://www.w3c.org/2001/sw

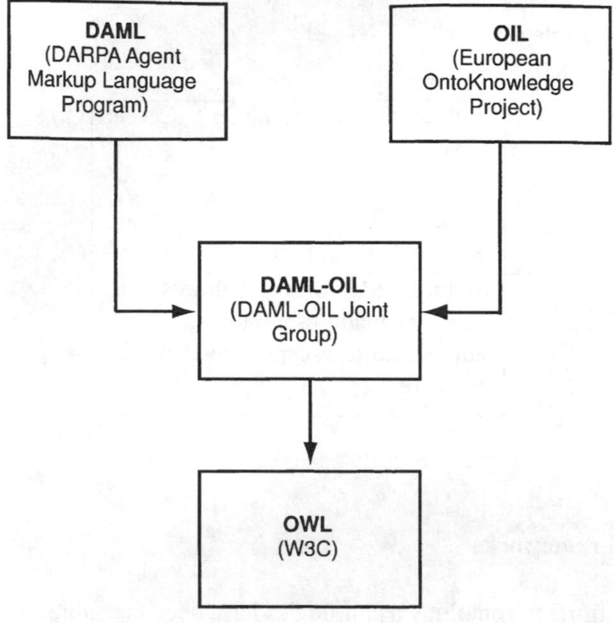

Figure 5.6 Progression of Semantic Web markup languages.

As described in Section 5.5.2, ontologies play a key role in agent communication, providing a shared reference point all agents in a system can use to interpret the meaning of messages. An example of how an ontology is relevant to something such as a FIPA message is given in the example of a FIPA message in Table 5.6.

For an agent to understand the message, it would need to able to parse and interpret the standard message elements (the performative, the sender, and receiver fields) and the meaning of the logical statement of content language expression (in this case in FIPA-SL). It would also need to have access to a domain ontology defining the elements in the world being referred to (such as the predicate "is-car" and the "car" object defined in a "car" ontology). In a single message, different ontologies are therefore in play:

- One or more domain ontologies defining notions of cars, color, registration, and so on;
- An ontology defining the notion of "agent-identifier" (in this case the FIPA Agent Management Ontology) and the values appearing as arguments to the other parameters of the message.

It is also possible to describe the components of the languages such as FIPA-ACL, FIPA-SL in terms of ontologies (creating language ontologies). For the message to be understandable, an agent must therefore match the message with the interpretation of each element, and their combination,

Table 5.6

FIPA Agent Message Example of a Possible Response to the Query Sent by Agent `i` in Table 5.2

```
(inform
 :sender (agent-identifier :name j)
 :receiver (agent-identifier :name i)
 :ontology car
 :language FIPA-SL
 :content
   ``((= (any ?x (is-car ?x))
     (car
       :color lightgray
       :registration VD 3651
       :make VW
       :type Golf
     )
   )''
)
```

based on its ontological and language models. There is also an implicit assumption that the ontologies used are precisely the same as those used by the sending agent. An accompanying piece of OWL to define the notion of *car* in the car ontology might be as shown in Table 5.7. This ontology fragment defines a "Car" class with several possible attributes:

- A color (which must be an object of type color);
- A make (which must be of type manufacturer);
- A type (which can be any string);
- A registration (also any string).

(Elsewhere, definitions of manufacturer and color classes would then completely specify the model.) The final two statements specify that any given car must have at least one and no more than one registration. An RDF representation of an instance of the car class given in Table 5.6 can be found in Table 5.8.

The significance of ontology standards for agent technology (in particular DAML-OIL and OWL) is difficult to overestimate, and they should be considered for all larger projects that envisage third parties accessing agent systems. More practically, the incorporation of such standards offers real benefits and is supported by existing tools.

Table 5.7

OWL Ontology Fragment for the Message in Table 5.6

```
<owl:Class rdf:ID=''Car'' />

<rdf:Property rdf:ID=''carColor''>
  <rdfs:label>color</rdfs:label>
  <rdfs:domain rdf:resource=''#Car''/>
  <rdfs:range rdf:resource=''#Color''/>
</rdf:Property>

<rdf:Property rdf:ID=''make''>
  <rdfs:label>make</rdfs:label>
  <rdfs:domain rdf:resource=''#Car''/>
  <rdfs:range rdf:resource=''#Manufacturer''/>
</rdf:Property>

<rdf:Property rdf:ID=''type''>
  <rdfs:label>type</rdfs:label>
  <rdfs:domain rdf:resource=''#Car''/>
  <rdfs:range rdf:resource=''&xsd;string''/>
</rdf:Property>

<rdf:Property rdf:ID=''registration''>
  <rdfs:label>registration</rdfs:label>
  <rdfs:domain rdf:resource=''#Car''/>
  <rdfs:range rdf:resource=''&xsd;string''/>
</rdf:Property>

<owl:Restriction>
  <owl:onProperty
 rdf:resource=''#registration'' />
  <owl:maxCardinality
   rdf:datatype=''&xsd;nonNegativeInteger''>1
  </owl:maxCardinality>
</owl:Restriction>

<owl:Restriction>
  <owl:onProperty
rdf:resource=''#registration'' />
  <owl:minCardinality
   rdf:datatype=''&xsd;nonNegativeInteger''>1
  </owl:minCardinality>
</owl:Restriction>
```

Table 5.8
An RDF Representation of an Instance of the Car Class Given in Table 5.7

```
<Car>
 <color rdf:resource=''#lightgray'' />
 <make rdf:resource=''#VW'' />
 <type rdf:datatype=''&xsd;string >Golf
 </type>
 <registration rdf:datatype=''&xsd;string>
 VD 3651
 </registration>
</Car>
```

- Available modeling tools (see Section 5.9) greatly simplify one of the major tasks in developing large-scale open systems: modeling the application domain, agreeing on the model, and sharing it between implementations.
- Ontologies make it much more likely that agents implemented by different parties will be able to interoperate. (Note, however, that the level of technology today means than *automatic interoperability* is still quite a way off!)
- There is a growing number of existing ontologies that can be reused for projects. Repositories containing such ontologies include http://www.daml.org and http://www.agentcities.net.

In large projects, much of this documentation must be done anyway, often in an ad hoc manner. Taking a formal ontological approach is likely to be more arduous initially, but pays dividends in the long run.

5.6 WEB SERVICES

The *Web Services* technologies are arguably one of the most important current trends in Internet, Web, and business application development. Various initiatives in this area are being led by major industrial organizations such as Microsoft, IBM, Sun, and HP. Lately, standards bodies such as the World Wide Web Consortium (W3C), the Organization for the Advancement of Structured Information Standards (OASIS), and the newly formed Web Services Interoperability Consortium (WS-I) have led to the development of a wide range of new technologies dedicated to enabling systems interoperability across intranet and Internet environments.

The combination of Web Services technologies is intended to allow developers to deploy software services in networked environments and expose their APIs for access by others. Technologies such as WSDL (Web Services Description Language[15] and UDDI T-models[16] (UDDI is Universal Description, Discovery, and Integration) can then be used to describe the service endpoints and UDDI directories can be used to locate useful services. Orchestration frameworks such as WSFL, XLANG, and BPEL4WS can be used to describe sequences of Web Services interactions. WSFL is the Web Services Flow Language[17] and XLANG[18] is Microsoft's extension of WSDL to capture sequences of Web Service executions. BPEL4WS is the Business Process Execution Language for Web Services, and represents the integration of WSFL and XLANG into a unique standard. Finally, communication with remotely deployed Web Services could be managed via the Simple Object Access Protocol (SOAP) protocol or one of several others. (A more detailed exploration of Web Services is provided in Chapter 6.)

While the current generation of Web Services technologies is aimed primarily at supporting human developers in integrating software systems, many of the technologies also provide tools useful in developing automated agents able to provide and access services deployed in the network. For this reason, Web Services are becoming increasingly relevant to agent development, in particular for industrial projects. The trend is further evidenced by the number of recent workshops covering Web Services and agent topics (examples include the WSABE workshop held at AAMAS in 2003). Many of the technologies being developed for Web Services applications can be closely related to work in the agent research community. Some illustrative examples are given here:

- Web Services Definition Language (WSDL) provides a simple representation of operations available via a given service access point (and how the operations can be called); through longer-term development (as in DAML-S, for example) these descriptions may form the basis for planning systems to dynamically compose Web Services.
- Business Process Execution Language for Web Services (BPEL4WS) allows the user to express workflows or patterns of interaction between Web Services, making them very similar to common agent interaction protocols and planning languages.
- Universal Description, Discovery, and Integration (UDDI) provides standardized directory interfaces for service discovery much as (for example) the FIPA directory facilitator does.

Although the levels of functionality of these technologies in general remain lower than, for example, FIPA agent standards, and many areas (such as higher levels of communication) are not covered, these developments are highly influential since they are being implemented in mainstream Web and system development tools. On the negative side, the tools available provide very few of the specific tools normally useful to build agent systems (threaded run-time environments, high-level language APIs, reasoning capabilities), leaving the developer with a great deal to do before work on the actual application can begin.

15 http://www.w3.org/tr/wsdl

16 http://juddi.sourceforge.net

17 www-4.ibm.com/software/solutions/webservices/pdf/WSFL.pdf

18 http://www.gotdotnet.com/team/xml_wsspecs/xlang-c/default.htm

There are also specific efforts to integrate more *agent* concepts into the Web Services world. These include DAML-S (see the next section), as well as FIPA and Agentcities Web Services Working Groups. It also seems likely that there will be an increasing convergence between the agents, Grid, and Web Services worlds as agent toolkits begin to integrate Web Services interfaces, and Web Services applications become more sophisticated. (For more examples and further discussion of these issues, see Chapter 6.)

5.6.1 DAML-S

The DAML Services (DAML-S) initiative[19] merges concepts from the Semantic Web and Web services arenas to develop a rich semantic markup language that can be used to describe services. The objectives of DAML-S go beyond current Web services languages such as WSDL in a number of ways:

- Making service descriptions machine processable: Descriptions are linked to ontologies written in the OWL ontology language with the long-term aim of enabling agents to parse and reason about them (rather than being aimed at human developers constructing interfaces as WSDL is).
- Including process models: DAML-S contains provisions for expressing not just interfaces to services that can be called but describing the functionality of the service in terms of preconditions and postconditions as well as information about its execution.
- Enabling reasoning and planning: The overall aim is therefore to enable agents to parse DAML-S statements and apply planning or reasoning techniques to dynamically compose services in an arbitrary fashion, creating new compound services.

The DAML-S ontology has three major parts:

- A *service profile* describes what the service provides. The functionality of a service is described through ontological terms for preconditions (the things should hold prior to service invocation), inputs (the necessary inputs to invoke the service), outputs (the results the requester can expect), and effects (the statements that hold true if the service is invoked successfully). In addition, there are several non-functional descriptors, such as service category, quality rating, and so forth.
- The *service model* describes how the service works. The aim is to facilitate the automated invocation of the service, its composition with other services, and the monitoring of its performance. DAML-S introduces different process types that can be used to describe the flow of operation of a service as well as the process control constructs.
- The *service grounding* describes how to access the service. It binds the abstract notions in the other parts of the DAML-S service description to protocols such as SOAP, HTTP, and so on. As such, it links a DAML-S service and a WSDL description of Web services (described in Chapter 6).

19 http://www.daml.org/services

The overall objective of the initiative is to enable the development of systems able to automatically discover published DAML-S descriptions, reason about how the services they describe might be composed, and thereby dynamically create new applications. The standard at the time of this writing was at version 0.9, released with DAML-S and OWL-S variations.

DAML-S has already been used with FIPA specifications in the Agentcities project and seems likely to become an important element in the agent standards toolkit. More information can be found at http://www.daml.org/services.

5.7 GRID COMPUTING AND THE OPEN GRID SERVICES ARCHITECTURE

The area of Grid computing has grown rapidly over recent years and has become a major focus of activity in the scientific computing community. Grid systems link distributed computing resources (processing machines, storage, specialist hardware, and so forth) to form large-scale virtual computing systems. Applications are many and varied, ranging from processing the results of particle accelerator experiments at CERN (such as those in the DataGrid Project [22]), to mass data mining over digital records of breast cancer scans [23].

In terms of standards, and particularly agent-relevant standards, there are two main areas of activity in the Grid community. The first revolves around commonly used Grid toolkits that can be used to create Grid systems, the best known of which is the Globus toolkit.[20] The second is through the activities of the Global Grid Forum[21] (GGF), which has taken on the task of setting standards for the development of Grid systems and interoperability between them. Potentially the most important aspect of this standardization is the development of the Open Grid Services Architecture (OGSA [24]) that brings together Grid computing concepts with Web services interfaces in a common framework. The OGSA is still at the draft stage but many of the components of the standard are already well advanced:

- Open Grid Services Infrastructure (OGSI), specifying the nature of Grid services, data, service properties, and many supporting elements;
- Open Grid Architecture Platform (OGSAP), specifying concrete behaviors, resource models, and interfaces required for building most Grid systems.

The Globus team is aiming to make the next version (3.0) of the toolkit compliant with the OGSA, which would then unify the two streams of activity. Figure 5.7 shows a current schematic diagram from the OGSAP specification with OGSAP components forming a layer between application and external access points.

The importance of Grid computing environments as an application area of agents looks set to grow, and as with Web services, Grid technologies potentially provide many of the lower-level communication and management features necessary to enable communication between agents. Therefore, although many aspects of the OGSA are not yet implemented, they should be considered

20 http://www.globus.org
21 http://www.globalgridforum.org

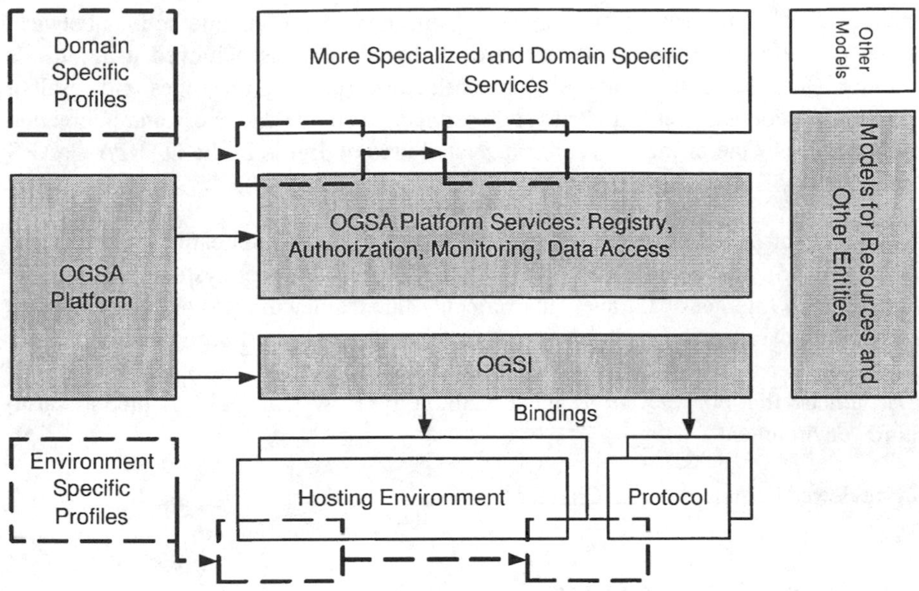

Figure 5.7 Schematic view of the Open Grid Services Architecture. OGSA Platform components (shaded) are related to host environment and domain-specific libraries via OGSI and OGSAP services. (*After:* [25].)

once tools become available. The Grid development should make it possible to develop agent systems on the basis of Grid infrastructures. The architectural similarities between Grids and agent systems (as remotely executing independent processes) also mean that the Grid environments could become natural candidates for the application of agent technologies.

5.7.1 Other Related Standards

Other standard or widely adopted technologies that provide potentially useful tools for developing agent systems come from the peer-to-peer computing and systems integration communities. In particular, these include the following:

CORBA The Object Management Group[22] Common Object Request Broker Architecture (CORBA) provides platform-independent programming interfaces and models for portable distributed object-oriented computing applications. The specifications and implementation are a widely used method for developing distributed applications and have also been used to develop agent systems. In particular, CORBA messaging underlies some of the FIPA agent standards.[23]

22 http://www.omg.org
23 http://www.corba.org

JINI The objective of Jini[24] is to provide mechanisms enabling spontaneous interactions between services deployed on different software or hardware platforms. This is achieved using Java's portability, remote method invocations, and object serialization (passing messages and results). Jini provides communication and message board style services to enable discovery and interaction between different services. One of the largest agent-related uses of Jini is in the DARPA CoABS Grid project (see Section 5.7.1).[25]

JXTA This provides a set of Java APIs for the development of distributed applications based on the peer-to-peer paradigm [26]. The core concept used in JXTA is that of a peer system that could be deployed anywhere in an Internet or Intranet environment—the framework provides mechanisms for communication, discovery, and simple service advertisement, making it a good candidate for experimentation with peer-to-peer-like agent systems.[26] (Note that there are other peer-to-peer computing environments that are relevant to agent technology. However, JXTA is the closest to being a "standard" environment.)

Jini and JXTA are reviewed in more detail in Chapter 6.

5.8 IMPLEMENTATIONS AND TOOLKITS

Standards rarely prove useful unless they are accompanied by available software toolkits, libraries, or at least APIs. This section introduces the major implementations for elements of the standards described in the remainder of the chapter. More detail on some of the systems can be found in Chapter 3 on agent toolkits and platforms.

5.8.1 FIPA Implementations

The number of implementations of the FIPA agent standard has grown significantly over the last few years, with many new platforms appearing and existing agent frameworks adding new functionality. The vast majority of the current compliant platforms implement the FIPA2000 generation of specifications and are in the process of updating to the 2002/3 "standard level" version of these specifications. Platforms generally implement the following major FIPA specifications:

- FIPA00023: FIPA Agent Management Specification;
- FIPA00061: FIPA ACL Message Structure Specification;
- FIPA00067: FIPA Message Transport Service Specification (MTS);
- FIPA00070: FIPA ACL Message Representation in String Specification;

24 Pronounced "Genie" and not in fact intended to be an acronym until Sun's Ken Arnold redefined it as an antiacronym "Jini Is Not Initials."
25 http://www.jini.org
26 http://www.jxta.org

- FIPA00084: FIPA Agent Message Transport Protocol for HTTP Specification (HTTP MTP);
- FIPA00085: FIPA Agent Message Transport Envelope Representation in XML;
- FIPA00075: FIPA Agent Message Transport Protocol for IIOP Specification (IIOP MTP).

A number of platforms also implement the abstract architecture (FIPA00001), most notably the reference implementation of the Java Agent Services Java Community Process (described in Section 5.2.6), and the University of Otago's OPAL platform.

Through the large number of available implementations, there are also a number of important trends that suggest that available tools should continue to provide useful starting points for different types of projects:

- Integration of agent platforms with industrial-strength software platforms. BlueJade [27], for example, was developed by integrating the Jade agent platform with HP's BlueStone application server, and the project is now being ported to the Open Source JBoss Enterprise Java Application Server[27] platform.
- Development of security tools and services for FIPA Agent platforms, including a more secure version of the JADE platform [28].
- Support for agent deployment on Mobile devices with LEAP[28] and MicroFIPA-OS.[29]
- Increasing integration of modeling tools. The OPAL platform [29], for example, is based on UML models that enable automatic code generation for many levels of an agent's behavior and communication.[30]

Several well-known FIPA agent platform implementations are listed in Table 5.9, but a more complete list of FIPA platform implementations can be found at http://www.fipa.org and http://www.agentcities.org.

5.8.2 Mobile Agent Platforms

As described in Section 5.4, mobile agent standards are unfortunately still not well advanced and the best policy at this stage appears to be to opt for one of the many existing toolkits. A number of these are listed in Table 5.10, but a Web search will also locate many more systems.

5.8.3 Other Useful Tools

A selection of tools available for the other standards described in this chapter are listed in Table 5.11. Implementations vary in terms of their maturity, completeness, and licenses (some commercial, some open source).

27 http://jboss.org/index.html
28 http://leap.crm–paris.com
29 http://sourceforge.net/projects/fipa-os
30 UML is the OMG's Unified Modeling Language.

Table 5.9

Selection of Well-Known FIPA Agent Platform Implementations

April Agent Platform (AAP) / Fujitsu Laboratories of America	
Description	Open-source (GPL) agent platform based on the April++ programming language.
URL	`http://www.sourceforge.net/projects/networkagent`
Comtec Agent Platform / Comtec	
Description	C++ based platform implementing both FIPA97 and FIPA2000 specifications.
URL	`http://ias.comtec.co.jp/ap`
FIPA-S / Emorphia	
Description	Open-source (Emorphia public license) Java-based implementation of the FIPA2000 standards.
URL	`http://fipa-os.sourceforge.net`
JACK / Agent Oriented Software	
Description	Commercial JACK agent platform with FIPA extensions to implement FIPA2000 specifications.
URL	`http://www.agent-software.com`
JADE / JADE Steering Board	
Description	Open-source (LPGL) implementation of the FIPA2000 and new standard level specifications.
URL	`http://jade.cselt.it`
LEAP / EU IST LEAP Project Consortium	
Description	Lightweight adaptation of the JADE platform (now part of Jade LPGL) for mobile devices.
URL	`http://leap.crm-paris.com` `http://sharon.cselt.it/projects/jade`
OPAL / University of Otago	
Description	Agent platform supporting both FIPA2000 and Abstract Architecture, and JAS standards.
URL	[29]
Zeus / BTExact	
Description	Open-source (BT Zeus License) FIPA platform implementation of FIPA2000 standards.
URL	`http://www.btexact.com/projects/agents/zeus`

Table 5.10

Selection of Well-Known Mobile Agent Platform Implementations

Aglets	
Description	Originally developed by IBM laboratories in Japan, Aglets is now open source.
URL	`http://aglets.sourceforge.net`
Beegents	
Description	A Java-based mobile agent system developed and maintained by Toshiba Corporation's Knowledge Media Laboratory, includes belief, desire, and intention reasoning capabilities.
URL	`http://www2.toshiba.co.jp/beegent/index.htm`
D'Agents	
Description	Developed by Dartmouth College (United States) Department of Computer Science, D'Agents was one of the first available implementations of a mobile agents toolkit.
URL	`http://agent.cs.dartmouth.edu`
Grasshopper	
Description	Developed by GMD Fokus and later IKV++, Grasshopper is a Java-based mobile agent platform aimed primarily at telecommunications applications.
URL	`http://www.grasshopper.de`
Hive	
Description	Hive is a GPL open source Java system for creating distributed applications using mobile components developed by MIT Media Lab.
URL	`http://hive.sourceforge.net`
Telescript	
Description	Arguably the original mobile agent language, defining many of the concepts of mobile code. Developed by General Magic.
URL	[30]
Voyager	
Description	Developed originally by Objectspace (now Recursion software), it is a CORBA ORB system that includes object mobility features.
URL	`http://www.recursionsw.com/products/voyager`

Table 5.11

A Selection of Tools for Agent-Related Standards

Standards	**Tools**
KIF	Available parsers include the Java KIF Parser (which is available from http://www.csee.umbc.edu/kse/kif/jkp and implements the SKIF subset of KIF equivalent to Horn Clause Logic), Stanford KIF parser (from http://piano.stanford.edu/concur/software/kifparser.html, which is implemented in C++ using Flex and Bison), ATOMIK (a Java-based LPGL multiple language API which also supports SKIF, available at http://liawww.epfl.ch/atomik). Reasoners that support subsets of KIF include EPILOG (http://logic.stanford.edu/sharing/programs/epilog, implementing reasoning for the SKIF subset) and JTP (developed by the Knowledge Systems Laboratory at Stanford University and available from http://www.ksl.stanford.edu/software/JTP).
DAML-OIL and OWL	While there are few OWL tools available (since the standard is still being finalized), there are a large number of tools available for various types of DAML-OIL processing. Good sources of tools include http://www.w3.org/2001/sw/WebOnt/#Tools and http://www.daml.org.
Web Services	With the current explosion in interest surrounding Web services, a large number of different tools have become available, including commercial offerings from Microsoft, Oracle, IBM, and others, as well as developer systems, such as the IBM Alphaworks series systems, Business Explorer for Web Services (BE4WS), and the Web Services Toolkit (now the Emerging Technologies Toolkit). Alphaworks tools are available from http://www.alphaworks.ibm.com. There is also a significant number of open-source activities implementing tools for each of the specific standards associated with Web services including UDDI, for example, and collections of functions such as the Apache Web Services Projects (http://ws.apache.org) and Enhydra's tools (http://www.enhydra.org).
DAML-S	DAML-S makes use of many of the DAML-OIL tools previously mentioned, but there are also specific DAML-S tools, such as matchmakers, that can be found at http://www.daml.org/services/tools.html.
Grid Computing	The best known and more widely used open-source Grid toolkit is Globus, updates of which can be found at http://www.globus.org/toolkit. There are also commercial offerings such as InnerGrid by GridSystems (http://www.gridsystems.com).

5.9 USES OF AGENT STANDARDS

While most of the standards discussed in this chapter remain in the research arena, many have been applied in large-scale prototype systems. This section outlines some of the major areas of standards use in agent systems.

5.9.1 DARPA CoABS Grid

The DARPA funded CoABS Grid activity in the United States is a long-running program to create architectures and an environment for federating heterogeneous agent systems. Large-scale demonstrations have been carried out integrating over 20 systems in different locations in military planning and recovery operations. More commercial uses are also planned.

The CoABS Grid uses adaptors for agent languages such as KQML and FIPA-ACL as well as Jini-based software components to enable run-time integration of agent-based systems running in distributed locations. The interoperability in the system is based on common software components that can be downloaded and installed by each of the participating nodes. Services on different nodes can then be located from descriptions registered in Jini directories. More information can be found at http://coabs.globalinfotek.com.

5.9.2 Agentcities

The Agentcities initiative is based on the development and deployment of a global open testbed environment for agent-based services. The project has been running since July 2001 with the testbed deployment launched with 14 platforms in late October 2001. Since then, the activity has grown rapidly and now includes around 100 deployed network nodes in over 20 countries worldwide. The testbed uses the following standard technologies:

- Standard Web and Internet technologies such as HTTP and XML to provide messaging infrastructures.
- The FIPA agent standards for semantic agent languages, interaction protocols, and agent management services, as well as the model for run-time environments to support agent services.
- Semantic Web technology in the form of DAML-OIL ontologies, enabling interoperability between agents and services deployed by many different organizations in the open environment.

The most important element of the deployment from a standards perspective is that there are currently around 20 different implementations of the relevant FIPA standards in use in the network. Applications developed in the network vary widely and include:

- E-business scenarios for the entertainment industry (linking services on 10+ of the deployed agent platforms—Agentcities.RTD project[31]);

31 http://www.agentcities.org/eurtd

- Healthcare services (with several groups including Universitat Politécnica de Catalunya, Universitat Rovira I Virgili, Tarragona/Spain; and Sheffield Hallam University, Sheffield/United Kingdom);
- Supply chain management (Gerstner Laboratory/Czech Republic, UMIST/United Kingdom);
- Recruitment and personal job search (Siemens, Munich/Germany);
- Knowledge Management (Aberdeen/United Kingdom);
- Business travel (France Telecom/France);
- Many more applications, some of which can be found listed on-line at the Agentcities Web site, http://www.agentcities.org/EUNET/Projects.

The testbed has been relatively successful both in providing a way to mature the standards involved (in part contributing to the growth in the number of FIPA-compliant platforms now available) and in creating a large user community that can benefit from the use of the standard technologies.

Most importantly, however, the development of Agentcities would not have been possible if it had not been for the availability of the FIPA standard; without these definitions and their implementations, it seems highly unlikely that such a large community could have integrated their systems in such a short time. More information can be found at http://www.agentcities.org.

5.9.3 Towards Commercial Uses of the FIPA Standards

FIPA standards and FIPA-compliant platforms have been used in a large number of projects. However, to date most of these have remained at the research stage and business use has yet to materialize. In the meantime, as mentioned in Section 5.6.1, there are positive trends towards making agent standards more viable for business use. These include:

- The emergence of platforms adapted to mobile environments;
- The development of security services;
- The integration of FIPA agent platforms with industrial-strength application servers.

With each of these steps, as well as increasing trends towards integration with Web services and Semantic Web technologies, it seems likely that commercial applications of agent standards technologies will become more feasible in the coming years.

5.10 CONCLUSIONS

Over the past couple of years, standards have become increasingly important for the development of agent systems, particularly for applications that involve data access and message exchange. Standards efforts such as FIPA have also matured, and there is now a wide range of both toolkit implementations and significant system deployments available. In addition to the dedicated agent standards, there are also significant numbers of associated standard technologies that potentially provide the agent developer with an armory of tools, links to developer communities, and formal specifications.

In conclusion, therefore, although there is without doubt significant development to be done, the standardization efforts of the past 5 years or so provide many useful starting points for agent development and should be seriously considered in any major project. The agents standardization world is still evolving, and the major question for the next 5 years seems likely to be to what extent agent standards remain separate and to what extent they fuse with mainstream software standards.

The work described here was partially supported by European Commission funded projects IST-2000-28384 and IST-2000-28385 as well as Spanish government grants SB2001-0122 and Agentcities.ES. The opinions given are those of the authors and do not necessarily reflect those of all project participants. The authors would like to thank the reviewers for their useful comments and Carlos Mérida Campos for his contribution of the OWL example.

References

[1] Dale, J., and E. Mamdani, "Open Standards for Interoperating Agent-Based Systems," *Software Focus*, Vol. 2, No. 1, 2001, pp. 1–8.

[2] Finin, T., Y. Peng, and Y. Labrou, "Mobile Agents Can Benefit from Standards Efforts on Interagent Communication," *IEEE Communications Magazine*, Vol. 36, No. 7, 1998, pp. 50–56.

[3] O'Brien, P., and R. Nicol, "FIPA — Towards a Standard for Software Agents," *BT Technology Journal*, Vol. 16, No. 3, 1998, pp. 51–59.

[4] FIPA, "FIPA00001 — FIPA Abstract Architecture Specification," http://www.fipa.org/specs/fipa00001/.

[5] FIPA, "FIPA00023 — FIPA Agent Management Specification," http://www.fipa.org/specs/fipa00023/.

[6] FIPA, "FIPA00067 — FIPA Agent Message Transport Service Specification," http://www.fipa.org/specs/fipa00067/.

[7] Sun Microsystems, "Java Community Process Version 2 documentation," http://java.sun.com/aboutjava/communityprocess/jcp2.html, September 2003.

[8] Chaudhri, V. K., et al., "OKBC: A Programmatic Foundation for Knowledge Base Interoperability," *Proceedings of the Fifteenth National Conference on Artificial Intelligence (AAAI'98)*, 1998, pp. 600–607.

[9] Finin, T., et al., "KQML as an Agent Communication Language," *Proceedings of the Third International Conference on Information and Knowledge Management (CIKM'94)*, 1994.

[10] Genesereth, M. R., "An Agent-Based Approach to Software Interoperability," *Proceedings of the DARPA Software Technology Conference*, 1992, pp. 359–366.

[11] Mayfield, J., Y. Labrou, and T. Finin, "Evaluation of KQML as an Agent Communication Language," *Intelligent Agents II: Agent Theories, Architectures, and Languages*, M. Wooldridge, J. Muller, and M. Tambe, (eds.), Volume 1037 of *LNCS*, New York: Springer, 1996, pp. 347–360.

[12] Tennenhouse, D. L., et al., "A Survey of Active Network Research," *IEEE Communications Magazine*, Vol. 35, No. 1, 1997, pp. 80–86.

[13] Version 98-03-09 Object Management Group, "The Mobile Agents System Interoperability Facilities Submission," *Specification Results*, at ftp://ftp.omg.org/pub/docs/orbos/98-03-09.pdf.

[14] Covaci S., "The First Reference Implementation of the OMG MASIF Mobile Agent System Interoperability Facility," http://www.omg.org/docs/orbos/98-04-05.pdf, September 2002.

[15] Milojicic, D. S., et al., "MASIF: The OMG Mobile Agent System Interoperability Facility," *Mobile Agents — Second International Workshop*, K. Rothermel and F. Hohl, (eds.), Volume 1477 of *LNCS*, New York: Springer, 1999, pp. 50–67.

[16] FIPA, "FIPA00005 — FIPA 98 Part 11 Version 1.0: Agent Management Support for Mobility Specification," http://www.fipa.org/specs/fipa00005/.

[17] Standard Upper Ontology Knowledge Interchange Format (KIF) Specification, http://suo.ieee.org/suo-kif.html.

[18] Farquhar, A., R. Fikes, and J. Rice, *The Ontolingua Server: A Tool for Collaborative Ontology Construction*, Stanford University, Knowledge Systems Laboratory Technical Report 1996, http://www.ksl.stanford.edu/software/ontolingua, September 2003.

[19] Foundation for Intelligent Physical Agents, "FIPA KIF Content Language Specification," http://fipa.org/specs/fipa00010, September 2000.

[20] Willmott, S., J. Dale, and P. Charlton, *Agent Communication Semantics in Open Environments: Issues and Challenges*, EPFL I & C Technical Report, #200240, 2002.

[21] Brachman, R. J., et al., "CLASSIC: A Structural Data Model for Objects," *Proceedings of the 1989 ACM SIGMOD International Conference on Management of Data*, 1989, pp. 59–67.

[22] CERN Openlab for DataGrid Applications, "Developing Solutions for the Data-Intensive Science of the Large Hadron Collider," http://proj-openlab-datagrid-public.web.cern.ch/proj-openlab-datagrid-public, September 2003.

[23] Worthington, T., "IBM Grid Helps Fight Against Breast Cancer," *eWeek Online*, October 14, 2002.

[24] Foster, I., et al., "The Physiology of the Grid," http://www.globus.org/research/papers/ogsa.pdf, September 2003.

[25] Foster, I., and D. Gannon, (eds.), "Open Grid Services Architecture Platform Specification Draft," http://forge.gridforum.org/projects/ogsa-wg/document/The_Open_Grid_Services_Architecture_Platform /en/1/The_Open_Grid_Services_Architecture_Platform.pdf, 2003.

[26] Oram, A., (ed.), *Peer-to-Peer: Harnessing the Power of Disruptive Technologies*, Sebastopol, CA: O'Reilly & Associates, 2001.

[27] Cowan, D., et al., "A Robust Environment for Agent Deployment," *Proceedings of the First International Workshop on Challenges in Open Agent Environments*, Bologna, Italy, http://www.agentcities.org/Challenge02/Proc/Papers/ch02_44_cowan.pdf, 2002.

[28] Vitaglione, G., "Jade Tutorial: Security Administrator Guide," http://sharon.cselt.it/projects/jade/doc/tutorials/SecurityAdminGuid.pdf, 2002.

[29] Purvis, M., et al., "Opal: A Multi-Level Infrastructure for Agent-Oriented Software Development," *Information Science Discussion Paper Series, Number 2002/01, ISSN 1172-6024*, University of Otago, Dunedin, New Zealand, 2002.

[30] White, J. E., "Mobile Agents," in *Software Agents*, J. Bradshaw, (ed.), Menlo Park, CA: AAAI Press/MIT Press, 1996.

Chapter 6

Agent Support Technologies

6.1 INTRODUCTION

One of the main implementation challenges for the agent-based systems application developer is to manage the large number of technologies that must be integrated to provide a working agent system. These range from the more "traditional" application development issues, such as object-oriented development, to the problems associated with distributed systems applications, through to the issues of communication, coordination, and cooperation that are introduced by agents. It is for this reason that appropriate methodologies, standards, and toolkits for agent systems are essential to ease the development process. In addition, another crucial component is the availability of mainstream technologies to support general distributed systems operation. In this chapter, we discuss this lower-level aspect of support for agent-based systems that deals with the technologies that enable distributed systems operation in general. There is a wealth of technologies available for developing distributed systems and they can also significantly aid in facilitating the development of agent-based applications. By exploiting these supporting technologies, developers can benefit from the efforts of a much larger community, and from the experience that community has had in implementing systems in real-world industrial settings.

This chapter reviews some of the best known and widely used distributed systems technologies, and discusses their suitability for agent-based systems. The aim is not to provide a detailed account of all the relevant technologies, but instead to describe the range of possibilities and provide some indications as to the kinds of agent-based systems that can be enabled by the different technologies. The reader is warned that the pace of technological development in this field is very fast, and as a result the best way to get an up-to-date account of the current state of the art is by accessing the Web resources referenced in the chapter.

The chapter begins with a consideration of the multitier enterprise application model, perhaps the most widely used model for describing enterprise applications. The model suggests some correlations with agent-based systems, and the technological solutions offered by the Java 2 Enterprise Editions and Microsoft .NET are investigated in this context. Then, Jini and JXTA are discussed as

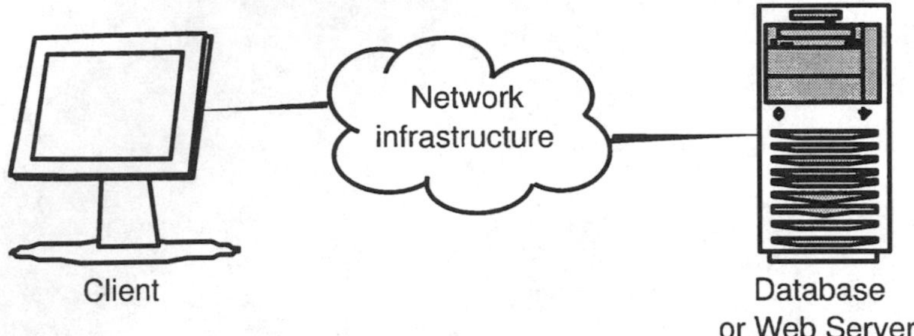

Figure 6.1 Two-tier application model.

representatives of two different models for enabling dynamic distributed systems, providing, respectively, a heavyweight and lightweight approach. Their relative benefits and disadvantages are outlined, and examples of their use in an agent-based systems context are suggested. Finally, the Web services model is examined in relation to its use in, for, and with agent-based systems. Some of this material is also covered in Chapter 5, which deals with standards, but a different perspective is taken here.

6.2 MULTITIER APPLICATION MODEL

The ways in which organizations structure their information systems have gone through numerous changes over the past decades, reflecting their changing needs and attempts to exploit new possibilities afforded by technological advances. One of the most significant changes has been the evolution from a single-tier enterprise model to the multitier (or n-tier) model. This section examines this evolution and relates it to agent systems development.

When automation through computer networks was first introduced in organizations, the typical situation was one in which a mainframe computer handled all the processing and retrieval of information from storage (such as tape drives) while users accessed data and applications through dumb terminals. This single-tier model was superseded in the 1980s, when it became possible to have personal computers that were able to both store and process some of the information locally. As a result, a two-tier model was introduced, in which the server was responsible for moving data to the client that could then perform the required processing and presentation operations. In this case, illustrated in Figure 6.1, a client directly accesses information on the server, and the logic of how the information is presented and dealt with is located on the client. The two-tier model was, however, limited when faced with the increase in prominence of networks at every level of organizations and the need to provide a much more varied range of services than originally envisaged. It quickly became evident that it would be too difficult to manage the large number of clients and to ensure that each client had installed locally the right kind of functionality for enabling the services that organizations wanted and needed to offer.

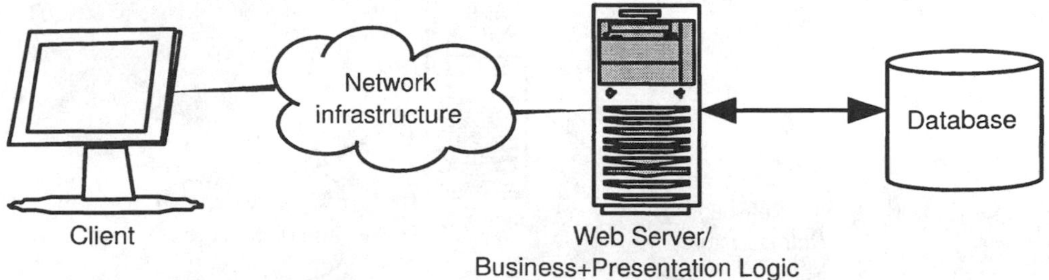

Figure 6.2 Three-tier application model.

A more efficient approach is to divide the process into its constituent components and deal with each separately. This is what the three-tier application model begins to do by separating the long-term storage and management of information from the logic by which it is accessed and presented, and the client application through which the services are accessed. The three-tier model places the logic for accessing data on a middle tier between user and data, as illustrated in Figure 6.2. This achieves two goals. First, it makes the management of access to information and the logic associated with that access easier, since it can be located on dedicated servers and directly accessed by administrators and developers. Second, it reduces the amount of administration end-user machines require, since their task is reduced to information presentation through generic browsers. As a result, different ways of presenting, and rules for accessing, information can be installed on the middle tier, without affecting the long-term storage in a database or requiring that clients install new software components each time a new service is required.

Despite the inherent benefits of the three-tier model over the two-tier model, there are still some problems to deal with. The three-tier model simply removes part of the functionality from the client and places it on servers. This has two disadvantages. First, clients (which are now powerful personal computers) are not exploited to their full potential. Second, placing most demands back on servers makes them difficult to manage and costly to maintain.

A more general solution to the problem that also enables other kinds of services is the multitier solution. In this case, functionality is spread out into different layers in a more flexible manner. A possible multitier scenario is shown in Figure 6.3. Depending on the kinds of tasks it must perform, the client can either access a Web server through a generic Web browser or through a dedicated Web application. The Web server deals with the presentation and business logic relating to Web-based interfaces, while the messaging server can allow communication with other users and take advantage of a dedicated application server to enable collaboration on common tasks between users. The multitier model enables system designers to have flexible configurations of components in a networked environment, with the clients being able to selectively choose which components to use to achieve their tasks.

From an agent perspective, the introduction of a multitier application model and its adoption in industry have been significant. This is because a lot of the infrastructure for enabling multitier applications, such as the management of transactions, dealing with different clients, and responding

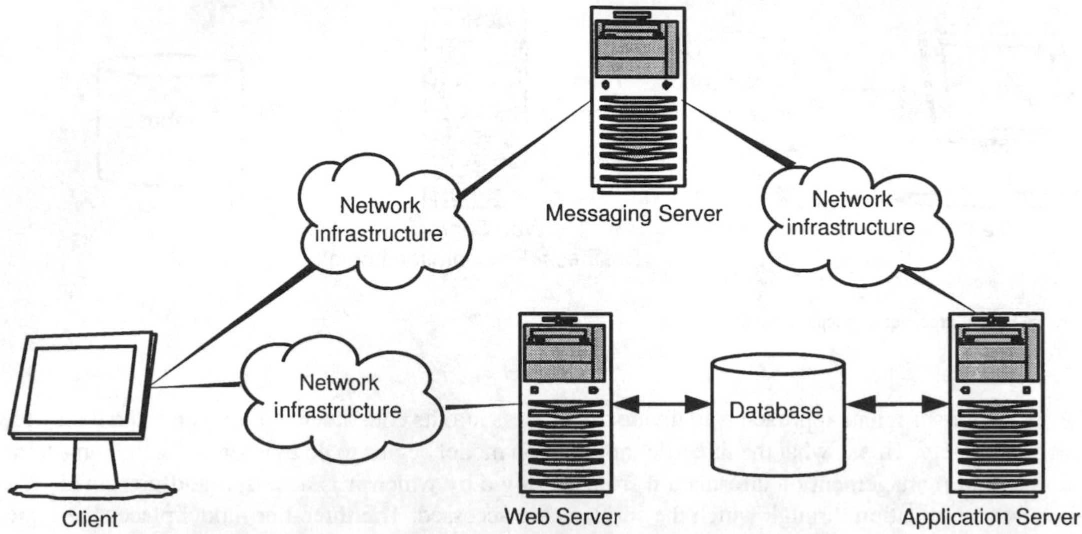

Figure 6.3 Multitier application model.

to changing demands, are issues that agent-based applications also need to tackle. Furthermore, from a conceptual point of view, the move of information technology infrastructure to a multitier model is, in many ways, a step closer to an agent perspective. The need for decentralization of functionality and a more dynamic allocation of tasks according to needs are hallmarks of the agent approach, while the different functionalities provided by different types of agents are in some ways similar to the different tiers in a multitier model, as illustrated in Figure 6.4. As suggested by some of the toolkits in Chapter 3, the general functionalities of agents can almost directly map to the variety of functionalities introduced by the multitier model. At the client there are interface agents that interact with the user and manage the user's tasks. Middle agents match task requirements to task agents and information agents. Task agents are able to work together to solve problems and enable collaboration between users, while information agents specialize in extracting information from databases and other information resources. Furthermore, the use of agents does not exclude the use of application servers or Web servers. Agent technologies can work alongside the more established enterprise technologies, offering a more dynamic level of decentralization and introducing new techniques for problem-solving such as negotiation.

Through industry uptake of the multitier model, agent-based systems can also benefit from well-developed and tested industry-grade technologies. However, not all technologies developed with the multitier application model in mind are ideal for agent application. Some of the relative benefits and disadvantages are discussed next.

The next sections examine two of the most popular sets of technologies, the Java 2 Enterprise Edition and the .NET Framework, for developing multitier applications, and discuss their relevance

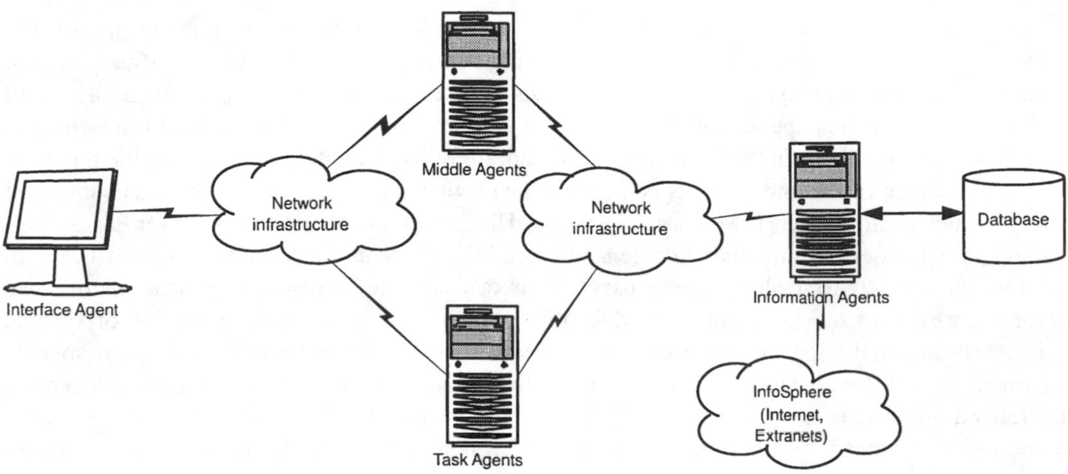

Figure 6.4 From multitier to agent tiers.

to agent-based systems. Note that that both of these technologies also support Web services but this is considered separately in Section 6.5 on Web services.

6.2.1 Java 2 Enterprise Edition

The Java 2 Enterprise Edition (J2EE)[1] is built on top of the Java programming language and development toolkit. Java is an interpreted language, which executes within a Java run-time engine that provides the specific interfaces to the underlying operating platform. In addition, the Java development toolkit provides a rich library of functionalities, ranging from basic input/output methods to extensive support for network protocols and parsing of XML documents.

The J2EE can be thought of in two, complementary, ways. On one hand, it defines a standard for a distributed applications platform based on the multitier application model. On the other hand, it can be thought of as a rich toolkit of technologies that can be combined in a variety of ways to develop distributed applications. The former provides a consistent vision of how the variety of technologies that come under the J2EE heading can be combined to produce an application. The latter is a consequence of the modular nature of J2EE, which is based on the exploitation of various technologies that can work independently of each other and have, therefore, been used in a variety of settings that do not follow the standardized application model. In this section, the standardized application model is introduced first before moving on to discuss how the various technologies in J2EE can provide useful pieces of functionality for an agent-based application.

The J2EE standard defines a J2EE platform as a set of APIs and policies for hosting J2EE applications, and a set of *compatibility tests* that can verify that an implementation of these APIs and policies is consistent with the platform. The central artifacts are Enterprise Java Beans, which

1 http://java.sun.com/j2ee

are components running within a dedicated container, and represent the various services provided to end users. EJBs follow a well-defined component model that specifies the exact interface with the container so as to ensure high portability. The container takes care of the management and access to the EJB services so that application developers can focus on developing business and presentation logic that is contained within the EJBs. An EJB could, for example, define the logic for the purchase of a book from an on-line store. Users can access the services through a variety of means, the most usual of which is through an HTML-based interface. This is facilitated by the Java Server Pages (JSP) technology, which enables the dynamic generation of Web content and can interface with EJBs. In addition, the *servlets* technology allows users to directly activate server-side applications that can perform a variety of tasks, including the dynamic creation of content, or the execution of specific logic. According to the application needs, a developer can choose whether to employ the more specific functionality of JSP, which is directly concerned with presentation, or servlets, which provide a more generalized server-side functionality. In any case, in the generalized J2EE application model, these technologies are meant to interface with EJBs, which define the exact business logic that allows access to the actual databases. However, servlets are also able to interface with databases, since they are nothing more than applications executed on the server, activated by the user. This simply means that a developer could bypass EJBs altogether and interface with databases and other systems through servlets, something that may be more appropriate in undemanding operating environments.

In addition to these technologies, there is wide support for various means of accessing information systems and coordinating between applications.

- Through the Java Database Connectivity (JDBC) API, EJBs, or servlets can perform SQL queries on a variety of databases, if provided with the appropriate JDBC *driver* (a specific implementation of the JDBC API).
- The Java naming and directory interface (JNDI) allows similar access to naming and directory services.
- The Java message service (JMS) allows sending and receiving of messages through a variety of enterprise message systems, such as IBM MQ Series[2] and TIBCO Rendezvous.[3]
- JavaMail defines an API for e-mail services.
- The Java transaction API defines support for handling transactions between components.
- JavaIDL is an API for the Interface Definition Language that allows access to CORBA services.

The links between J2EE technologies and agent-based applications can more easily be seen if J2EE is viewed as a technological toolkit rather than an application model. Technologies such as JDBC, JMS, and Java Transactions can be used directly to satisfy a range of middleware support needs (or low-level services as described in the toolkits chapter). There are several examples of use, such

2 http://www.ibm.com/software/integration/mqfamily
3 http://www.tibco.com/solutions/products/active_enterprise/rv

as the JACK toolkit that supports the use of JDBC APIs for accessing databases, and the Tryllian[4] component-based agent development toolkit that uses JNDI.

On the surface, the J2EE application model has several similarities to generic models for agent-based systems. The containers for EJBs and servlets could be considered as similar to agent platforms, which offer the basic management and resource access functionality. EJBs and servlets can be thought of as the equivalent of agents running within the containers, and using the various supporting technologies for communication and discovery. However, a direct implementation of agents as EJBs is not straightforward because the component model for EJBs is too limiting when used for agent applications. EJBs and servlets are designed as reactive components that respond to user initiated events and, as a result, the containers have been designed with that in mind. Agents, on the other hand, are also proactive entities which, independently of any user action, could decide to perform an operation. Furthermore, EJBs cannot start their own threads of execution, they cannot each dynamically load classes, and they share the same namespace with all the other EJBs in the container.

Nevertheless, as mentioned earlier, it is useful to develop technologies that allow agents systems and J2EE to operate alongside each other. One example already mentioned in Chapter 3 is the *living markets* toolkit, which provides EJB connectors for enabling agents to make use of, and interact with, EJBs. Alternative approaches have been developed and used by Whitestein Technologies[5], who have investigated both solutions with agent platforms that work alongside EJB containers, and the integration of agents into EJB containers by adding the missing functionality. In the first case, developers are provided with the benefits of a custom-made agent platform but lose in terms of solution portability and vendor choice. In the second case, developers retain use of the more familiar EJB platforms for developing agents and deal with the limitations through the added functionality provided by the Whitestein solution.

6.2.2 Windows Server System and the .NET Framework

In 2001, Microsoft introduced the first beta version of the .NET Framework, which represents a significant evolution of the programming model for the Windows OS. A new language has been introduced, C# (C sharp), which is an object-based language that is more similar to Java than C++. Furthermore, the various technologies available for developing applications in Windows have been restructured, and some rewritten, so that they all became accessible through a carefully arranged library structure. Finally, all the compilers that accompanied the Microsoft languages now compile to a common underlying byte-code language called the Intermediate Language, which is interpreted by a Common Language Run Time. The Windows Server System (WSS) is the latest name given to the family of server technologies that enable enterprise systems development using the .NET Framework. In this section, we discuss the set of technologies that enable such development, based on the multitier model described above.

The central infrastructural components of the Windows Server Systems are the Internet Information Services, which is a set of services that form the actual server engine. Presentation is handled

4 http://www.tryllian.com
5 http://www.whitestein.com

by ASP.NET (Application Server Pages), which enables the dynamic creation of Web pages. It encompasses the kinds of functionality that Java Server Pages and servlets allow with specific functions for presenting pages as well as accessing capabilities or performing server-side processing. The handling of identities and relationships between network components, in terms of directory services, is provided by the active directory service. Thus the .NET Framework provides a component-based model for encoding business logic and applications and can use the component object model (COM+) services, for instance management, transactions, activity-based synchronization, granular role-based security, disconnected asynchronous queued components, and loosely coupled events.

The technologies provided by the Windows Server System and the .NET Framework could provide for most of the infrastructural needs of an agent-based application. However, there are practically no well-known examples of agent-based applications developed using these technologies. One reason for this may be that .NET is a relatively new technology. More significant, however, may be the fact that .NET technologies are essentially single-platform technologies and, since agent development has traditionally taken place in research labs or within the context of integrating different platforms and legacy software through an agent-based system, such single-platform solutions are not ideal. With the advent of Web services, which abstract beyond such issues, Microsoft technologies can be expected to be used more and more to also develop agent applications.

6.3 JXTA

The JXTA project[6], originating from, and managed by, Sun Microsystems, is an open-source, community-based project that develops the specifications and a reference implementation of a set of protocols for enabling peer-to-peer computing. Its name is derived from the word "juxtapose," meaning placed side by side.

The peer-to-peer model is the logical alternative to a client-server model. Nodes in the network are considered peers because each can initiate communication and receive and provide services. Although practical applications of this model have existed for a long time (for example, the first incarnations of the Internet were essentially peer-to-peer systems), it has only caught on in the mainstream since 1999. That was the year that the Napster file-sharing program was released, which illustrated in a very powerful way how the combination of improved network capabilities and powerful personal computers could enable users to exchange information, in Napster's case predominantly music, on unprecedented scales. Other systems, such as SETI@home[7], which employs a peer-to-peer network to analyze radio signals reaching Earth in the search for extraterrestrial intelligence, illustrate how large-scale process-intensive applications can take advantage of redundant cycles on workstations accessible via the Internet.

The JXTA project is an attempt to enable peer-to-peer computing through a set of protocols that are platform and application neutral, so that developers can use them in a variety of settings. As a result, the protocols for communication between peers are based on XML messages and the reference implementation is in Java. In addition, there is an implementation in C for both the Windows and

6 http://www.jxta.org
7 http://setiathome.ssl.berkeley.edu

Linux operating systems, while work towards a .NET implementation is under way. Furthermore, since JXTA has been engineered as a lightweight protocol, there is also a version that is able to operate on mobile devices through the Java 2 Mobile Edition[8] (J2ME) technologies.

The JXTA model defines peers as any entity that can communicate using the six basic protocols of JXTA [1]. These protocols work together to allow peers to discover each other, communicate, organize into the necessary structures and monitor activity. A peer is identified by a JXTA ID. This is a virtual address given to a peer in order to abstract beyond the underlying network topology, and is resolved to a physical IP address as late as possible in the communication process, through *late binding*. The aim is to enable maximum flexibility for peers to move within the network topology, something that is crucial for peer-to-peer and mobile networks. There is no need for centralized mechanisms for resolving addresses such as a domain name server, making the network much more flexible and dynamic. When a query is sent to a peer it is relayed from one peer to another, each having partial knowledge about the physical addresses of peers, until a route is established from the querying peer to the responding peer. At this point, a *virtual* route between peers using their JXTA IDs can be established to send messages between the two peers.

Peers send messages through *pipes*, which are an abstraction over the actual network layer. Pipes are unidirectional, so there are in and out pipes, and *endpoints* can be bound to multiple peers. Pipes are identified by their endpoints, which are, once more, not the physical IP addresses but the IDs of the peers. As a result a peer can refer to a pipe between one peer and another (or a group) and the underlying JXTA infrastructure takes care of establishing the appropriate route to the physical location of that peer. Endpoints can also be used to differentiate between the communication protocols used to reach the peer. One endpoint may indicate HTTP communication while another may indicate that the TCP protocol should be used. Finally, peers can be grouped in order to form logical organizations of peers. JXTA takes a very liberal approach to peer groups and does not enforce rigid structures for them. Peers can belong to any number of peer groups and groups can have any number of peers within them.

The kind of behavior described above is supported by the JXTA protocols. As mentioned earlier, in order for a peer to participate in a JXTA network, it must be able to understand these protocols. A brief description of each follows:

- The *Peer Resolver Protocol* is a generic query/response protocol that is used by any other protocol or service requiring this basic functionality. A query is addressed to a specified *query handler*. Any peer registered as the specified query handler can generate a response, so the query handler defines a group of peers rather than any individual peer.
- The *Peer Discovery Protocol* defines how peers advertise their own capabilities and discover others. Advertisements are XML documents, which can be used to describe single peers or a group of peers and the available services. The description of services is application-specific, since the protocol only defines how concepts that are native to JXTA are described.
- The *Peer Information Protocol* specifies how peers can obtain information about other peers, relating to attributes such as uptime, traffic, and capabilities.

8 http://java.sun.com/j2me

- The *Endpoint Routing Protocol* defines how a peer finds a route to other peers if no direct link exists. It defines a set of query/response messages that can be processed by a peer acting as a router to aid in finding a route to the destination.
- The *Rendezvous Protocol* enables the propagation of messages through JXTA peers by allowing them to act as Rendezvous peers, which can then propagate messages they receive to subscribers.
- The *Pipe Binding Protocol* defines how a pipe's input and output ends bind to a peer's endpoint.

Along with these protocols JXTA provides a vision of how peer-to-peer environments should be organized from a technological point of view. This is based on a three-layer model, in which the bottom layer, the JXTA core, is made up of the concepts and protocols described above. Over this enabling layer JXTA services operate to provide generic functionality such as file searching and indexing. Finally, at the top are the JXTA applications that make use of the various services to provide well-defined end-user functionality.

Peer-to-peer technologies such as JXTA are well suited to agent-based applications since the peer-to-peer model is, essentially, a subset of the agent-based application model. JXTA, with its *light* communication model based on XML, is particularly appealing for situations in which peers may operate from significantly heterogeneous environments (such as applications including mobile devices) and where it is necessary to ensure that the devices will have the required processing power and network capability to receive the messages. Nevertheless, JXTA does not provide every aspect of the required infrastructure for an agent-based system. Although there are tools for creating peer groups and discovering peer capabilities, some agent applications will require more robust mechanisms using service registries or middle agents. Such services can, of course, be built on top of the JXTA core layer.

An example of incorporating JXTA middleware with other technologies is the Tryllian framework, which uses the functionality of JXTA for agent communication while also employing J2EE technologies for more sophisticated services such as database access and directory services.

6.4 JINI

As outlined in Chapter 5, Jini is a set of network protocols and APIs that define a middleware infrastructure developed with the aim of enabling the dynamic discovery and use of services over distributed computing networks. Services, in this context, are anything that a user could consider useful, ranging from access to storage and printing services, to the use of processor cycles for scientific computation. Jini makes use of the Java programming language and Java RMI. As such, it takes full advantage of an object-oriented approach to middleware for dynamic networks, using RMI to enable the movement of objects from one Java virtual machine to another. It was introduced in 1999 and was developed by Sun Microsystems, but is now administered as a community-based project under the Sun Community Source License.[9]

9 http://www.jini.org

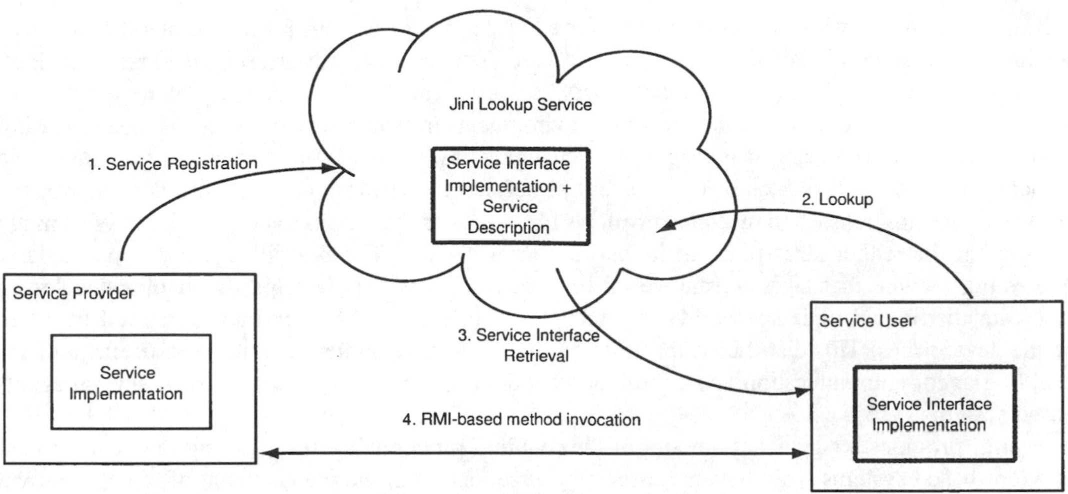

Figure 6.5 Jini service discovery.

Jini is based around three protocols that enable services to discover, register, and join in federations of Jini services [2]. Since Jini is designed as a decentralized, network-centric middleware it is only through the *federation* of services, dispersed across the network, that a Jini system takes form. However, this form of decentralization and loose coupling of services, which deals with the location of services of a computer network, should not be confused with loose coupling at the semantic level. Jini services can only access each other through precisely defined Java interfaces (a set of method signatures). We discuss this issue further on.

A Jini federation begins with the use of the discovery protocol to discover other services. Through the discovery protocol, a Jini service announces its presence in a network by multicasting a message with some basic information about how the service can be contacted. A specialized Jini service, called a *lookup* service, listens for such announcements. Note that, in principle, any Jini service can also act as a lookup service, but for obvious reasons relating to more efficient administration and management of federations of services it is more logical to allow only lookup services to perform this service. The lookup service uses the information contained within the message to contact the service and retrieve from it a description of the service and an implementation of the interface that allows access to that service. This process is defined by the *join* protocol. Now, other services can use the lookup protocol to interrogate lookup services about the availability of required services. This interrogation can be done by specifying either the Java object type of the service interface that has been uploaded to the lookup service, the service attributes, or both. Once the required service has been discovered, the interface implementation is downloaded to the client that can then access the service using Java RMI. The process in illustrated in Figure 6.5.

In addition to these basic enabling protocols, Jini provides a range of mechanisms for the administration and more effective operation of Jini federations. The most important is the Jini leasing mechanism, which provides means for services to register and make use of other services for limited amounts of time defined through a lease. This is especially useful for lookup services. Every service that registers with a lookup service must renew its lease or the lookup service will remove the registration. In dynamic network environments in which services may disappear, leasing provides an effective means of managing this changing environment. Jini distributed events provide a means for events that take place at one Jini service to be propagated to listeners across the network. The Jini transaction mechanism allows for groups of operations to be considered as a unique transaction that either takes place in its entirety or is not considered at all. Finally, a particularly interesting service that takes advantage of Jini is JavaSpaces [3]. JavaSpaces enables developers to create distributed tuple spaces [4] in which Java objects can be stored and retrieved by users of the JavaSpaces. This distributed information exchange environment can prove a useful tool for enabling agent communication and coordination and has been used in the context of several agent-based systems [5, 6].

Jini provides a significant amount of the required functionality for enabling the development of agent-based systems. The dynamic discovery of services and the management of registration via the lookup services and leasing mechanisms represent key infrastructural components for agent-based applications in heterogeneous dynamic environments. However, Jini is severely limited in an agent application context by the use of RMI and the dependence on Java interfaces. Although such technology makes sense in a situation in which the aim is to administer well-known services such as storage and printers in a closed environment with well-defined and unchanging interfaces, often the same cannot work effectively in open agent applications. In such open environments in which the available services cannot be known beforehand, the options are either to define a very basic interface that is so open it could represent any service or use the reflection mechanisms provided with the Java language for examining the method signatures that are available. In both cases, the result is using an inefficient mechanism for dealing with a situation that is fundamentally ill-suited to agent systems. A much better solution could be to use some of the concepts of Jini within the context of a better suited infrastructure such as JXTA.

Nevertheless, Jini has been used extensively within mainly academic settings for agent-based systems (for example, [7–9]). As described in Chapter 5, the most notable example is the CoABS project, which uses Jini to provide a common infrastructure to enable agent applications that have been developed using a number of different agent toolkits to work together. CoABS uses Jini as the underlying enabling infrastructure and defines a generic interface that should wrap around agents derived through a variety of agent toolkits. Agents discover each other using the Jini services and communicate through this wrapper interface. One of the benefits of this approach is that alternative implementations of the wrapper interface can be provided to deal with the peculiarities of each agent system. However, as a general solution to the issue of interoperation between heterogeneous agent systems, it is unclear whether this is a better approach towards establishing a common standard for communication languages and interoperation at the semantic level (such as applying the FIPA approach). Furthermore, the whole system is forced to use the heavyweight RMI technology for communication. Although some basic experiments on scalability [10] have shown that the system is able to support several hundreds of agents relatively well, they did not consider agents operating in realistic, complex settings.

Jini represents a type of middleware that can provide solutions for a wide range of problems when dealing with the administration of services in dynamic environments. There are several similar efforts (for example, Salutation[10]), and all have their place in providing enabling infrastructure. With regard to agent applications, Jini is certainly useful but perhaps not ideal. Clearly, though, some of the technologies contained within it, such as leasing and dynamic discovery, provide useful lessons of how certain key issues should be addressed.

6.5 WEB SERVICES

The term "Web services" has been used in a variety of contexts, and often out of context, to describe any sort of service that is accessible over the Internet. As a result, there is considerable confusion about what exactly a Web service is. It is in turn referred to as a standard, a way of developing distributed applications, or a specific set of technologies. The reason for this apparent confusion is that there is considerable interest in Web services and the term has been heavily marketed by all the major software companies. For the purposes of this chapter, Web services are considered to be the set of technological standards that are developed by the W3C, with the aim of enabling the publication, location, and invocation of services over a network by defining a programmatic interface for that service, and providing mechanisms for its description and discovery. The W3C Web Services Architecture Working Group provides the following definition for a single Web service:

> A web service is a software system identified by a URI (Uniform Resource Identifier), whose public interfaces and bindings are defined and described using XML. Its definition can be discovered by other software systems. These systems may then interact with the Web service in a manner prescribed by its definition, using XML based messages conveyed by internet protocols.[11]

Web services technologies have emerged out of a realization that alternative approaches, such as CORBA or Java RMI, were too tightly coupled to enable truly open distributed systems. What is really required is a set of technologies that provide a platform and programming language independent solution. In order to achieve this, Web services technologies need to deal with the exchange of messages, the description of Web services, and their publication and discovery. As such, there are three central roles that perform the respective *behavior* within the Web services architecture. The *discovery agency* holds descriptions of available services and makes it possible to search these descriptions. A *service provider* needs to make available to the discovery agency an appropriate description of its service so that *service requestors* can locate it, verify whether it is an appropriate service, and use it through the programmatic interface provided along with the service description.

The W3C definition of the Web services architecture does not bind any specific technological solutions to the issues of message exchange, service description, and the discovery agencies. This is in recognition of the fact that there are a number of technologies that could deal with these issues.

10 http://www.salutation.org
11 http://www.w3.org/TR/ws-arch

However, in practical terms, there is a well-defined set of technologies, which represent technological standards in their own right, and are used by the majority of Web services development toolkits for these tasks. In the following sections we briefly describe these technologies.

6.5.1 Message Exchange

Message exchange is achieved using the Simple Object Access Protocol[12] (SOAP), which defines a lightweight message exchange mechanism and the encoding of messages in XML. A SOAP message consists of a message envelope, which contains a header and a body. The header is used to define the encoding style for the message, indicate who is the ultimate recipient, and whether there are intermediate recipients of the message, specifying which parts of the message must be understood by a recipient.

The encoding style is usually defined by providing a URI that refers to the specification for the structure of the body. For example, the encoding style defined by the SOAP standard itself is referred to as:

```
SOAP-ENV:encodingStyle="http://schemas.xmlsoap.org/soap/encoding/".
```

Other commonly used encoding styles are the Web Distributed Data Exchange (WDDX)[13] and XML Remote Procedure Call (XML-RPC).[14]

A SOAP message can travel through different recipients before reaching its ultimate destination. Each recipient can be instructed to refer to a particular part of the SOAP message body. By enabling the handling of a SOAP message through a variety of intermediate recipients before it arrives at its final destination, the SOAP standard allows for developing flexible communication mechanisms that can reflect the usual flow of information between departments in an organization.

The SOAP body must include the appropriate method calls for interacting with the various recipients and any other relevant information. Along with application-specific information, the SOAP body can also contain fault information that includes a fault code, an explanation of the fault, an indication of where the fault originated, and, possibly, further application-specific details about the fault.

6.5.2 Service Description

Service description uses the Web Service Description Language[15] (WSDL), a W3C working draft, which provides an XML grammar for defining network services and specific bindings to a transport protocol, such as HTTP, and an encoding, such as SOAP.

In WSDL, services are described as sets of endpoints that exchange messages. For each service a WSDL definition must indicate how to access the service, the types of information the service can accept, the methods the service can perform, and the types of information that will be returned. To

12 http://www.w3.org/TR/SOAP
13 http://www.openwddx.org
14 http://www.xmlrpc.com/spec/
15 http://www.w3.org/TR/wsdl

this end, WSDL defines a set of constructs that allow such descriptions to be built. Some of the more relevant elements are described here, so as to provide an understanding of the kinds of concepts used:

`<types>` The `types` element allows different data types to be defined. The developer can build on basic types already defined such as integers, strings, floats, and booleans to develop arbitrarily complex application-specific type definitions. The available building blocks for types come from another W3C standard, the XML Schema specification.[16]

`<message>` The `message` element is used to group data elements, based on the type definitions, and binds them to a name in expectation of network transmission. The name of the message is used to reference the data within an operation.

`<portType>` *and* `<operation>` Messages can then be grouped, under the `operation` element, where input and output messages are defined, as well as possible fault messages. Groups of operations are placed under the `portType` element which, by acting as a container of different operation definitions, can be thought of as an interface.

`<binding>` The `binding` element is used to bind the abstract definitions above to a specific messaging protocol, such as SOAP.

`<service>` The `service` element is used to define the network process through which the service can be reached, usually a URI defining a network address and a port number.

6.5.3 Service Discovery

The discovery of services can be achieved through a variety of means, the most well known of which is via Universal Description, Discovery and Integration[17] (UDDI) of Web services. UDDI is a technological standard supported by the UDDI Specification Technical Committee, which operates under the auspices of the Organization for the Advancement of Structured Information Standards[18] (OASIS), an industry-driven consortium that is dedicated to the development of e-business-related standards.

The main concepts behind the UDDI architecture are those of a *businessEntity* that is used to represent businesses or providers within a UDDI registry, *businessServices* that act as logical groupings of Web services, a *bindingTemplate* that represents individual services, and *tModels* that allow the representations of unique technical models for the purposes of reuse and standardization within a software framework. Examples of possible tModels are WSDL or XML Schema.

At the time of writing, UDDI Version 3 was the latest installment of UDDI. It has introduced a variety of improvements that make registration and querying about services more flexible. Included in the features available is the identification of registered entities through a unique key, even across multiple registries. Registries can also be better structured into particular configurations to enable a

16 http://www.w3.org/XML/Schema
17 http://www.uddi.org
18 http://www.oasis-open.org

better distribution of the data, and replication between registries is possible. Complex queries can be performed, with queries that previously required multiple steps now supported through single queries.

Applications can interact with a UDDI registry through a number of standardized APIs, according to the task at hand. The most significant API sets are listed here:

- The *Inquiry* API defines methods for locating and identifying entities in a registry.
- The *Publication* API defines methods for publishing and updating information.
- The *Security Policy* API defines methods for handling authentication.
- The *Custody and Ownership Transfer* API is used for determining who is the owner of data and which registry is responsible, or has custody, of the data as well as the transfer or ownership and custody.
- The *Subscription* API allows for clients to register their interest in a particular subject, and as a result, receive notification of changes that may concern the *Value Set* API that supports the validation.

Other registry technologies include the ebXML Registry[19] and UN/CEFACT.[20] Applications that need to make use of Web services may eventually be able to access a variety of registries, something that the Java Web services toolkit acknowledges by providing the Java API for XML registries, which is an API for accessing a variety of XML registries, including those mentioned so far.

6.5.4 Service Orchestration

The technological vision for Web services, beyond the fact that they will provide services over the Internet to any operating platform and through a variety of programming languages, is that clients will be able to employ a number of Web services together in order to gain functionality that cannot be achieved through a single Web service. This use of multiple Web services coordinated to achieve a single goal has been called *Web services orchestration* and is even supported by standards that define how Web services can be used together. The Business Process Execution Language for Web Services (BPEL4WS)[21] is one such effort developed by IBM, BEA Systems, Microsoft, Siebel Systems, and SAP AG. It is a language that enables the specification of business processes and interaction protocols and, as such, complements the functionality provided by UDDI and WSDL by providing the missing piece of how to define the semantics through which a number of Web services can be orchestrated to support a complete business process.

19 http://www.ebxml.org

20 http://www.ebtwg.org

21 http://www-106.ibm.com/developerworks/webservices/library/ws-bpel

6.5.5 Use of Web Services in Agent Systems

Web services technologies represent the realization by industry of the need for technological standards for distributed computing that will enable a more dynamic networked environment in which service discovery and use are achieved through a model that recalls the *just-in-time* manufacturing model. In other words, service provision should closely reflect changing demands and needs. However, Web services lack the autonomy that agent technologies can offer, since Web services are essentially user driven. *Coupled* with agent technologies, Web services technologies can provide effective solutions to a number of problems, such as the provision of powerful coordination mechanisms that can indicate how diverse Web services can be harnessed to achieve the required application goals. Web services are a relatively new technology so there are as yet few examples of their application in an agent technology setting.

The Queensland University Faculty of Information Technology has a research project under way for developing Web services using the .NET Framework to *integrate* mobile agent computation with Web services communication, both between agents, and between agents and static Web services.[22]

Some of the most exciting work, however, comes from the unification of Web services with the Semantic Web, and standardization efforts that build on that. For example, researchers at the Carnegie Mellon Intelligent Agents Laboratory have developed discovery technologies that are integrated with their RETSINA toolkit for Web services using DAML-Services[23] (DARPA Agent Markup language[24]). (The Semantic Web, DAML, and DAML-S are discussed in more detail in Chapter 5.) They have developed a matchmaker agent that is itself a Web service to facilitate the discovery of other agents [11, 12], using similarity matching algorithms to match service requests to service providers. This work has also been complemented by the introduction of some basic security semantics, to allow agents to search for those services that support an appropriate level of security [13]. The Intelligence, Agents, Multimedia research group of the University of Southampton has also combined Web services technologies and agents within the context of a Grid project[25] to investigate the synergies between these technologies [14–16].

Although Web services are still a relatively new technology the initial indications are that they can provide appropriate solutions to a number of problems in distributed computing; technologies such as SOAP and WSDL are sufficiently flexible to allow their application in a variety of settings. Particularly exciting, however, is that the next generation of agent-based systems can employ these technologies and enhance them by providing solutions to the various problems of discovery and coordination that have been addressed within the context of agent-based systems for a number of years. In this way, they will add a level of context-awareness, proactivity, and semantic reasoning that is not supported by the Web service standards.

22 http://www.citi.qut.edu.au/research/plas/projects/web_services.jsp
23 http://www.damlsmm.ri.cmu.edu/index.html
24 http://www.daml.org
25 http://www.mygrid.info

6.6 CONCLUSIONS

During the 1990s, agent research evolved in relative isolation from developments in mainstream distributed computing. To a large extent, this was because distributed computing technologies at that point did not satisfy the requirements of agent researchers. The advent of Java in 1995, and subsequent developments, presented the first viable mainstream technology that agent researchers could adopt directly when building systems. Now, the overwhelming majority of agent technologies are implemented in Java.

Since 1999, however, there has been a marked change in the kinds of software technologies from mainstream distributed computing. Technologies such as Jini provide robust solutions to long-standing problems for agent researchers. More recently, technologies such as JXTA have enabled the kinds of lightweight peer-to-peer systems that in many ways were originally envisaged. This means that agent developers no longer need to address the lower-level infrastructure issues of dynamic, distributed systems, since they can be obtained through mainstream, often open source, technologies. In the most recent developments, Web services have begun to provide the glue that can enable service access across organizational domains, and on a much larger scale than previously envisaged.

The work done so far is now empowering new conceptual developments for computing environments such as computational Grids [17] in which the sharing and coordinated use of computing resources is supported. Furthermore, Web services that are supported by the annotation semantics of languages such as DAML+OIL can enable agents to automatically discover them. Finally, the convergence of the semantic Web and Grid technologies has led to the definition of a *Semantic Grid*, in which Grid services carry semantic annotation so that they can better be used by agents [18]. Accordingly, the new technological challenges relate to dealing with these new scales of interacting services, across organizational domains, and enabling new kinds of services while supporting semantic interoperability. In this respect, new issues of security, trust, and reputation will become paramount.

References

[1] Oaks, S., B. Traversat, and L. Gong, *JXTA in a Nutshell*, Sebastopol, CA: O'Reilly & Associates, 2002.

[2] Arnold, K., et al., *The Jini Specification*, Reading, MA: Addison-Wesley, 1999.

[3] Freeman, E., S. Hupfer, and K. Arnold, *JavaSpaces Principles, Patterns, and Practice*, Reading, MA: Addison-Wesley, 1999.

[4] Ahuja, S., N. Carriero, and D. Gelernter, "Linda and Friends," *IEEE Computer*, Vol. 19, No. 6, 1986, pp. 26–34.

[5] Checn, G., et al., "Coordinating Multi-Agents Using JavaSpaces," *Ninth International Conference on Parallel and Distributed Systems*, New York: IEEE Press, 2002, pp. 63–74.

[6] Cabri, G., L. Leonardi, and F. Zambonelli, "MARS: A Programmable Coordination Architecture for Mobile Agents," *IEEE Internet Computing*, Vol. 4, No. 4, 2000.

[7] Ashri, R., and M. Luck, "Paradigma: Agent Implementation Through Jini," *Eleventh International Workshop on Databases and Expert System Applications,* A. M. Tjoa, R. Wagner, and A. Al-Zobaidie, (eds.), New York: IEEE Computer Society, 2000, pp. 453–457.

[8] Furmento, N., et al., "A Component Framework for HPC Applications," *Euro-Par 2001 Parallel Processing,* R. Sakellariou, et al., (eds.), Volume 2150 of *LNCS*, New York: Springer, 2001, pp. 540–548.

[9] Juhasz, Z., A. Andics, and S. Pota, "JM: A Jini Framework for Global Computing," *Second International Workshop on Global and Peer-to-Peer Computing on Large Scale Distributed Systems at IEEE Symposium on Cluster Computing and the Grid*, 2002.

[10] Kahn, M. L., and C. D. T. Cicalese, "CoABS Grid Scalability Experiments," *Infrastructure for Agents, MAS and Scalable MAS, Workshop in Autonomous Agents 2001,* T. Wagner, and O. F. Rana, (eds.), 2001, pp. 145–152.

[11] Paolucci, M., et al., "Semantic Matchmaking of Web Services Capabilities," *International Semantic Web Conference,* I. Horrocks and J. A. Hendler, (eds.), Volume 2342 of *LNCS*, New York: Springer, 2002, pp. 333–347.

[12] Payne, T. R., R. Singh, and K. P. Sycara, "Importing the Semantic Web in UDDI," *Web Services, E-Business, and the Semantic Web, CAiSE 2002 International Workshop,* C. Bussler et al., (eds.), Volume 2512 of *LNCS*, New York: Springer, 2002, pp. 225–236.

[13] Denker, G., et al., "Security for DAML Web Services: Annotation and Matchmaking," *Proceedings of the Second International Semantic Web Conference (ISWC2003)*, F. Fensel, K. Sycara, and J. Mylopoulos, (eds.), Volume 2870 of *LNCS*, New York: Springer, 2003, pp. 335–350.

[14] Lawley, R., et al., "Automated Negotiation for Grid Notification Services," *Ninth International Europar Conference (EURO-PAR'03)*, H. Kosch, L. Boszormenyi, and H. Hellwagner, (eds.), Volume 2790 of *LNCS*, New York: Springer, 2003.

[15] Moreau, L., "Agents for the Grid: A Comparison for Web Services (Part 1: The Transport Layer)," *Second IEEE/ACM International Symposium on Cluster Computing and the Grid (CCGRID 2002),* H. E. Bal, K. P. Lohr, and A. Reinefeld, (eds.), New York: IEEE Computer Society, 2002.

[16] Dialani, V., et al., "Transparent Fault Tolerance for Web Services Based Architectures," *Eighth International Europar Conference (EURO-PAR'02),* B. Monien and R. Feldmann, (eds.), Volume 2400 of *LNCS*, New York: Springer, 2002, pp. 889–898.

[17] Foster, I., and C. Kesselman, (eds.), *The Grid: Blueprint for a New Computing Infrastructure*, San Francisco, CA: Morgan Kaufmann, 1998.

[18] de Roure, D., N. R. Jennings, and N. Shadbolt, "The Semantic Grid: A Future e-Science Infrastructure," in *Grid Computing: Making the Global Infrastructure a Reality*, F. Berman, G. Fox, and A. J. G. Hey, (eds.), New York: Wiley, 2003, pp. 437–470.

Chapter 7

Agent-Based Development Resources

7.1 INTRODUCTION

As this book should clearly demonstrate, after 15 years of work in the area of agent-based computing, and with the recent rapid advances in supporting technologies, a degree of maturity in this area is becoming manifest. This is true at the level of technologies, systems, toolkits, and methodologies, as the book has shown, but it is also true for supporting resources that are available to assist the community by enabling the dissemination and sharing of results. In this chapter we review the various resources available.

7.2 MAILING LISTS

There are several e-mail lists that provide information relating to current and forthcoming events in the area of agent-based computing, including conferences and workshops, new books, resources, and so on.

7.2.1 DAI-List

The DAI-list is a mailing list concerned with distributed artificial intelligence, now generally focused around the area of agent-based computing, which includes agent-oriented software engineering. The list is moderated, so that all mail to the list is filtered for relevance. Submissions should be sent to `DAI-List@ece.sc.edu` and requests to join the list `DAI-List-request@ece.sc.edu`.

7.2.2 AgentLink E-Mail Update

The AgentLink E-Mail Update is a regular monthly mailing that provides moderated, edited information about the activities of the AgentLink Network of Excellence for Agent-Based Computing, including events, publications, and resources. To join the list, mail `coordinator@agentlink.org`.

7.2.3 Software Agents List

The Software Agents Mailing List is concerned with all aspects of agents and agent technology. Although it is a general list, it is restricted to software agents as opposed to hardware (robots) and human agents. It is currently run by the University of Maryland Baltimore County.

The list is also available in digest form, in which messages are batched and sent periodically. To join the mailing list send a message to `majordomo@cs.umbc.edu` with `subscribe agents` or `subscribe agents-digest` in the body of the message. Confirmation of the choice of lists then follows.

7.3 EVENTS

There are a significant number of events that focus squarely on agent issues. Some of the most relevant for agent-based software development are presented below. However, these are by no means the only ones, and agent research and development does not find exposure in just purely agent-related events. Due to the large number of application areas in which agents can be used, agent-related results can be found at conferences dealing with issues ranging from ubiquitous computing and robotics to human-computer interaction and social simulation.

AAMAS The International Joint Conference on Autonomous Agents and Multi-Agent Systems series was initiated in 2002 as a merger of three highly respected individual conferences, ICMAS (International Conference on Multi-Agent Systems), Agents (International Conference on Autonomous Agents), and ATAL (International Workshop on Agent Theories, Architectures, and Languages). Its aim is to provide a single, high-profile, internationally renowned forum for research in the theory and practice of autonomous agents and multiagent systems.

The first AAMAS conference was held in Bologna, Italy, in 2002, the second in Melbourne, Australia, in 2003, and the third in 2004 will be in New York, United States.

IJCAI The IJCAI (International Joint Conference on Artificial Intelligence) series of conferences is held biennially since 1969. It is the dominant event in artificial intelligence. The amount of agent papers being published in this conference has grown over the years, clear proof of the maturity of agent research in the past 15 years, and it currently features several tracks dedicated to agent research.

WI/IAT The Intelligent Agent Technology conferences started in 1999, focusing on agent-related research stemming from the Asia-Pacific region, while the Web Intelligence conferences started in 2001 focusing on the use of artificial intelligence on and for the Web. The two events are now handled by the Web Intelligence Consortium (`http://wi-consortium.org/`) and are co-sponsored by IEEE. Several WI/IAT-related books have been published or will be published by Springer, World Scientific, CRC Press, and IOS Press.

ECAI The European Conference for Artificial Intelligence has a history dating back to 1974. It is organized by the European Coordinating Committee for Artificial Intelligence and takes place biennially. The number of agent papers in the conference has increased over the years, and a number of the workshops attached to the conference deal with agent subjects as well.

CIA The Cooperative Information Agents (CIA) workshops have been running for the past seven years, with the proceedings published each year by Springer. The focus of the workshops is on the use of agent technologies for intelligent information application for the Internet and the World Wide Web. The papers cover subjects such as mobile agents for information management, intelligent interfaces for information agents, agent-based knowledge discovery, and advanced theories of collaboration.

AOSE The Agent-Oriented Software Engineering workshops have been taking place since 2000, and have quickly gained a reputation as an authoritative workshop in relation to the software engineering issues related to agent software development. Past proceedings have been published by Springer.

MA Mobile Agent events have been running since 1997, starting out as workshops before turning into the current Mobile Agent conference format sponsored, among others, by the IEEE Computer Society. The proceedings of the events have been published by Springer.

ESAW The Engineering Societies in the Agents World workshop series has been running annually since 2000. The focus is on the practical engineering issues that arise when dealing with agent systems development in open, heterogeneous environments. Proceedings have been published by Springer.

Coordination The International Conference on Coordination Models and Languages has been running annually since 1999. It has become an active forum for the presentation of work concerned with both theoretical and application-specific issues on coordination models and component-based software. The conference proceedings are published by Springer.

UKMAS The UKMAS (UK Multi-Agent Systems) workshops are organized by the United Kingdom special interest group on Multi-Agent Systems and have been running since 1996. The aim is to bring together people for academia and industry (mainly from around the United Kingdom) to discuss relevant issues and present new work. A collection of the best papers from the past five years has been published by Springer:

d'Inverno, M., et al., (eds.), *Foundations and Applications of Multi-Agent Systems*, Volume 2403 of *LNCS*, New York: Springer, 2002.

EUMAS The European Workshop on Multi-Agent Systems was established in 2003, with the aim of providing a forum in which European researchers can present work and promote activity in the research and development of multiagent systems, both in industry and academia.

ISWC The International Semantic Web Conference was established in 2002 and takes place annually. It is the main forum in which research and development relating to Semantic Web issues is presented. The participation of agent researchers in the conference has been significant from the start, reinforcing the links between the Semantic Web research and agent research and development.

7.4 FURTHER REFERENCES

Throughout this book, numerous references have been provided as pointers to further reading on the specific subject matter of the different chapters and on the general area of agent-oriented development. The book has also sought to start from a position of almost no knowledge of the field at all, and to build only on a general awareness of computing. However, there are several general reviews and introductory texts that may be useful background sources, as follows:

Luck, M., P. McBurney, and C. Preist, *Agent Technology: Enabling Next Generation Computing (A Roadmap for Agent Based Computing)*. Southampton, England: AgentLink, 2003.

Wooldridge, M., and P. Ciancarini, "Agent-Oriented Software Engineering: The State of the Art," *Agent-Oriented Software Engineering*, P. Ciancarini and M. Wooldridge, (eds.), Volume 1957 of *LNCS*, New York: Springer, 2001, pp. 1–28.

Shen, W., and D. H. Norrie, "Agent-Based Systems for Intelligent Manufacturing: A State-of-the-Art Survey," *Knowledge and Information Systems*, Vol. 1, No. 2, 1999, pp. 129–156.

Jennings, N. R., K. Sycara, and M. Wooldridge, "A Roadmap of Agent Research and Development," *Autonomous Agents and Multi-Agent Systems*, Vol. 1, No. 1, 1998, pp. 7–38.

Nwana, H. S., "Software Agents: An Overview," *The Knowledge Engineering Review*, Vol. 11, No. 3, 1996, pp. 205–244.

Wooldridge, M., and N. Jennings, "Intelligent Agents: Theory and Practice," *The Knowledge Engineering Review*, Vol. 10, No. 2, 1995, pp. 115–152.

7.4.1 Texts

The following books provide a good general introduction to the area of agent technology:

Weiss, G., (ed.), *Multiagent Systems: A Modern Approach to Distributed Artificial Intelligence*, Cambridge, MA: MIT Press, 2000.

Wooldridge, M., *An Introduction to MultiAgent Systems*, New York: Wiley, 2002.
Although not an agent book in the same sense, this book is an excellent general artificial intelligence text, covering material relevant to agents, and with an agent perspective.

Russell, S., and P. Norvig, *Artificial Intelligence: A Modern Approach*, 2nd ed., Upper Saddle River, NJ: Prentice Hall, 2002.

In addition to these introductory texts, there are many other books that are directed at more specialized audiences in focusing on particular aspects of agents and multiagent systems. The following books can offer more details of particular aspects as a follow-up to the material covered in this book:

d'Inverno, M., and M. Luck, *Understanding Agent Systems*, New York: Springer, 2001.

Garcia, A., et al., (eds.), *Software Engineering for Large-Scale Multi-Agent Systems: Research Issues and Practical Applications,* New York: Springer, 2002.

Kraus, S., *Strategic Negotiation in Multiagent Environments*, Cambridge, MA: MIT Press, 2001.

Jennings, N., and M. Wooldridge, (eds.), *Agent Technologies: Foundations, Applications and Markets*, New York: Springer, 1998.

Omicini, A., et al., (eds.), *Coordination of Internet Agents: Models, Technologies, and Applications*, New York: Springer, 2001.

Wagner, T., and O. F. Rana, (eds.), *Infrastructure for Agents, Multi-Agent Systems, and Scalable Multi-Agent Systems: International Workshop on Infrastructure for Multi-Agent Systems, Revised Papers*, Volume 1887 of *LNCS*, New York: Springer, 2001.

Wooldridge, M., *Reasoning about Rational Agents*, Cambridge, MA: MIT Press, 2000.

7.4.2 Agent-Based Software Engineering Collections

A particularly good assessment of recent research and development efforts can be drawn from the *Agent-Oriented Software Engineering* series of books, published by Springer. These books are effectively the post-proceedings of the workshop series by the same name, which covers all aspects of agent engineering, development, and methodology.

Ciancarini, P., and M. Wooldridge, (eds.), *Agent-Oriented Software Engineering, First International Workshop, AOSE 2000*, Limerick, Ireland, 2000, Revised Papers, Lecture Notes in Computer Science 1957, New York: Springer, 2000.

Wooldridge, M. J., G. Weiss, and P. Ciancarini, (eds.), *Agent-Oriented Software Engineering II, Second International Workshop, AOSE 2001*, Montreal, Canada, 2001, Revised Papers and Invited Contributions, Lecture Notes in Computer Science 2222, New York: Springer, 2002.

Giunchiglia, F., J. Odell, and G. Weiss, (eds.), *Agent-Oriented Software Engineering III, Third International Workshop, AOSE 2002*, Bologna, Italy, 2002, Revised Papers and Invited Contributions, Lecture Notes in Computer Science 2585, New York: Springer, 2003.

The proceedings of AOSE 2003, which took place in Melbourne, Australia, were under preparation for publication by Springer at the time of this writing. Finally, two other relevant books are also in preparation:

Padgham, L., and M. Winikoff, *Developing Intelligent Agent Systems: A Practical Guide to Design*, New York: Wiley, 2004.

Bergenti, F., M. P. Gleizes, and F. Zambonell, (eds.), *Methodologies and Software Engineering for Agent Systems*, Boston, MA: Kluwer, 2004.

7.4.3 Journals and Magazines

Agent-related articles are published in a wide range of journals and magazines. The following is a list of publications that feature articles on agent-related issues on a regular basis.

Autonomous Agents and Multi-Agent Systems Published by Kluwer Academic Publishers, this journal publishes articles on all aspects of agents and multiagent systems. It is the premier academic journal for the area, and has featured several articles on agent-oriented development.

Artificial Intelligence A well-known journal, published by Elsevier and with a history of over 30 years, *Artificial Intelligence* often features agent-based articles as well as several issues that are tightly related to agent research.

The Knowledge Engineering Review Published by Cambridge University Press, *The Knowledge Engineering Review* often features several articles that are concerned with reviews of agent-specific topics, including an annual account of the UKMAS meetings.

Communications of the ACM This offers magazine-style articles of general interest, and has featured numerous articles related to agent technologies over the years, with several special issues dedicated to the subject.

IEEE Internet Computing This is a good source of up-to-date information on Internet technologies, and is especially relevant for anyone interested in infrastructures for agent-based systems.

IEEE Intelligent Systems Articles in *Intelligent Systems* are often very generally relevant to intelligent autonomous agents and multiagent systems.

International Journal of Cooperative Information Systems Published by World Scientific, the scope of this journal covers the issues of communication and coordination between distributed information systems.

Journal of Artificial Intelligence Research This is both an electronic and print journal (by Morgan Kaufmann Publishers) and often contains papers relevant to agent-based systems.

Web Semantics: Science, Services and Agents on the World Wide Web Published by Elsevier, this is an interdisciplinary journal whose scope incorporates work at the intersection of the Semantic Web, agents technology, and Grid computing.

7.5 WEB RESOURCES

7.5.1 UMBC Agent Web

`http://agents.umbc.edu/`

The UMBC Agent Web is probably the first dedicated portal to be created specifically for agent technologies, beginning in 1995. It provides a comprehensive set of links to agent-related material;

a new initiative is an attempt to provide a list of FIPA services from around the world. The portal is maintained by the UMBC Laboratory for Advanced Information Technology, with Tim Finin acting as editor and Yannis Labrou as associate editor.

7.5.2 MultiAgent.com

`http://www.multiagent.com/`

The `multiagent.com` portal contains a comprehensive set of links relating to multiagent systems, such as conferences, groups, companies, and people. It is maintained by Jose Vidal of the University of South Carolina, director of the Multiagent Dynamics Laboratory.

7.5.3 Agents Portal

`http://aose.ift.ulaval.ca/`

A recent addition is the *Agents Portal*, which includes discussion forums. The site is maintained by Sehl Mellouli, of Laval University, and Houssein Ben-Ameur, a researcher of CIRANO, and Montreal University.

7.5.4 KTweb

`http://www.ktweb.org`

KTweb is a project funded by the European Commission under the Information Society Technologies program, and aims to act as a community-building and awareness service for digital content, media, and knowledge technologies. It publishes articles on issues related to knowledge technologies, has an up-to-date news service for funding issues from the European Commission, news related to knowledge technologies and links to projects, people, and products. KTweb is run by ERIN S.A., INBIS Group and Vrije Universiteit Amsterdam, through its Division of Mathematics and Computer Science.

7.5.5 SemanticWeb.org

`http://www.semanticweb.org`

The Semantic Web portal provides links to the majority of resources related to Semantic Web issues, such as events, projects, groups, companies, and so on. Many of these resources are also tightly connected to agent development issues. The portal is managed by the Onto-Agents and Scalable Knowledge Composition (SKC) Research Group at Stanford University, the Ontobroker Group at the University of Karlsruhe, and the Protege Research Group at Stanford University.

7.5.6 AgentLink

`www.agentlink.org`

AgentLink is the European Commission's Network of Excellence for Agent-based Computing, which has been running since 1998. It offers numerous links, just as the sites listed above, but also commissions and develops its own resources and reports, as well as running events including an annual summer school. More details of AgentLink are provided next, but the site includes the following set of resources:

- *Research database*
  A research database is available, mapping areas of research within the scope of AgentLink to nodes within AgentLink that have expertise in these areas. The database is available via the AgentLink Web site, and provides at-a-glance information on the major areas of strength within AgentLink. The database is kept up-to-date as new organizations join the network and as new areas of research and development activity emerge.

- *Publications clearinghouse*
  The on-line clearinghouse allows researchers to keep such materials in a single, central place. Materials are submitted electronically via the Web site or e-mail, and are classified according to the AgentLink taxonomy, with the goal of allowing users rapid, easy access to relevant materials.

- *Curricula database for agent-related teaching*
  The curricula database offers a repository of agent teaching materials and curricula, covering all aspects of agent-based computing. Each curriculum summarizes the teaching aims of the course, teaching plans, and pointers to reading material.

7.6 ORGANIZATIONS

7.6.1 IFMAS

The International Foundation for Multiagent Systems (IFMAS) is a nonprofit corporation whose purpose is to promote science and technology in the area of artificial intelligence and multiagent systems. The IFMAS Web site states that it undertakes the following kinds of activities:

- Coordinating and arranging seminars on artificial intelligence and multiagent systems;
- Becoming a representative forum for experts within the field of artificial intelligence and multiagent systems;
- Distributing, and making available, knowledge about multiagent system technology through publications, organizational seminars, courses, and conferences;
- Collaborating with scientific and other institutions, organizations, and other societies, including industrial companies, governments, and international bodies with similar or related purposes.

Despite this broad range of activities, IFMAS is primarily known for organizing regular conferences. From 1995 until 2000, these conferences were the International Conferences on Multi-Agent Systems, which merged with the International Conferences on Autonomous Agents in 2002 to form the International Joint Conference on Autonomous Agents and Multi-Agent Systems. With income generated from these events, IFMAS regularly supports the community with grants for student travel to conferences and for educational event organization, among other things.

7.6.2 FIPA

The Foundation for Intelligent Physical Agents (FIPA) is an organization that was established in 1996 with the aim of developing and promoting software standards for heterogeneous software agents and agent-based systems. As described in Chapter 5, FIPA is recognized as the premier body for standardization in the agents arena, and has already developed specifications for agent communication languages, interaction protocols, content languages, agent management, and message infrastructure.

FIPA undertakes its work at meetings that are held four times a year; it also has close working relationships with other standards organizations, such as the Object Management Group (OMG).

Since FIPA and its work have been described at some length in Chapter 5, it is unnecessary to add more here. Further details of FIPA and its specifications are available from `www.fipa.org`.

7.6.3 AgentLink

AgentLink is Europe's IST-funded Network of Excellence for agent-based computing. As such, AgentLink coordinates research and development activities in the area of agent-based computer systems on the behalf of the European Commission. AgentLink supports a range of activities aimed at raising the profile, quality, and industrial relevance of agent systems research and development in Europe.

IST is a research and development program together with a number of related industrial take-up measures funded by the European Commission. IST operates in the area of information society technologies.

AgentLink divides its activities into five main areas:

- *Industry actions:* Facilitating technology transfer through a program of industrial meetings, workshops, standardization updates, and working groups;
- *Research coordination:* Promoting excellence in European agent research through support for workshops, special interest groups, and dissemination of research results;
- *Teaching and training:* Establishing agent-related skills throughout Europe by support for summer schools and courses;
- *Special interest groups:* Focusing on the development of communities around areas of strategic importance and providing input to the management committee from the SIG members, as well as developing the technological *roadmap*;

- *Information infrastructure:* Providing an infrastructure through which AgentLink can do its work, including a WWW site, regular newsletter, e-mail list, and an awareness program.

7.7 AGENT-BASED SOFTWARE DEVELOPMENT

`www.agentdevelopment.com`

This book has its own Web site, which contains pointers to all of the various resources mentioned here. There are also pointers to all the relevant Web sites mentioned throughout the book, organized by the structure of the book, for easy reference. Finally, there are a number of readily accesible resources relating to the book and updates on the various topics covered.

About the Authors

Michael Luck is a professor in the Intelligence, Agents, Multimedia Group in the School of Electronics and Computer Science at the University of Southampton, United Kingdom. He has worked in the field of agent technology and multiagent systems for more than 10 years, having previously led the Agent-Based Systems Group at the University of Warwick for 7 years, and having obtained his Ph.D. from University College London in 1993 for work on agent-based discovery. Professor Luck is a member of the Advisory Boards of FIPA (the agent standards body), EUMAS (the European agent workshop), and CEEMAS (the Central and Eastern European agent conference). He has served on numerous program committees for agent conferences and workshops and has organized and chaired several international conferences in the area of agents, including those for industry. Professor Luck has contributed to policy-making forums for national and European agencies and has published extensively in this area (with more than 100 publications, including seven books). From 2000 to 2003, he was the director of AgentLink, the European Network of Excellence for Agent-Based Computing, and is currently a member of its Executive Committee. His e-mail address is mml@ecs.soton.ac.uk.

Ronald Ashri is a research fellow in the Intelligence, Agents, Multimedia Group in the School of Electronics and Computer Science at the University of Southampton, United Kingdom. His interests lie in agent infrastructure, semantic Web technologies, and pervasive computing. His main research focus is currently on the representation and establishment of security policies at the semantic level in heterogeneous domains. His work was previously concerned with investigating agent infrastructures, also at the University of Southampton, where he undertook his Ph.D. research. He has published several academic papers in relation to agent infrastructure as well as writing more generally on middleware and mobile-device technologies. His e-mail address is ra@ecs.soton.ac.uk.

Mark d'Inverno obtained his B.A. in mathematics in 1986 and his M.Sc. in computation in 1988, both from Oxford University. In 1998 he obtained his Ph.D. from University College London, and is now professor of computer science at the University of Westminster. His research focuses on the application of formal methods in providing theoretical and foundational formal frameworks in emergent technological fields of computer science, including agent-based systems, hypertext systems, and algorithmic and interactive music systems. He is the coauthor of *Understanding Agent Systems* (Springer-Verlag, 2004) with Michael Luck, and was the general cochair of the First European Workshop on Multi-Agent Systems held at Oxford University in 2003. His e-mail address is dinverm@wmin.ac.uk.

Index

Recent Titles in the Artech House Computing Library

Action Focused Assessment for Software Process Improvement, Tim Kasse

Advanced ANSI SQL Data Modeling and Structure Processing, Michael M. David

Advanced Database Technology and Design, Mario Piattini and Oscar Díaz, editors

Agent-Based Software Development, Michael Luck, Ronald Ashri, and Mark d'Inverno

Building Reliable Component-Based Software Systems, Ivica Crnkovic and Magnus Larsson, editors

Business Process Implementation for IT Professionals and Managers, Robert B. Walford

Data Modeling and Design for Today's Architectures, Angelo Bobak

Developing Secure Distributed Systems with CORBA, Ulrich Lang and Rudolf Schreiner

Future Codes: Essays in Advanced Computer Technology and the Law, Curtis E. A. Karnow

Global Distributed Applications with Windows® DNA, Enrique Madrona

A Guide to Software Configuration Management, Alexis Leon

Guide to Standards and Specifications for Designing Web Software, Stan Magee and Leonard L. Tripp

Implementing and Integrating Product Data Management and Software Configuration, Ivica Crnkovic, Ulf Asklund, and Annita Persson Dahlqvist

Internet Commerce Development, Craig Standing

Knowledge Management Strategy and Technology, Richard F. Bellaver and John M. Lusa, editors

Managing Computer Networks: A Case-Based Reasoning Approach, Lundy Lewis

Metadata Management for Information Control and Business Success, Guy Tozer

Multimedia Database Management Systems, Guojun Lu

Practical Guide to Software Quality Management, Second Edition, John W. Horch

Practical Process Simulation Using Object-Oriented Techniques and C++, José Garrido

A Practitioner's Guide to Software Test Design, Lee Copeland

Risk-Based E-Business Testing, Paul Gerrard and Neil Thompson

Secure Messaging with PGP and S/MIME, Rolf Oppliger

Software Fault Tolerance Techniques and Implementation, Laura L. Pullum

Software Verification and Validation for Practitioners and Managers, Second Edition, Steven R. Rakitin

Strategic Software Production with Domain-Oriented Reuse, Paolo Predonzani, Giancarlo Succi, and Tullio Vernazza

Successful Evolution of Software Systems, Hongji Yang and Martin Ward

Systematic Process Improvement Using ISO 9001:2000 and CMMI®, Boris Mutafelija and Harvey Stromberg

Systematic Software Testing, Rick D. Craig and Stefan P. Jaskiel

Systems Modeling for Business Process Improvement, David Bustard, Peter Kawalek, and Mark Norris, editors

Testing and Quality Assurance for Component-Based Software, Jerry Zeyu Gao, H. -S. Jacob Tsao, and Ye Wu

User-Centered Information Design for Improved Software Usability, Pradeep Henry

Workflow Modeling: Tools for Process Improvement and Application Development, Alec Sharp and Patrick McDermott

For further information on these and other Artech House titles, including previously considered out-of-print books now available through our In-Print-Forever® (IPF®) program, contact:

Artech House
685 Canton Street
Norwood, MA 02062
Phone: 781-769-9750
Fax: 781-769-6334
e-mail: artech@artechhouse.com

Artech House
46 Gillingham Street
London SW1V 1AH UK
Phone: +44 (0)20 7596-8750
Fax: +44 (0)20 7630-0166
e-mail: artech-uk@artechhouse.com

Find us on the World Wide Web at:
www.artechhouse.com